LAMBETH PAST

First published 2006

by Historical Publications Ltd
32 Ellington Street, London N7 8PL
(Tel: 020 7607 1628)

ISBN 1 905286 12 0
British Library Cataloguing-in-Publication Data
A catalogue record for this book is available from the British Library

Typeset in Book Antiqua by Historical Publications Ltd
Reproduction by Gilderson's, Pitfield Street, London N1
Printed by Edelvives, Zaragoza, Spain

The Illustrations

The following have kindly given permission to reproduce pictures:

British Library: *45*
British Museum: *56*
Graham Gibberd: *41, 93*
Guildhall Library, Corporation of London: *18, 28, 30, 39, 47, 54, 60, 61, 68, 86, 91, 98, 108*
London Borough of Lambeth Archives Department: *14, 20, 32, 57, 63, 67, 75, 76, 77, 78, 80, 96, 103, 104, 105, 106, 118, 132, 134, 135, 136, 143*
London Metropolitan Archives: *13, 127*
London Transport Museum: *114*
National Portrait Gallery: *24, 40, 65, 66, 74*
Hannah Renier: *144, 145, 146, 147, 148*
Robert Opie Collection: *139*
Royal Bethlem Hospital: *71*
Sainsbury's: *133*
Stephens Collection: *73*
Surrey County Cricket Club: *115*
Lawrence Wright/Fine Art Gallery: *138*

Other illustrations were supplied by Historical Publications

LAMBETH PAST

Kennington Vauxhall Waterloo

Hannah Renier

HISTORICAL PUBLICATIONS

To Meir

"Some people never come across the river," said he to Charles, and Charles had to confess that he had very seldom done so; also that he had never been in the streets they were passing through at all, and didn't know their names.
Alice-for-Short, A Dichronism, William de Morgan, 1907.

Acknowledgements

With thanks for the magnificent resources of the British Library and Lambeth Archives and their staff, and to Mr and Mrs Marsh at the Stephens Collection. Gratitude also to the creators of the Vauxhall City Farm and the lavender garden in Vauxhall Park.

Contents

Beside the river

LAMBETH

Lambeth now, at the start of the 21st century, generally implies the entire enormous borough, encompassing just about everywhere between Southwark and Norwood. This book deals only with the three villages of its northern part which, until Victorian times, were what Londoners meant when they spoke of Lambeth: Waterloo, Kennington and Vauxhall. These are the flat lands across the Thames from Pimlico, Westminster and the Temple. Waterloo and Vauxhall occupy the shoreline from Blackfriars Bridge to some little way upstream beyond Vauxhall Bridge. Kennington is their hinterland.

Much of this 'south' side of the river is not south, but east, of Westminster. Its long stretch of riverbank is like a letter *f*, with the National Theatre on the eastward curve at the top and the barges of Nine Elms bobbing west at the base. More confusingly still, two of its villages have changed their names. Lambeth Marsh became Waterloo in the middle of the nineteenth century when the railway station (named after the bridge, which had been named after the battle) came to dominate the area. Water Lambeth straggled along the Thames from Lambeth Palace until the upstream end developed its own identity and became known as Fulk's Hall, later Vauxhall.

BRONZE AGE RELICS

Stand on Vauxhall Bridge and today's London is deafeningly present. Emergency services wail and bellow as they race to an accident, crowded buses swerve into the middle of the road, helicopters growl across the sky, and office workers scuttle along the pavements to meetings.

Yet it is here, of all places, that you can see the remains of a modest jetty or bridge built by our predecessors over three thousand years ago. When the tide goes out, you can spot it as you go past on the bus. Still better, stand on the Thames Path outside the St George's Wharf apartments and you will see two rows of waterlogged black stumps on the gritty beach below. As artefacts, their intrinsic value is not impressive, but there are 27 stumps and they are the most visible, tangible record we have of London before the city was here.

These are said to be all that is left of the first London bridge. This is probably wrong, although there is a theory, impossible to disprove, that since the Effra River emerged here from the south bank, and the Tyburn from the north, this may have been a bridge to an islet in the middle. Another theory holds that it was a jetty, perhaps used for the ceremonial deposition of corpses and votive offerings like the two superbly worked spear heads which were found close to it.

When Channel 4's *Time Team* and the Museum of London removed one of the waterlogged stumps for analysis they were able to identify it as a pile, rather than a post. Posts are inserted into a hole dug out of dry land; piles are driven by force into mud, such as a muddy river. So we know that the river flowed here 3,200 years ago. We also know, from microscopic analysis, that the head of the salt water tides was somewhere between Vauxhall and Westminster Bridge. But it was creeping inland; today you can smell the sea right up to Battersea.

THE FIRST SETTLERS

The south bank of the Thames, which in the Stone Age had been very cold and largely underwater, was slowly draining and drying out. Since there was no embankment, people would have lived and farmed on higher ground in case of flooding, and harvested the flood plain for reeds, waterfowl and fish. Deer were hunted among the trees inland.

With agriculture affecting the environment, the river gradually deepened, defined itself and settled into its familiar course. In 1,000BC (when the ancient jetty was already two hundred years old) the Thames was much wider than it is now, with shallow mud flats, alders and willows on the south bank, and a steeper declivity scoured by faster-flowing water on the north. And by 500BC the locals were using iron tools, weapons and wheels, happily oblivious that inquisitive descendants would label theirs the Iron Age.

Lambeth – we have to call it that, since we don't know what it was called at the time – was a flat part of the London basin and as such, of little interest to Iron Age Britons. In this southern part of England, the most defensible places were hill forts with a water supply, and there are traces of many like that, high along the ridgeways to Avebury, eighty miles west. Further west was the nexus of trade. Tin and silver were exported to southern Europe through ports in Devon and Hampshire; pack animals carried goods north from there. The Thames basin, which was too big and too flat to defend, much too close to Continental marauders for comfort, and soggy underfoot on the south side, was not the most favourable of sites. Boggy ground meant leeches and malarial swamps and bronchitic fogs.

But the Thames itself was indispensable to the people of the riverbank, as it had been for hundreds of years. Most were Britons; that is, the type of Celt found in Northern Gaul, and speaking the same language as those people – although newcomers arrived from Europe all the time. They travelled along the Thames and across it in shallow-bottomed boats, they used it for transporting goods in quantity, they ate the fish from it, drank water from streams that ran into it, irrigated their land with it and relied on it for dyeing and tanning. Where they found higher ground behind the marshes, they farmed cereals on its fertile alluvial residue and raised stock and horses. They built circular mud-and-wood houses on the gravel ridges over the marsh, they wove wool, made cheese, and intermittently squabbled with their neighbours. They shifted goods by cart and pack animal on well-worn tracks, and where a useful route crossed boggy ground, they reinforced it with tightly packed bundles of twigs or reeds, sawn planks or split logs. They shared their space with a huge variety of wildlife: great flocks of birds, especially on the marshes.

The more populous defensible settlements were in the west of England, but on the banks of the Thames traders flourished nonetheless, for the river was accessible from the north and the Low Countries. Pre-Roman artefacts from the continent, especially the Rhine valley, have been found in the riverbed. An Iron Age helmet was unearthed when Waterloo Station was being extended in the 1860s. Coins, a continental innovation, were in widespread use. Bone and metal tools and weapons have been found under County Hall and Iron Age pottery in the Lambeth Palace kitchen garden.

VENI, VIDI, VICI

The Roman expedition that arrived in the Thames basin in 55BC was not the first invading force, but they were simply years ahead technologically and politically of those that had come before, and the first to leave us a record.

Thorney Island (where Westminster Abbey stands) still was an island, and close to the tidal head. Tides, and river depth, would be important reasons for the Romans to locate a heavily defended frontier town well upriver on the higher ground of the north bank.

But the pre-Roman Thames was also a boundary between tribes. The Catuvellauni and the Trinovantes had their headquarters up in the North Downs while the Arebates and Cantii claimed the land south of the river. The Romans arrived to discover that all of them, forewarned by a first Roman invasion the previous year, had joined up to confront the enemy under a single chieftain. This valiant attempt at self-defence was a failure. Caesar's troops hounded Cassivellaunus and his united tribes north across the Thames and extracted the promise of tribute before retreating to Rome.

We know of no great destruction of livestock or property. Except for taxes paid to an unimaginably distant ruler, nothing much changed until 43AD, when imperial forces returned to build the capital city of this new colony.

1. A Roman galley found during the excavations for the foundations of the new County Hall in 1911. The exact location was 40 feet below the Council chamber. The boat was about 60 feet long and from the evidence of coins found on board, dated to about the end of the third century. It is exhibited at the Museum of London.

LONDINIUM CHANGES EVERYTHING

Gaul was now firmly within the Roman Empire and an occupying force could reliably be supplied, on both sides of the Channel. Order was imposed. Traders who had previously struggled across heaving seas from Normandy to Hengistbury Head and points west were able to send goods up the Seine and the Rhône and along the French coast to a point near Calais, from which Kent, and the coastal route to the Thames, were a shorter voyage. Londinium was the gateway to new Roman Britain and the seat of its Governor, and merchants and administrators were busy constructing a major trading post there.

For the next four centuries under the Empire, land throughout the entire colony was held only by gracious consent of the Imperial power. Those tribal chieftains who had owned it before the Romans came were the only ones who didn't have to pay tax; other classes paid in cash or kind. This established the principle that land ownership was granted by favour, not by right. By extension there emerged hundreds of years later 'knight service' – the feudal lord's obligation to raise a force for the king in wartime.

Lambeth, as an unhealthily marshy, sparsely inhabited sprawl of hovels several miles upriver from London, was of little interest to the Roman incomers, except as a place from which freshwater fish and farm produce could be got for sale in the town. The north side of the river offered higher and drier land. So far as we know the Romans largely ignored Lambeth; they didn't even have a name for it – and yet, they did use it as a local through route. One of the earliest known roads was a cut across Lambeth from Southwark to the ferry to Thorney Island. Marked on a map, its split-log remains lie roughly under the railway lines that link Waterloo to London Bridge. Like most non-military local roads used by Roman settlers, this was a solid thoroughfare laid on a pre-existing track. Travellers followed the raised gravel outcrop along Lambeth Marsh, roughly along today's Royal Street and that short curve of Albert Embankment where it has passed behind St Thomas's Hospital and heads for the river. At Stangate ferry (Stangate means 'stone lane'), boatmen would take travellers across to the settlement on Thorney, and thence towards Watling Street, the main route north-west (today's Edgware Road). Goods crossing the marsh in convoy were probably safer from raids than they would be on the well-wooded, hillier north shore. Also, throughout the history of Stangate ferry, which existed for over fifteen hundred years, it was usually cheaper than crossing London Bridge. A Roman flat-bottomed boat sixty feet long was found during excavations for County Hall at the start of the twentieth century.

In their 350 years of occupation the Romans built two great roads that intersected east of the boggy heath that lay behind the riverbank. One road ran from north to south along the east side of Lambeth. It was Stane Street (again meaning a stone road), and it ran from a timber bridge (at London Bridge) to Chichester, a key Roman camp and port. Stane Street lies beneath Kennington Park Road, at the eastern extremity of the flood-prone riverside. The other was the Walworth Road, which met Stane Street at Newington, where the Elephant and Castle is today; it is in Southwark, beyond the area covered in this book.

The Thames was not the only watercourse. Two of its local tributaries, the Neckinger and the Effra, used to be wide and deep enough to obstruct foot traffic all the year round, and were bridged at key points. The Neckinger rose near today's Imperial War Museum and meandered untidily in two directions before debouching in Bermondsey to the east, and under the present Waterloo Bridge to the west; the Effra, from Norwood, ran downhill through what became Brixton, and veered west to join the Thames close to today's Vauxhall Bridge. But there were streams and ditches all over the place. Knowing what we do about the prevalence of ague (a form of malaria) which survived in the eastern English counties as late as the twentieth century, we may suppose that most of Lambeth, away from the better-drained riverbank, was unhealthy.

LAMBETH MARSH AND WATER LAMBETH

When the Roman armies departed, lawlessness reigned and claims to land ownership were precarious. And there was no longer any effective defence from invaders. It is said that the first Saxons had been invited by Romano-British leaders to Londinium in about 450 to help repel the Picts, but once their masters were weakened they took control of resources for themselves. As a result civil war smouldered until the middle of the sixth century. The more prosperous Romano-British defended their estates as best they could, but over hundreds of years shifted west as Anglo-Saxon immigrants populated the Thames Basin.

The Saxons didn't build cities. Some squatted in the old Roman houses until the fabric disintegrated, but most lived in homesteads or hamlets west of the Roman city on the north bank. Their settlements straggled along close to the Thames, some of which was fortified by a timber embankment, all the way to Thorney Island. Lambeth, opposite, got its name, Lambhythe, from the Anglo-Saxons. It is said to mean a landing place (think of Queenhithe or Rotherhithe) for sheep. One imagines flocks bobbing along the river on rafts, and scrambling up a gently sloping shore.

Saxon tribal leaders apportioned some land to their most loyal henchmen, some to themselves and some to the group. The principle has descended to us as private land, royal estates and common land. The new settlers' language became a mixture of Latin, British (Gaulish Celtic), and Anglo-Saxon, as over time they mixed and interbred with the people who already lived here. These earlier settlers would have been Celtic, Scandinavian and Southern European, interspersed with a few dark faces, the descendants of Roman soldiers from North Africa.

They can't have been very cheerful. Evidence from Roman burial sites indicates that most Londoners were shorter than people today, and more likely to suffer chronic pain from parasites, abscesses, or what for us would be curable disease. People upriver in Lambeth are unlikely to have been much different. They were probably worse off, since Lambeth was low-lying, cold and damp, and anyone unfortunate enough to live in it would have been subject to fever in summer, and rheumatism and chronic sinusitis (from living in smoky, chimneyless huts) in winter.

Long before the Romans left, Londinium had been designated head of one of the four provinces into which the early Church divided England. Better-off Romano-British families were often Christian, but the late-Roman Christian communities of which traces have been found have all been north of the river. The country folk of Lambeth probably resisted change and stuck to the old pagan ways.

DESTINY BECKONS

When, in 597, Augustine and his missionaries arrived to Christianise the rest of the recalcitrant English, they quickly obtained the support of the Saxon King Ethelbert, and set up a new church structure. This annoyed the existing Romano-British Christians, who continued to support the bishops to whom they had been loyal before; many joined the westward exodus.

Augustine's church controlled a diocesan structure and a monastic one, and during the seventh century a monastery was instituted on Thorney Island. There had probably been a market on Thorney for generations, and now, with the community there growing, the crossing at Stangate in Lambeth was more commercially useful than ever. An eighth-century record from the archives of King Offa dismisses Thorney as a slum (it was surrounded by marshes and unhealthy). But it was destined for greater things, and Lambeth, across the river, would benefit.

Mediaeval glory

Lambeth crept to a position of national importance in the Middle Ages. Thanks to its significance in the power triumvirate (London financiers, Royalty and the Church) it grew politically and socially prominent in the lives of the rich and famous.

KING CANUTE

In Lambeth, the Dark Ages were inappropriately colourful. By the tenth century, London and the south-east were prosperous again and invaders were attracted by rich pickings. The Danes, with their motley crew of royal hangers-on and Scandinavian and Russian mercenaries, were relentless and determined, but since Londoners were vicious in retaliation, exchanges of bloodcurdling violence continued for decades.

Legend has it that when Canute decided to attack London from the east in 1016 he had a channel dug between the Effra and the Neckinger at Kennington, so that his army could sail all the way from Bermondsey to Nine Elms and avoid the fierce defenders of London Bridge. This tale appears in just about every book about the area, and there is even a map showing three different versions of the ditch's route. The legend appears to have begun with a vague reference in the Anglo-Saxon Chronicles. It is not in books about Canute. Sceptical local historians doubt the capacity of either river to support an army and to this author it seems more likely that a body of men sailing up the Neckinger would simply heave their boats out of the water and drag or carry them the few miles overland through the woods, as Scandinavian traders crossing Russia did for many centuries, rather than dig channels between rivers.

At least one specialist contemporary historian,

2. A map (taken from Nicholas Barton's Lost Rivers of London*), showing the courses of the Neckinger (rising near the Imperial War Museum), and to the south the Effra.*

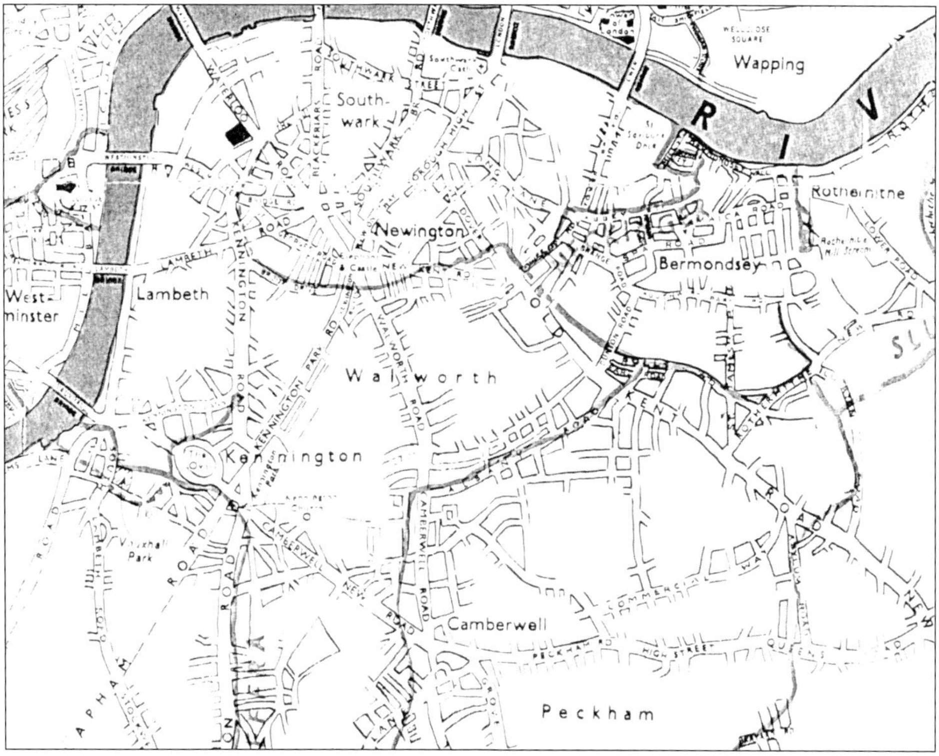

in a book about Canute's magnificently named father Swein Forkbeard, ignores the story entirely. Ian Howard tells us that Viking raiding parties, in shallow-bottomed boats of all sizes, harassed the south-eastern seaboard from 990 onwards. From 1013 London's merchants paid Danegeld to make the invaders go away. King Ethelred the Unready (meaning ill-advised) died in 1016, and this left his brother Edmund and Ethelred's Norman widow Emma to confront Canute when he attacked London a few months later. Edmund fled, and Emma married Canute, possibly by pre-arrangement. The mystery of Canute's conquest seems solved, with no digging.

EDWARD THE CONFESSOR

Around 1050 Lambeth Marsh, straggling along today's Lower Marsh and Upper Marsh, was a trading post on the way to the Stangate Ferry. The riverside further south, close to the parish church of St Mary, supported a hamlet called Water Lambeth. Ferries carried people and goods downriver to long-established markets behind the Strand embankment, while other boats transported wood and hay, building materials and fruit, bacon and livestock from the Wandle river and the Thames Valley to the city and the market that sprawled around the religious settlement on Thorney.

But it was Edward the Confessor who really put Thorney Island on the map and increased the traffic to and from Water Lambeth. Thorney was now landlocked, and since he was a pious man, he decided to endow a magnificent church there – and, more importantly for Lambeth, to relocate his royal household (and government) to a site close by. If you wanted to take your goods from the City of London to this new centre of population, Lambeth Marsh and the Stangate Ferry would be an alternative to the north bank route – in daylight.

After dark, south of the river, the boggy heath, ponds and unlit woods were menacing, and robbers lay in wait for lone travellers along Stane Street (now Kennington Park Road). The old Roman roads were used for long journeys by day and by wagon train. The lanes and tracks that criss-crossed the north bank, Southwark and parts of Lambeth were ill-maintained and muddy in wet weather. If you were a City merchant, a senior cleric or a courtier, you kept your own boat and staff to convey you by water between London and Westminster and up into the Thames Valley. Everyone else hopped into a rowing-boat and paid a fare.

WHO OWNED WHAT?

Scholars argue about how and when reigning monarchs began to claim land, by sneaky appropriation rather than outright bullying or purchase, with the Witan or council of elders turning a blind eye. A plausible theory is that around the end of the ninth century, by which time all the attractive, fertile bits had been taken, kings began quietly to take over scrub, river and woodland. By the time of the Norman Conquest, the Anglo-Saxon royal family owned extensive estates and hunting grounds, including much of Lambeth with the buildings upon it.

In 1066 William, the first Norman king, defeated Edward's successor Harold at Hastings. After the Conquest, land ownership reverted to the tidy Roman system whereby everything belonged to the King/Emperor as of right, unless declared otherwise. William allowed inoffensive local nobles to hang onto their estates so long as they paid him for the privilege. His Norman lords were rewarded with rent-free land, often on condition of 'knight service', while the Church, oddly enough, ended up better off even than the Norman nobility.

DOMESDAY

Not long after the Domesday survey was made in 1086, William's son William Rufus completed the change begun by Edward the Confessor; he began to build the first Westminster Hall on Thorney Island and Lambeth's eventual assimilation into the metropolis became inevitable. But at Domesday, Lambeth and Kennington were still provincial, and part of Surrey.

The Domesday Book, besides recording the

extent of property owned and by whom, exists also as testimony to how they came by it. London was especially favoured; a charter, granted by William the Conqueror to the secular and ecclesiastical authorities in place when he arrived, reassures them that:

> I give you to know that I will that ye be all those laws worthy that ye were in King Edward's day. And I will that every child be his father's heir after his father's day, and I will not suffer that any man offer you any wrong.

William's benevolence did not quite extend to Lambeth. Surrey was divided into fourteen 'hundreds', and the Brixton Hundred included three local manors belonging respectively to the King, a particularly well-connected Norman nobleman and the Church. The three manors were covetable; not exactly prime land, but prettily located nonetheless.

Domesday shows that the King owned Kennington, having inherited it from his Anglo-Saxon predecessor, but that he leased the entire manor to Theodoric the Goldsmith. A silver coin in the National Portrait Gallery bears the image of Harold, the King who died at Hastings in 1066, and the image is ascribed to Theodoric. He somehow managed to keep a Kennington roof over his head despite having served the wrong side. He got a rent reduction, too. A translation of the Domesday entry reads:

> Theodoric the Goldsmith holds of the king Kennington. He himself held it of King Edward. It was then assessed at five hides; now at one hide and five ingates. That is land for two and a half ploughs. In demesne is one plough; and four villeins and 3 bordars with two ploughs. There is one slave and four acres of meadow. It was and is worth £3.

The 'demesne' in which farmland was held represented an obligation to work the land for the Lord of the Manor. Villeins were bound to the land: if they decided to leave, they could be brought back. All of these men probably supported families, and Theodoric's household would have included servants and their children. Bordars were peasants of an inferior class, and ploughs, hides and ingates were measurements of land and, implicitly, the produce due from it. Almost everyone depended for their living on either the lord of the manor or the Church. Domesday records fisheries, mills, and other potential tax-revenue producers in other places but there appear to have been none here to speak of.

In the manor of Lambeth, the Count of Mortain was tenant in chief and held his part (the Vauxhall end) rent free.

> The Count of Mortain holds Lambeth. The canons of Waltham held it off Harold. It was then assessed at six and a half hides; now at nothing. There is land for six ploughs. In demesne is one plough; and five villeins and twelve bordars with three ploughs. There is one slave, and six acres of meadow. TRE [in the time of King Edward] it was worth 100/-; and afterwards, as now, £4.

The third local Manor was closest to London: Water Lambeth and Lambeth Marsh.

> There is a manor of St Mary's which is called Lambeth. Countess Gode, sister of King Edward, held it. It was then assessed at ten hides; now at two and a half hides. There is land for two and a half ploughs. In demesne are two ploughs, twelve villeins and 27 bordars with four ploughs. There is a church, and 19 burgesses in London who pay 36/-, and there are three slaves and 16 acres of meadow and woodland for three pigs. TRE and afterwards it was worth £10; now £11.
>
> Of this manor the Bishop of Bayeux has a piece of arable land, which before and after the death of Gode belonged to this church.

Bishop Odo of Bayeux was a highly unpopular land-grabber, half-brother of King William and brother of the Count of Mortain, and was at the time of Domesday in jail. He was the richest man in England after the King. The church that temporarily lost its piece of arable land to him stood on land still occupied by the old parish church of St Mary's, east of Lambeth Palace. This part of Lambeth had fallen in and out of Royal hands and from Domesday onwards most of it belonged to the Bishop of Rochester.

Perhaps we can identify proud Theodoric the Goldsmith, Lord of the Manor of Kennington, as

3. A coin depicting a portrait of Hardicanute, who died at Lambeth.

the first local celebrity. Until he came, everything of note seemed to take place elsewhere. The inhabitants must have been grateful for their quiet lives, since Southwark, so much more often traversed by the predatory and inquisitive, had been burned down and blockaded in its time. Lambeth was remarkable for only one incident, and that not much to be proud of. Hardicanute, son of Emma and Canute and half-brother of Edward the Confessor, had died at Lambeth back in 1042. He was in his early twenties, and is ignobly remembered as a binge drinker who fell into a fatal stupor at a wedding. An historian of 1795 states that 'Hardicanute died at the wedding of Canute Prudan with Githa the daughter of Efgod Clape a Saxon nobleman' and that the Saxon bride was whispered to have poisoned him; also that Hardicanute had it coming, since he had revived the Danegeld, sacked Worcester, and exhumed his dead brother and tipped the corpse into a bog.

Many writers have supposed that the horrid youth died at Kennington Palace; where else in the district, it is argued, would royalty have been seen – even dead?

KENNINGTON PALACE

The original Kennington Palace is not easy to place, since over many generations it was extended, renovated, rebuilt, modernised, robbed of its useful materials and finally left to crumble gently away. Nothing remains of it now, but it stood for six or seven hundred years at the north-west side of today's Kennington Cross, close to the corner of Kennington Lane and Kennington Road. There was a large pond less than half a mile away, next to the old Roman road to Chichester.

This is the drier side of Lambeth and its location suggests that the house was erected at a time when river-flood defence was inadequate and the main Roman road still a magnet for thieves and cattle-rustlers. There was certainly a manor house on the site of Kennington Palace early in the eleventh century: probably a long barn-like timber building – the sort of communal banqueting hall with associated sleeping accommodation occupied by prosperous lords at the time – most likely with outbuildings. There is no record that royalty occupied it before the Conquest, although when Hardicanute's even more vicious brother Harold Harefoot proclaimed himself king in 1037 he is said to have done so at Kennington.

At Domesday Theodoric held the manor and manor house on a 40-year lease from William and his successors. It was a convenient and salubrious place with a straight road to London Bridge close by, fertile well-watered land all around to supply the household with fruit and vegetables, deer-hunting in the hills to south and east, and pleasant walks across flower-filled meadows in dry weather. In 1189 it passed from King Richard on a long lease to Sir Robert Percy; but it later reverted to royalty, for Henry III held the Lambeth Parliament there, and kept Christmas there in 1231. It must have been a place of significant size, as a king to keep Christmas must hold open house for days or weeks, with every day feasting, mummers, jesters, minstrels and dancing, and merriment enjoyed by hundreds of finely dressed courtiers and attendant retinues. A small on-site brewery, corn-mill, bakery, fishponds, stables, laundry and so on would have been necessary to support gatherings of this size.

THE BLACK PRINCE

In the fourteenth century Edward III granted Kennington Palace to his son, Edward Duke of Cornwall. The estate has been inherited as part of the Duchy of Cornwall by first-born sons of the monarch ever since.

Edward Duke of Cornwall, later Prince of Wales, and still later known as the Black Prince, was born in 1330, and would join his father in a series of campaigns in France from the age of thirteen. He was extravagant, and like his father keen to improve the property. Edward III had been adding to the old house since his son was ten, but when Prince Edward came of age the young man demolished part of it and commanded a home fit for his eventual bride.

Ten more years passed; and by the time he married (for love) rich young twice-widowed Joan of Kent in 1361, the new Kennington Palace was almost complete. They would spend their first summer there with her three children. Much of the palace consisted of a hall, nearly ninety feet long and fifty wide, by Henry Yevele, the famous master mason responsible, over thirty years later, for the renovation and extension of the old Norman Westminster Hall. Yevele's Kennington hall had walls of Reigate stone and a tiled roof and floor. A more elaborate private chamber, almost as big, adjoined it, and the whole was flanked by a line of half-timbered kitchens and bakeries, sculleries and stables and servants' quarters. The window-panes were probably small leaded lights of Sussex glass (which was rather dim) or even squares of the latest Normandy glass, which offered a greenish, distorted view but at least you could see out. The Prince owned magnificent tapestries with which walls would be draped in winter. The palace would have had its own kitchen gardens and a fishpond; and a vine grew in a small sunny garden outside the private chamber. (This was the Mediaeval Warm Epoch, a couple of hundred

4. Kennington Manor in 1636. From a plan in the possession of the Duchy of Cornwall.

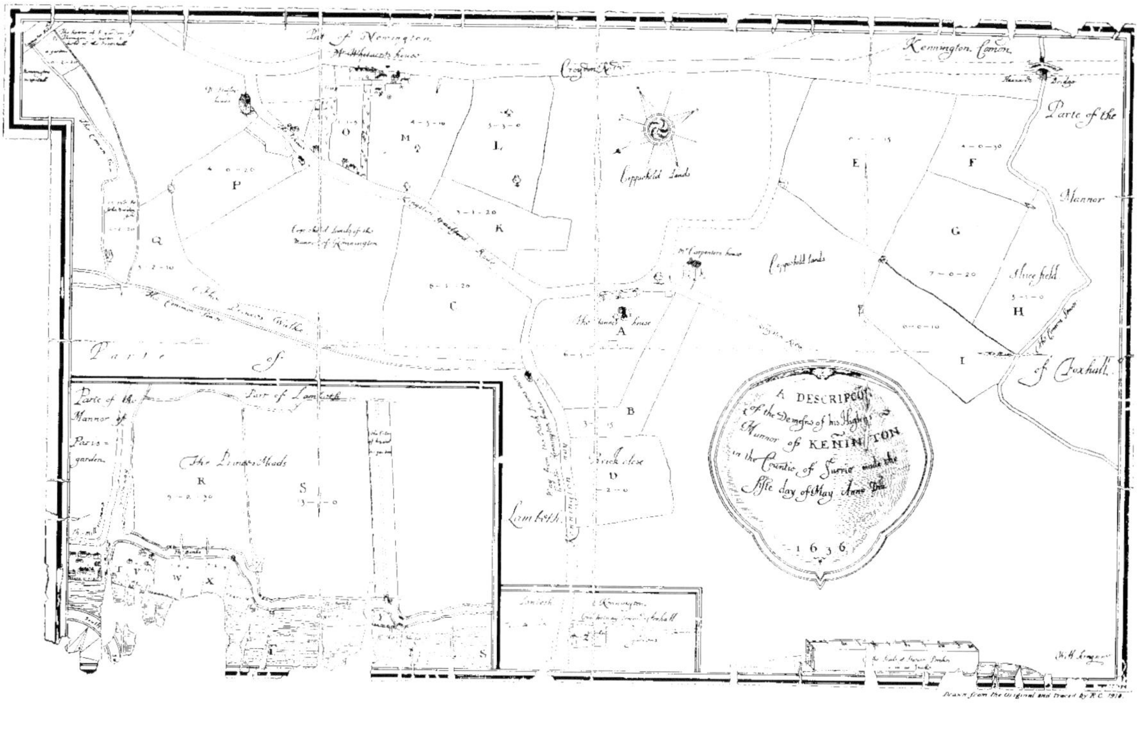

years in which the Thames basin had a half-decent climate.)

For the next fifteen years, Prince Edward and Princess Joan stayed often at Kennington between his many excursions to fight in France and later, in Spain. Kennington was Prince Edward's London home, as Westminster was the King's, and his last months were spent there before his death at Westminster in 1376.

The Black Prince predeceased his father. His own sons, Edward, who died in childhood, and Richard – later King Richard II – were brought up at Kennington Palace.

It remained a royal palace, albeit a neglected one, for generations. Katherine of Aragon stayed there on her way to marry Prince Arthur, who left her a widow (after which she married Henry VIII). Much of the main building is said to have been demolished by Henry VIII in 1531 in order to provide materials for his upgrading of Whitehall Palace. And Reigate stone, especially allied with lime mortar, is notoriously prone to crumble. Walter Besant, writing in 1899, claims that Kennington Palace was all gone by 1607. However, he mentions a moat and a 'long barn' which remained on the site nearly a hundred years later, and an indefinable huddle of buildings marked 'Black Prince' appears on Faden's wonderful map of 1785.

THE ORIGINS OF LAMBETH PALACE

Canterbury had become the superior Archbishopric only in 1072, and York continued to seethe. So did the Benedictine monks and nuns of the Priory of Christ Church Canterbury, who had the support of Rome and who saw successive archbishops as a threat to the way Rome wanted to run things. There was open suspicion between the two sides. Twelfth-century archbishops therefore performed some of their ecclesiastical duties away from Canterbury in a chapel belonging to the diocese of Rochester, at Lambeth.

The Christ Church monks remained unable to find common ground with the more independent-minded archbishops. Their resentment had festered for a hundred years when, in the second half of the twelfth century, Archbishop Baldwin set up a collegiate chapel of his own for secular canons. At first, it was sited just outside the Canterbury walls. Then it was moved by papal decree further and further away, until in the summer of 1189 he found a permanent home for it. He negotiated a swap: in exchange for the Kent parish of Darenth, the Bishop of Rochester handed over Lambeth.

Having signed off on the exchange, Archbishop Baldwin joined a crusade to Jerusalem, and was dead by Christmas. In 1190 his successor Archbishop Hubert gritted his teeth and began building, aware that there would be papal fallout. Successive Popes in Rome had never been keen that the Archbishop of Canterbury should build an ecclesiastical power base in London. Edward the Confessor had founded the Dominican Abbey at Westminster, the Norman kings had moved their residence there from the Tower, and to allow the most powerful priest in England to live five minutes away from royalty by rowing-boat seemed like asking for trouble (as indeed proved to be the case).

And now Archbishop Hubert was setting up an independent establishment opposite Westminster. With King Richard I away at the Crusades he was soon acting as the unofficial Regent.

In 1199 with the accession of King John, the Christ Church monks got the Pope's backing to have the threatening new collegiate chapel at Lambeth razed to the ground. Archbishop Hubert retained the site and the office of Archbishop, but only on condition that the next building he erected there should be a residence, rather than a mutinous cloister.

LAMBETH MANOR HOUSE

The first version of Lambeth Palace, with its outbuildings, Chapel and Great Hall, was called the Manor House. It was constructed from about 1207 when Stephen Langton became Archbishop. In its essentials, the property was complete by 1300. Like today's residential section of the palace it was constructed at right-angles to the river, well north of the gateway where Morton's Tower stands today. The river flowed much closer to the walls of the property than it does now, for there was no Albert Embankment.

A gateway and wharf for the horse-ferry stood at the south end of the grounds beside St Mary's parish church. From 1357 important visitors were borne in their own sumptuously decorated barges to land at a quay slightly further north, closer to the house itself. Between the south gate and the house a Great Hall arose alongside the river; and close to the house, a Chapel. This, much altered, is still there. It was built around 1225, though the crypt below it appears to be a couple of decades older. The walls of the crypt are four feet thick and its marble pillars support a roof of vaulted ribs. The chapel that Archbishop Langton built above, much of which we still have, was as austerely beautiful as he could make it without inciting ecclesiastical opponents to burn it down again.

The Great Hall was used for banquets to celebrate consecrations, ordinations and feast days. It could rise to any occasion; after convocations at St Paul's, black-capped bishops and their retinues would sail with some pomp upriver to Lambeth for dinner there. We do not know what the mediaeval Hall looked like for it was much altered before its eventual destruction and rebuilding. Something like Westminster Hall, a cavernous oblong spanned by mighty roof timbers, is the general idea. It may, like the later Great Hall, even at this early date have had a bell in a lantern tower on top. A pealing bell welcomed visiting bishops, celebrated royal birthdays and weddings and announced news of victories abroad.

In time a cloister and library were added between the Archbishop's house and the Great Hall, and later still a guardroom. This was so far as we know the only sizeable complex of stone, and possibly brick, buildings in the parish. Brick was too expensive for domestic use and stone had to be brought from Surrey or Kent, via the Wandle or the Thames. At this time there was still plenty of English oak for building. Wealthy people lived in oak-framed lathe and plaster houses, but humbler dwellings were set on rubble foundations and erected out of a timber frame insulated with mud and straw, clad with rough planks and roofed with reed thatch or clay tiles. Oiled cloth took the place of window-panes; window glass was imported, and expensive.

From the start Lambeth Manor House had its own bakehouses, sculleries, almonry and poultry room, wardrobes and other offices. The house and grounds were as self-sufficient as possible, considering the number of people who must be catered for. Chickens were kept and vegetables grown close to the manor house; there was a fishpond and beer and honey were made on the premises. A smelly ditch ran around the land (which extended further east and north than the grounds of Lambeth Palace do now) and a mill stood next to the wharf by the south gate. Both the brewer and the baker needed a mill. What this one was used for, and what powered it, are matters for speculation, although there is evidence of local windmills in later centuries. In the middle ages a mill could also have been powered by water (unlikely here), or a horse. The sight and sound of a blindfold pony laboriously circling a mill-wheel, hour after hour, were common enough.

Horses, in this prosperous, flat part of the world, also carried people and burdens - most importantly water - to those households furthest from a clean supply. Where there were working horses, there was a need for hay, brought by barge from meadows further upstream. By the time the horse ferry was established close to the south gate, watermen and their families had come to live in a huddle of cottages close to the foreshore of Water Lambeth. They mainly offered a river-taxi for foot passengers to and from the many river stairs between Lambeth and London Bridge. The Archbishop of course kept his own barge, with private access to its moorings through the Post Room.

No doubt the sound of plainsong drifted from the Chapel over the bustle of the estate. An anxious visitor, awaiting an audience with the Archbishop, would have been aware of elderly

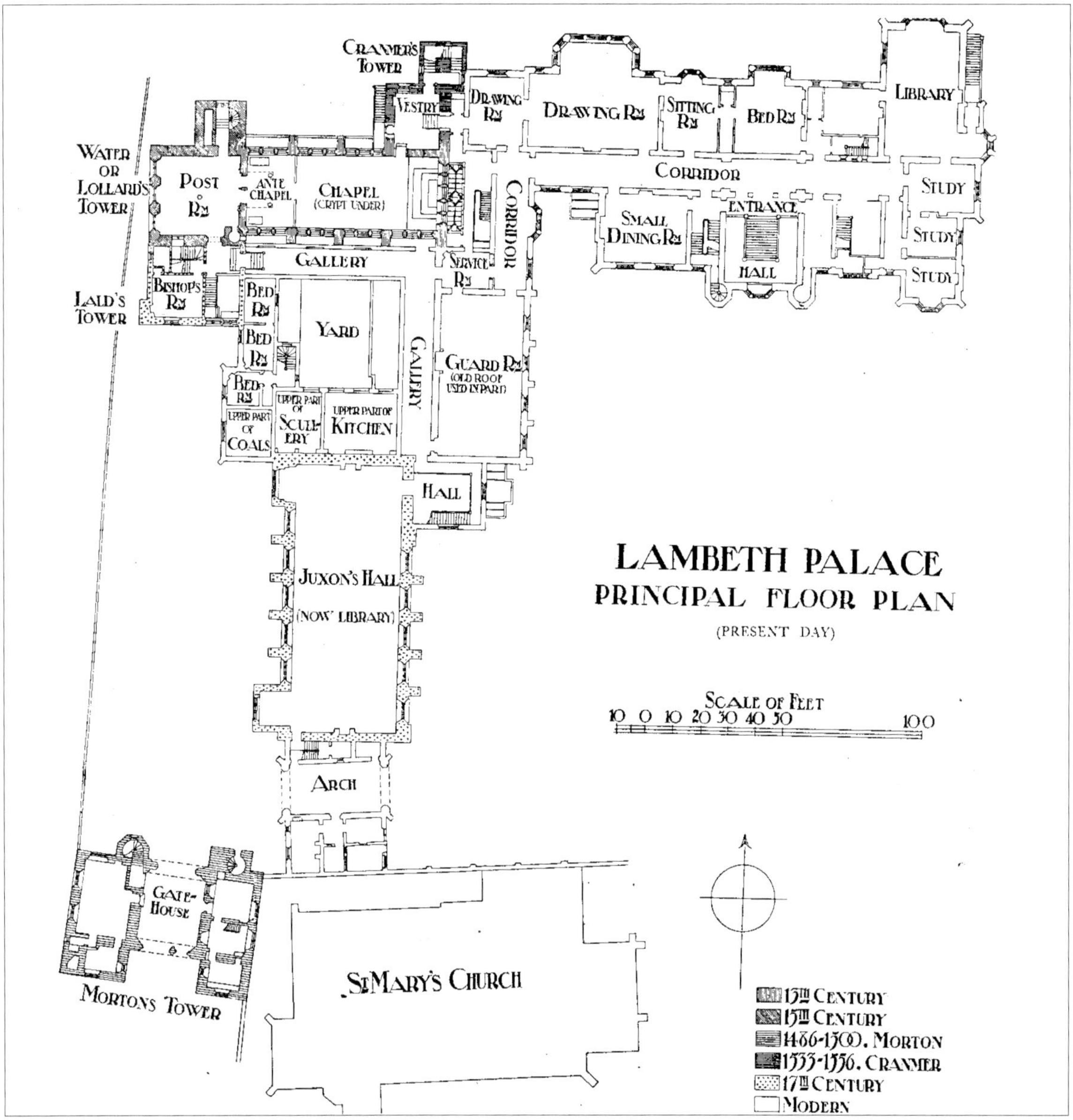

5. *An historical principal floor plan of the present Lambeth Palace, showing the development of the buildings.*

clerks and scholars, some resident for years, strolling in the gardens; of well-dressed stewards and doctors and barge attendants going about their business; of cheeses and fish, hops and corn and wine and bolts of cloth being carried in at the south end off a boat or an iron-wheeled cart; of cooks salting, butchers slaughtering, smiths forging, millers grinding, gardeners clipping, carpenters hammering, and labourers forever digging holes or mixing mortar – for there was always something being built or made, and the kitchen garden to be drained and fertilised.

MURMURINGS OF DISCONTENT

From the end of the thirteenth century, the south gate became important as the place where the dole was distributed. This began with leftovers from the banquets donated to people in need, and was later formalised into a regular dole of bread on Fridays and Sundays, with generous alms on feast days. Vagrants and fugitives joined infirm and aged local people in waiting for the great oak doors to open. The sick always came here to plead for help, for physicians (who understood certain mysteries) were drawn from the religious, and there was no hospital closer than St Thomas's on Bankside.

In the deep midwinter, Christmas celebrations went on for weeks. Within the walls the feasting would seem endless, punctuated only by this twice-weekly distribution for the clamouring maimed or destitute, leprous or mad or lost. In the safety of the Manor House and grounds lived men who wore ermine and sable, richly dyed warm wool and silk and linen and jewels. They spent their days in prayer and intrigue. Outside the gates, paupers in hessian and fustian and rabbit fur shivered and scratched and died in intermittent plagues. Anger slowly mounted.

The dole was not enough. The Church was even more corrupt than the King was greedy. The fourteenth century brought the terrible Black Death with its aftermath of anger and frustration, and in 1381 Archbishop Sudbury, like his predecessor, would meet a ghastly end. He supported the poll tax and resented John Wycliffe's criticisms of papal greed – for the rich revenues of the English church were being shipped back to Rome. The peasants revolted and Archbishop Sudbury was a prime target. The mob failed to find him at Lambeth Manor House and roared onward into the City, where they dragged him from his prayers, beheaded him on Tower Green and stuck his head on a pole.

6. The prison room in the Lollard's Tower, a drawing published in 1791. The artist records that on a chimney in the room 'there are scratches of half sentences, and letters, cut out with a knife by some of the unhappy persons who are supposed to have been confined here.'

John Wycliffe was condemned as a heretic and died a few years later, but his theological and social teachings would live on. Those who shared his views were known as Lollards, and in 1425 Archbishop Chichele, having constructed a tower out of Kentish ragstone near to the Chapel, prudently secured the upper floor as a jail for those of suspect beliefs. The Lollards' Tower stands today, and so does the jail, with a door three inches thick impregnable behind another door, and great iron rings set into walls lined with inch-thick oak boards. Outside, high up, is a tall niche in the wall overlooking the river. This used to contain an image of Thomas à Becket, and a tradition arose later whereby Thames watermen would stand and doff their caps to it as they passed.

8. Henry Chichele, Archbishop of Canterbury.

MORTON'S TOWER

The late-mediaeval addition most familiar today is Morton's Tower, the beautiful brick gatehouse east of Lambeth Bridge. Cardinal Morton

7. The Morton gatehouse at Lambeth Palace c.1896, with St Mary's church to its side.

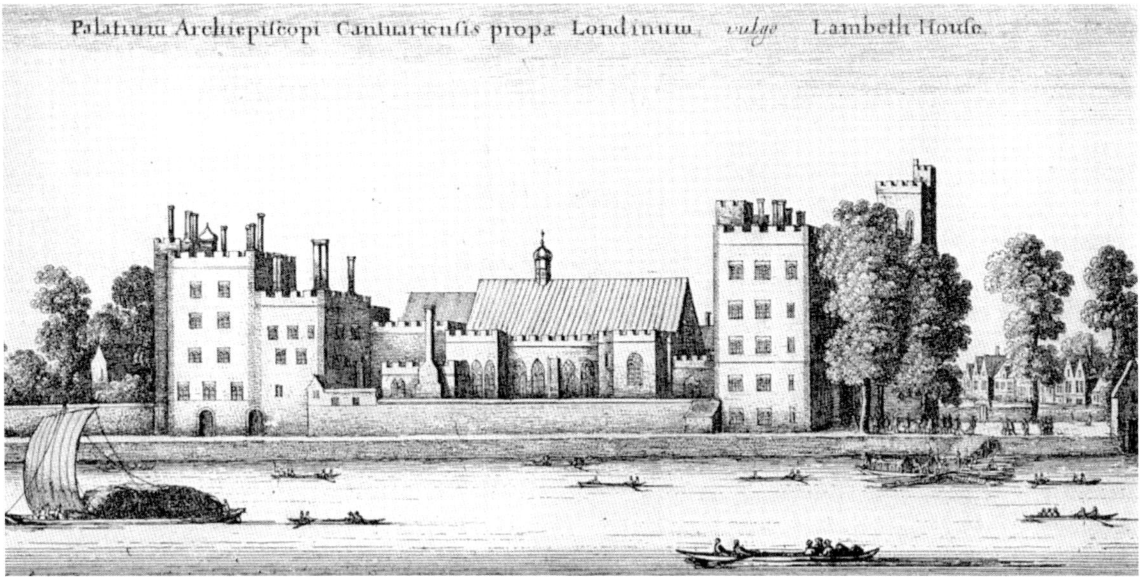

9. Wenceslaus Hollar's river side view of Lambeth 'House' in 1647.

constructed it in the second half of the fifteenth century in place of the existing south gate; the colours of the diapered brickwork, red and blue-black, indicate that they were imported from areas with a high iron content in the soil, perhaps coal-baked at high temperature, rather than dug and made locally – burning Newcastle 'sea coal' was officially prohibited in the London area because it made the air so dirty. There is a room above the entrance which was used as an audience chamber. Here too there was a prison, and two iron rings are still firmly embedded in the wall of a cell on the ground floor of the eastern tower. Lambeth Manor House was, if not yet a fortress, at least a visibly defended seat of power. It was far from being the only ecclesiastical grand house in the London area – there were several dozen of them – but it was towards the end of the middle ages the most magnificent. (Morton himself was an advisor to Henry VII who earned regal gratitude and everyone else's dislike for raising Morton's Fork, a tax to pay for the Wars of the Roses.) There were cloisters and a library behind the Great Hall, the Chapel would soon be provided with a new and more fashionable ceiling, the armoury was secure and well stocked with firearms and swords, and relationships with the Rochester clerics were equable enough. Before the Reformation, Lambeth Manor House and grounds stood as visible evidence of the Pope's firm hold over the English Church and, by extension, its monarch.

LA PLACE

Meanwhile, the Bishops of Rochester may have swapped Lambeth for a few Kent villages, but they did not budge very far, for they had negotiated the right to lease part of the land and right of access to the river. The part occupied by Canterbury was the riverside property we know as Lambeth Palace and gardens today, but extending further north. The Rochester household and seminary were parallel to it on the east side, on what is now Carlisle Place, commanding access to the Stangate ferry road (pretty well where Royal Street is). On Rochester's part of the land there were at first some dilapidated buildings, all that remained of Hubert's collegiate chapel that had been burned down. This would now be developed and extended. The grand house that Rochester built was named La Place. The significance of naming it a 'place' was that it would be the episcopal seat and location for probate and consistory courts, and as such did not have to submit to the Archbishop or pay tithes to the incumbent of St Mary's next door, which was in the diocese of Winchester. Winchester was a wealthy diocese with a Bishop's Palace at Southwark, and in the 1370s it arranged the complete reconstruction of St Mary's ancient parish church. Lambeth was no mean borough, ecclesiastically speaking, and a capacious and prestigious church was called for.

Bishops of Rochester made themselves locally unpopular by trying to restrict access to Stangate, where the jetty belonged to Canterbury. The 'way granted by Archbishop Hubert was in a straight line from the great gate of La Place to Stangate, and continued to be an open passage' but over the years the Rochester Bishops asked tolls from the public and put barriers across the Bishop's Walk, the riverside path which ran outside the Manor House walls from Morton's Tower to Stangate. In the end 'Archbishop Moore, in order to enlarge his garden, inclosed it, by a writ of *quod damnum*, the jury allowing to the public highway a quantity of land in lieu of it.' In other words, Canterbury confiscated access to the Stangate ferry and what we now have is a public right of way along the Westminster Bridge Road. Much of Stangate, the old Roman road to the ferry, was later buried under St Thomas's and the Albert Embankment.

DANGEROUS TIMES

The Bishop of Rochester, whoever he happened to be, never had an easy time in Lambeth, as the following stories illustrate.

In 1326 the middle classes in the City, furious with King Edward II, had offered the crown to Queen Isabel instead; she accepted. None of the bishops, muttering anxiously in the Great Hall at Lambeth, would have this, and they declared that one of them must to go to St Paul's and take control of the mob. But which one? Nobody dared go. Finally the Bishop of Exeter volunteered. Within hours, news reached Lambeth that he had been murdered. At La Place, the Bishop of Rochester made a prudent decision. He called for his horses. But there were no horses; the Archbishop of Canterbury had made a hasty departure, and had taken Rochester's horses along with his own. Rochester had to leave on foot, and he trudged a good thirty miles into Kent before he dared stop.

According to Stow, another Bishop of Rochester made enemies in the late fifteenth century. One day a man appeared at his cook's door, and hung around talking in the kitchen until the cook was otherwise occupied, when he slipped some poison into the gruel. This was being prepared for the bishop's dinner, but the bishop did not eat that day so the servants ate it. Two of them died. The person who had allegedly committed this wicked act was 'boyled alive at Smithfield'.

THE MEDIAEVAL PARISH

St Mary Lambeth, the parish church next to Lambeth Palace, was rebuilt in the late fourteenth century under the auspices of the Bishops of Winchester. On religious festivals, local people would process from it, singing and playing instruments, drinking and wearing garlands, along the Marsh to St Mary Overie at Southwark, which was the mother church of the diocese of Winchester.

The entire population was no more than a few thousand, and it shrank in time of plague, but business was good because strangers constantly passed through from London and the south. The markets and riverside were the commercial focus. People lived and worked along the riverbank from Stangate northwards to what is now Blackfriars Bridge, and in houses along Lambeth Marsh (today's New Cut and Lower Marsh) to Stangate. Along the Marsh there would have been market stalls and street entertainers and inns, often run by women, where ale was brewed. This was the part of Lambeth to which miscreants from the stews of the Borough would eventually gravitate. Southwark and London had vigilant and efficient constables and courts and rules that did not apply in Lambeth, so cutpurses and rapists could flee across St George's Fields (a great wetland occupying most of Lambeth inland from Southwark to Kennington) and for legal and practical reasons evade capture. It was

10. St Mary's church, depicted in the 18th century.

certainly worth evading. Outright criminality did not result in a fine, but in a long list of punishments that ended in death and included such mild chastisement as pulling out the tongue (for slander), branding on the face, and cutting off the 'privie parts' (for counterfeiting).

KENNINGTON

Along the river, from the thirteenth century onwards the marsh was systematically drained and embanked to the best of the villagers' ability, although it remained prone to disastrous floods from time to time (the river flooded six miles inland at Lambeth in 1242). The few people in Kennington remained more dispersed, on the old Anglo-Roman model of isolated farms, than those closer to the river. There were settlements near Kennington Palace and houses dotted along Kennington Lane and on the west side of Newington. A great part of the parish, from Southwark southwards to Kennington, was occupied by St George's Fields, owned and ignored by the Bridge House Estates (an arm of the Corporation of London dating from 1097, today a Trust with responsibility for all the City bridges). By custom and practice St George's Fields were common land, with ponds and streams slowly drying up, and the Neckinger meandering or flooding, depending on the weather.

In the south, people began to cluster in a newer riverside community.

VAUXHALL GETS ITS NAME

In 1207, King John had been essentially blackmailed by the Papal authorities into recognising Stephen Langton as Archbishop at Lambeth. The King therefore had an opponent with a power base across the river from Whitehall and could do nothing about it. However the manor south of Water Lambeth along the riverbank (once the Count of Mortain's estate) was held by the Earl of Devon, who was on King John's side in his ongoing argument with most of his barons. This was some comfort; but then the Earl died, leaving the manor to his widow, Margaret Redvers.

Strategically placed land occupied by a marriageable woman gave King John his opportunity. He ordered her to marry again. Her new husband, she was informed, would be Fulk de Breant. Fulk was a Gascon mercenary, allegedly a murderer and a looter of churches, who had already been rewarded with official posts by the King. 'He being a bastard of mean extraction, and a profligate rogue', Margaret did not want to marry him, but she was in no position to argue. He moved in and built a manor house on her land, at a point convenient to keep a boat – on the river north of where MI6 now stands. Fulk's Hall stood for several centuries, and was the house after which Vauxhall is named.

Margaret had to put up with Fulk the royalist hatchet man as husband and claimant to her property for a good few years yet. King John died in 1216, but his son and heir Henry was only twelve, and Fulk was among the barons who were determined to take advantage of the boy by seizing a fortress and holding onto it. Eight years later when King Henry III was twenty and a force to be reckoned with, Fulk's brother and about a hundred men held a royal retainer hostage in Bedford Castle. Royal forces besieged the castle until the occupiers gave in; all, including Fulk's brother, were hanged. Fulk, who had been behind the whole thing, was pardoned for 'former services to the King and his father' but Margaret Redvers asked King Henry to let her divorce him. She said she had been taken by violence in a time of hostility. So far as we know she got her divorce. The Manor reverted in due course to the Duchy of Cornwall.

WELFARE IN LAMBETH

On the whole, people in Lambeth led healthier lives than those in overcrowded London. Plague was always present to a greater or lesser extent, but epidemics did not take hold as they did in the city. Wise women would pick sage and woodbine, henbane and viper's bugloss and a myriad other herbs from the meadows to cure any malady. While pollution by dirty trades, Newcastle sea-coal and waterborne sewage was rife in London proper in the thirteenth and fourteenth centuries, in Lambeth there was clean air and water and space in which to launder and bleach, make rope and dry timber. Horse-dung and night-soil were collected in the crowded city and carted upstream by barge to fertilise Lambeth land close to the river and provide marketable produce.

So there was also generally something to eat, and usually work and shelter for the able-bodied and honest. Lambeth Manor House, by far the biggest establishment, provided employment for a small community outside its south gate. There must have been opportunities for casual work all the way upstream from Southwark. Sailmakers, ropemakers and boatbuilders, watermen and ferrymen were members of guilds, proud of their skills, which they passed on to their sons; but they would need adult helpers from time to time, just as men were needed to offload goods at the docks. Fulk's Hall attracted other houses, enough to have a wharf beside it. Market gardeners and poulterers and dairymen supplied the food market that thrived along Lambeth Marsh. The warden pears of Lambeth were famous, and surplus crops from the Archbishop's garden were sold. From Surrey and Hampshire arrived more fruit and vegetables and livestock, which were ferried across to Westminster, the Strand and the market outside the Convent Garden, and of course downriver to London.

IMPORTANT RESIDENTS

In Water Lambeth, east of Morton's Tower and the church and across the lane that led to the river, the Archbishop of Canterbury had powerful neighbours: the Howard family, descendants of a younger son of Edward the Confessor, whose head was the Duke of Norfolk, Earl Marshal of England. They owned a considerable acreage of Lambeth close to today's Waterloo Bridge.

Norfolk House – their London home in the Middle Ages – was on a plot which is today occupied by the police HQ between Pratt Street and Old Paradise Street, just along the road from Lambeth Palace. The family had taken up residence late in the 1300s and are said to have contributed to the rebuilding of the parish church. They employed local staff who sometimes, as the Plantagenets faded from view and the Tudors came to power, must have regretted that they'd ever got involved.

Turbulence: 1500 - 1700

In the sixteenth and seventeenth centuries Lambeth was the stage on which events of national importance were played. The effects of Reformation, Revolution, and Restoration would be visible and palpable. They directly affected the daily lives of Lambeth people because at the start of the period so many of them were dependent on clerics and noblemen who struggled, and failed, to retain their wealth and power.

The weather was changing - getting colder. There would be no more vines at Kennington; several times in the next two centuries the Thames would freeze solid from the great multi-piered obstacle of London Bridge right back to Westminster, and the watermen of Lambeth would be reduced to dragging customers in sledges along the ice. At Frost Fairs drums and pipes and squeals of pleasure made a cheerful din on the ice, and torches blazed among stalls gay with streamers; in 1684 there was an ox-roast and a royal fox-hunt, and a printing press was set up on the frozen river to print people's names. You could walk, according to John Evelyn, from Lambeth Stairs across to the horseferry landing at Westminster. With the exception of women's upper chests, nothing of the person, of either sex, remained unclad - everyone, even the poorest, wore layers and layers of fabric to keep out the cold.

But there were consolations, and one of them was alternative local employment. It began with the rise of Lambeth as a place of entertainment: a resort from life's dull care.

THE PARIS GARDEN

Maps of the 1500s either don't include Lambeth at all, or show it only as far south as what we now call Lambeth Palace. People who lived there were socially insignificant, and much land east of Lambeth Marsh was uncultivated. Mapmakers

11. Detail from Visscher's Panorama of London (1616) showing the Bear Pit at Paris Garden.

(who made little pictures of the details) did not waste their energies on delineating Lambeth, but got busy drawing the myriad boats on the river.

But at the far north end of Lambeth was Paris Garden - Bankside - a manor with menace. It was too close to Southwark, that was the trouble; Southwark with its brothels and drunks spilled over into Lambeth's countryside here, so that there were rough sports and vice of a kind uncommon in the rest of the parish.

Crowds, in the sixteenth century, must have been offensive in themselves. Nobody bathed or brushed their teeth, almost everyone wore wool unwashed for years, lice and fleas were rampant and people were not fastidious about where they performed bodily functions. In Paris Garden the bye-laws of Southwark did not apply and nor did those of Lambeth. This was part of its attraction. Legally, Paris Garden was a separate manor, situated (like Lambeth) in Surrey and belonging to Christ Church. It was surrounded by a ditch and occupied land both east and west of where Blackfriars Bridge Road runs now.

In the sixteenth century, Paris Garden contained London's best-known bear-pit. The place was effectively lawless, and customers could easily fall prey to gamblers and thieves. A contemporary picture shows that the bear-pit

12. *The Frost Fair on the Thames in the winter of 1683/4. The view, drawn at Temple Stairs, is from the west looking towards London Bridge.*

was a circular, windowless, tall building, thick-walled at the bottom and narrowing towards the top, like a stumpy version of an early skyscraper. Inside, people stood on scaffolding to watch what was happening below. It was accessible by Paris Garden Stairs or Holy Ghost Stairs from the river, and had once been a playhouse.

The Paris Garden bear-pit collapsed in 1550, when eight people were killed, but was quickly rebuilt. The bears were known by name to the public: 'Harry Hunks' and 'Sackerson' were two of them. Dogs were kept for bear-baiting – both bears and dogs would be tethered to trees in St George's Fields, and brought to the Garden, terrified, to roar and snarl before a grinning crowd. This was in the time of Elizabeth, and it was not long before courtiers became involved. Some kept packs of dogs for bear-baiting, and many dogs were mauled to death. Or, men would gather around a blinded bear, whip it into a frenzy and dodge it for sport. An account written in 1598 describes such a night's entertainment, with nuts and apples, wine and ale, for sale among the crowd and onlookers smoking that new import, tobacco, in long clay pipes. In and around Paris Garden were mummers and jugglers, street entertainers and musicians, as well as beggars and prostitutes.

At least once, a bear escaped; one can only cheer the poor beast's memory. Bear-baiting was just one of many vile amusements. Ponies and monkeys were baited by dogs as well, and bulls, in St George's Fields; and there was cock-fighting in a number of pubs. All these entertainments required a human infrastructure. Everyone from animal keepers to ticket collectors and the managers who hired the acts would eventually settle in Lambeth. They did well when there was money about, but in years when the plague raged they suffered. People stayed away.

BARGE-HOUSES AND INDUSTRY

London and Westminster, connected by the line of noble palaces along the Strand, became more crowded and expensive, and wealthy residents began to look across the river for cheap land to rent. In the 1530s Henry VIII had a barge-house

13. Boat building near the Stangate ferry was still in operation c.1840, when this drawing of Roberts' Boat House was made.

on the river at the Paris Garden end of Lambeth: Barge House Stairs, near the Oxo Tower, mark the site. In Tudor times any significant building on the riverbank had its own wharf, or Stairs. Half a century later, barge-houses – the royal one, John of Gaunt's and others – were being built further upstream towards Lambeth Palace. Lime-burners had started to move to Paris Garden, as well as boilers of bones and dyers, and all the unpleasant industry that London had ejected. The aldermen of London no longer wanted nose-wrinkling, mucky trades on their side of the river and legislated against them, so smoke and stink and dirty water began to pollute Lambeth at the Southwark end. A great sandbank had built up between Paris Garden (Bankside) and the point where Waterloo Bridge now stands. This was further embanked with an earthwork, and people called it the Narrow Wall and could stroll along the top of it. From today's Waterloo Bridge to Stangate (by St Thomas's now) were barge-houses and timber yards.

THE PARISH REORGANISED: THE VESTRY

Around 1500 Lambeth's social and bureaucratic structure was essentially vertical. If you were poor and destitute of family, there was no common pot to dip into: you begged from the rich. It has been said that in hard times of plague or flood or famine four or five thousand people would be waiting for the dole when the great gate opened in Morton's Tower. Yet the population of all Lambeth – including new hamlets like Stockwell and Norwood – was still under ten thousand altogether. A Chantry Commission in the mid-century counted 712 houseling people (householders) so even allowing for dependants, the population was small. Needy people swelled the numbers; they came from far and wide to Lambeth Manor House. It was now a fortress with strong walls and an armoury, an institution separate from the local people.

All over England the Manor, as a bureaucratic structure framing people's lives, was demoted in the next half-century under the Tudors. The Parish, represented by a group of prominent laymen from the community, became the central

14. A detail from the 'Agas' map of c. 1570, showing the Paris Garden area, copied and painted, somewhat inaccurately, in 1749 by Joseph Jones. St Mary's church is centre with Lambeth Palace to its left. Bishop's Walk, on the bank of the Thames, lies along the left edge and the river is just seen in the top corner. Though it is a fairly true copy of the old map, the clock has been added by the artist.

unit of control. Responsibility became collective in a way it had not been under feudal Lords of the Manor. By 1605, a century later, at Lambeth there were fewer mendicants at Morton's Gate and more charitable disbursements noted in the Parish Register, such as 'item payed to George Page he being sick of the plague and confined within his howse.'

In practice, the secular parish of Lambeth was represented by a group of about a dozen churchwardens annually chosen from prominent attenders at St Mary's Lambeth; they met in the vestry, the enrobing-room in the church, so they came, as in other parishes, to be called The Vestry. A middle class and a trading class grew up in the latter half of the 1500s, and the churchwardens were men of substance, successors to those 'burgesses' from London who had supported St Mary's at Domesday. Many Londoners owned land in Lambeth but let it out for market gardening, while others divided their time between the city and the pleasant Lambeth countryside. The churchwardens were usually tradesmen; the local vintner (for many years in the latter part of Elizabeth's reign, Anthony Vaux) or brewer, builder and butcher would generally be among them. One among them was chosen to fill in the registers, which is why Lambeth records of the period are less tidily kept than they were in the Middle Ages. Literacy, beaten mercilessly into children at that time, was haphazardly acquired and spelling consistent only in its inconsistency.

St Mary's was part of the diocese of the Bishop of Winchester. He made a Visitation to the church from time to time, took note of any deterioration in the fabric of the place and looked at the books. Churchwardens could be excommunicated for any malfeasance, and this had secular as well as religious repercussions so they were generally kept on their toes. In any case there was a long tradition of astute vicars at Lambeth; the very first had been chaplain to Thomas à Becket, and although he held the parish as a formality, that was no longer the case with Lambeth vicars. So no lay member who was not of good reputation would be allowed to have any authority.

PARISH INCOME AND HOKETIDE

Lambeth's parish records date back to 1504. They show that there was a poor box at St Mary's from the 1530s onwards. Donations for the alms chest were collected every month from wealthy citizens, and the churchwardens distributed poor relief when necessary. They also noted down fees received from parishioners – extra for baptising a child born out of wedlock – and

15. The old 'Pedlar Window' in the church of St Mary Lambeth.

fines: 'received of some that were tipling in time of divine service', for instance. The parish coffers took in fees for tolling bells, for hire of the hearse cloth, for selling candles, annual payments for pews ... Parishioners were expected to contribute according to their evident wealth; thus the burial of 'a waterman's child' would cost less than the 'beryall of My lady of Norfolke's gentlewoman'. There were also processions, with streamers and garlands and music, to St Mary Overie, the cathedral at Southwark, on religious festivals. Every parishioner was expected to take part and the parish paid a fee, sometimes called smoke money.

Demands such as these could be enforced by the Bishop if necessary, at a consistory court, even (from 1589) upon an absentee landlord.

Lambeth was among the richest and most important parishes in the country. It was fortunate in that when a subscription was required, the Archbishop of Canterbury and Lord Burgh or the Duke of Norfolk or the Leighs of Stockwell could generally be relied upon to head the list of contributors. Many baronets attended the Church, and the Leigh and Norfolk chapels had been built within it in the 1520s. There were several altars dedicated to different saints – it was common at the time to have more than one altar – and the church owned a great deal of plate. It owned Pedlar's Acre, a big tract of grazing land on the South Bank. (Lambeth parishioners had been told that it was left to the parish in gratitude by a passing pedlar. His image was commemorated in stained glass in the Church – there is a modern depiction of him in stained glass there now.) It received income from its land and buildings, such as Sir John Argall's rent for his house, and from herds that it owned, and it held other charitable endowments which paid for maintenance of certain roads and bridges and the upkeep of almshouses.

There was also the annual revenue from Hoketide. Hoketide was rapidly becoming unmanageable, at any rate by the churchwardens of Lambeth. Hoketide was a leftover from the Middle Ages which would no longer do in the new, vaguely humanist and more po-faced atmosphere of the 1500s. It had always taken place on the Monday and Tuesday after the second Sunday after Easter. On the Monday, men trapped women, tied them up and refused to release them unless a forfeit was paid. In theory, the forfeit was money for the church; in practice, it was other favours. But the highlight was Binding Tuesday, when the women got their revenge in kind. And Hoketide became a way for bills to be paid, and women had a tendency to go Too Far, and none of these people were married to each other (in fact most were married to other people) and everyone got disgracefully drunk. The women were what made it notorious: their immodesty, and the way they took advantage of their single day of power.

Hoketide went on in Lambeth, according to the churchwardens' accounts, well into the sixteenth century, by which time it had been stopped in most other places. Lambeth's excuse was that it had begun as a celebration of the death of Hardicanute, the horrid Dane. But it was all over in Lambeth by the Reformation, the parish having decided it made more trouble than money.

PARISH EXPENSES

The Bishop ordered what was required by the Church – a new bell, at least once in the sixteenth century, besides 'a new makynge of ye clocke and ye dyalle' – and if there was no other source of revenue the parish paid; they held a 'benyvolence' to raise money for 'ye clocke'. On top of immediate needs (candles and communion wine, cleaning, gravedigging, upkeep of the churchyard, repainting and 'church ornaments') came parish disbursements and obligations like 'paid to the sexton for tolling the bell when a corpse came through the town, and to him that brought word of the corpse', hirings and purchases of all kinds. There were good works, although usually the church was paid for services such as burying 'a corpse brought over the water' or 'Diana Posthuma Theaber, buried in the night, ground knell, and black cloth'.

In a parish with many wealthy parishioners like Lambeth, it was of course argued that parish demands were less of a burden than elsewhere. The rich contributed massively, and the local tradesmen benefited, since so many goods and services were bought from them.

The churchwardens were empowered to oblige local men into road building and maintenance, each providing tools, beasts of burden and carts according to his ability. If a man failed to help, he had to pay a fine or find a substitute. The parish was responsible for the roads that went through it and bridges, too; Lambeth was a big parish. A 'bridge' meant jetties and probably stairs, such as the several landing places along the river, as well as the hundreds of little bridges and culverts over Lambeth's streams and ditches. London Bridge, in Southwark, was still the only Thames bridge, but Cox's Bridge in Vauxhall over the Effra had three arches and took a lot of traffic, as it stood at the junction where the Kingston Road (Kennington Lane) converged with Fore Street. What was later called Cuper's Bridge, over the Neckinger where Waterloo Bridge now stands, must have been busy enough to require upkeep; and watercourses up to three metres wide and a metre deep ran under the Marsh, and the Effra was bridged as it coursed through Brixton. Many roads would have had ditches and little culverts between the houses and the cart-track.

The churchwardens had to chivy a local militia, or 'trained band', into action, and arm it. Those men who were liable to be called up had to be provided with a uniform and trained by the parish. The present-day Black Prince Road used to be called Lambeth Butts, and Butts usually meant a plank-covered earthwork used as target practice, but the parish records don't record archery there. They show that two or three fellows would regularly be sent off to St George's Fields for a day or to Croydon for three days in order to drill and shoot, perhaps in a larger company of men drawn from elsewhere. Travel and subsistence must be paid for and, later on, firearms were kept by the parish for use in an emergency. The parish was also responsible for vermin control – rat-catching and otter-trapping and netting of cormorants and crows; for employing a constable; and for conveying committed offenders to jail.

Further, it was the churchwardens' duty to keep the population informed of what they were and were not allowed to do. Regal proclamations and new statutes must be copied out and nailed up on the parish door or hung in a frame inside. It seems unlikely that many people saw or cared about these notices. Even in the mid sixteenth-century, church attendance was far from universal, and worthy public information probably never got south of Stockwell. Besides, humble people had to find someone to read things out to them, which could mean waiting for the Vicar to turn up.

CHURCHWARDENS' PERKS

The civic duties of a churchwarden increased until the middle of the seventeenth century. Consolation came in two forms. One was contracts. The accounts include scores of notes like 'item for 11 gallons and a quart of wine for ye communion ye 9 of May.' Anthony Vaux the vintner supplied it. (In 1592: 'item paid to Mr Vause for wine for the whole year £53 and 8 pence.' There were at least five variants of the way he spelled his name.)

The baker (Mr Wilson) who provided communion bread was also a churchwarden, as might be the chandler with his candles, the silk merchant who provided vestments and so on. In other parishes as the years passed, significant sums were invested in getting the plum job of churchwarden.

The second consolation for parish responsibilities was feasting. Churchwardens were required to beat (mark) the bounds of the parish a couple of times a year, and they made a day of it in Lambeth, because the long walk to the Vicar's Oak in Norwood required many pauses for refreshment and a slap-up meal on their return. 'Item for a drinking for certaine honest men of ye parishe when we went our perambulacion to vicar's oke' would be entered in the records. All year round, every opportunity was taken for a celebration: 'item laid out at ye kinges head when we were chosen new churchwardens' was followed by 'item for our dinner their *[sic]* ye same time'.

LAMBETH AND THE REFORMATION

'Who is there among Englishmen who does not profess to know all and sundry matters concerning the Reformation?' asked the Reverend H. Bedford Pym, MA, introducing his lantern slide lecture on Lambeth Palace in 1898.

'I wish', might be the response of a present-day Archbishop. History is no longer taught in terms of Kings and Queens, and yet the Middle Ages were driven by powerful people, their greed for money, their jostling for position, their superstitions and terror of retribution, divine and otherwise. Many of us have the haziest idea of what the Reformation was, and of the thousands of present-day Lambeth inhabitants educated abroad, most have probably never heard of it.

It made a difference, though, to the place where they live. One difference was in the way Lambeth looked and the sort of people who lived there. Because Archbishop Cranmer supported the King, Canterbury's lands in Lambeth were not confiscated. On the north side of the river, lands belonging to the great monastic orders and the convents would be seized and in due course sold freehold or awarded to favourites; so in the next century the Dukes of Bedford would be in a position to commission architects including Inigo Jones to start laying out Covent Garden and Bloomsbury, and London's terraces and garden squares and shopping arcades would spread across the meadows. Over in Lambeth, which was unsatisfactory building land anyway, nothing of the kind took place.

THE HOWARDS OF NORFOLK HOUSE

Henry VIII knew Lambeth well – at least, he knew its religious and aristocratic centres of power. One was at Norfolk House, opposite St Mary's Church; it was the London home of the Howards, who with the Percys of Northumberland were England's leading Catholics after the Reformation.

Henry VIII took a mistress and two wives from Norfolk House, and beheaded both the wives. As the sixteenth century progressed his terrifying presence must have felt much too close for comfort, glowering, as he was, at Lambeth Palace and Norfolk House from Whitehall and his palace at Chelsea.

By the late 1520s, no senior churchman could keep his head unless he did what he was told. The king wanted a male heir. He wanted the Pope to grant him a divorce from Katherine of Aragon (she who had stayed at Kennington, and had been his brother Arthur's widow). He would then marry Anne Boleyn, whose sister had once been his mistress; Anne was an ambitious Howard cousin. The Pope refused to grant the divorce and when Henry married Anne in 1533, the King was excommunicated. With the help of Thomas Cromwell, Henry promptly took over the English Church and most of its estates and property.

Within three years duplicitous Anne Boleyn was kneeling in the crypt of the chapel at Lambeth, pleading with Archbishop Cranmer to have her sentence commuted from burning at the stake to decapitation.

At La Place, the Rochester clerics had other things on their mind. They probably wouldn't have been too bothered by Anne Boleyn's ghastly fate anyway, since her father had once shot a playful cannonball across the river and it crashed through the Bishop's study window while he was sitting there, but now something much worse had happened: they had been thrown out of La Place after the Bishop of Rochester refused to take the Oath of Supremacy. Like Sir Thomas More, he just couldn't convince himself that the king was God's representative on Earth; and like Sir Thomas More, he was executed. His clergymen scuttled off to Southwark, where they had to pay rent to the diocese of Winchester. La Place was conveyed to the Bishop of Carlisle, like Cranmer a lackey of the King. He already had a palace in the Strand, but he let that out and came to live in Lambeth. La Place - on what is now Carlisle Lane - became Carlisle House.

Once the monasteries were dissolved and looted Henry turned his attention to the churches. They were all too Popish. The incense, candles, superstitious images and stained glass must go. Vestries were responsible for this, and at Lambeth they made haste to clear out St Mary's.

By the 1540s the King was ill and obese and prematurely aged, and after a couple more marriages and the birth of his frail son Edward, the Howard family, scheming for power, correctly judged him ready for another bride. There was a quite a crowd of young cousins living in rambling old Norfolk House, preparing for their turn at court; all the Duke of Norfolk had to do was select the prettiest and instruct her in how to behave. So Archbishop Stephen Gardiner was encouraged to invite Henry to Lambeth Manor House to dine, and tripping daintily across the lane to join them came Anne Boleyn's nineteen-year-old cousin Katherine. The charming and well-connected local girl was a niece of the Duke of Norfolk. Her mother was Joyce née Culpeper, who had been, before marrying into the Howards, the widow of Ralph Leigh, Lord of the Manor of Stockwell and Under-Sheriff of London.

16. Carlisle House, formerly La Place.

The King found her irresistible. Unfortunately for both of them, Katherine Howard was not the virtuous maiden of Henry's fond imaginings. The Duchess, her step-grandmother, preferred to ignore the creaks and rustles and suppressed laughter from the dark dormitories and corridors of her mansion, but it was common knowledge that young Francis Dereham had been Katherine's lover for some time. The Howard elders were not about to tell Henry this, and as they had planned, he whisked the girl off to Whitehall and married her.

The new Queen's amorous skills did wonders for the King's temper, but she caused talk. She flirted openly with Thomas Culpeper, a distant cousin, at court and took Francis Dereham to be her secretary. Within two years she met her downfall. Humiliated and broken-hearted, Henry had Katherine beheaded along with many of her circle from Norfolk House.

The Duchess survived, and returned to Lambeth after a short incarceration in the Tower. So did the Duke, who hastened to restore his reputation by victories abroad. Two royal brides sacrificed on the altar of ambition spelled disaster for him nonetheless, personally if not emotionally. Henry became more than ever convinced that the Howards were plotting to rule from behind the throne after his death. He ordered the Duke's execution, but died the night before the sentence was due to be carried out.

The Duke (and later his son) were not beheaded until the reign of Elizabeth I, when much of their large estate at the Lambeth end of today's Waterloo Bridge was broken up and sold.

With the Duke's execution, the Norfolks lost their title and for several generations were mere Earls of Arundel. In the next century the family would live at Arundel House in the Strand rather than at Lambeth. Norfolk House had unpleasant connotations.

A REVERSAL: QUEEN MARY

Edward, the frail child king, reigned only from 1547 to 1553. Upon his death Mary Tudor - Henry VIII's only child with Katherine of Aragon - became Queen, and her shadow fell over Lambeth Palace. Archbishop Cranmer, who had allowed her father to divorce her mother, was burned at the stake. Since Mary Tudor disliked all that Henry had stood for, the parishioners of Lambeth, like others up and down the country, had to replace - at their own expense - all the 'superstitious images' and chalices, communion cups, ornate candelabra and hangings and vestments, special service books and bibles and other evidences of Catholicism that they had sold off in the previous decades.

There was no shirking this; St Mary's was on the doorstep of Cardinal Pole, the new Archbishop of Canterbury, and Cardinal Pole was among the Queen's closest friends and her cousin, to boot. She and her husband, Philip of Spain, had awarded Pole a patent to retain a retinue of one hundred personal servants at Lambeth - Cranmer had had only sixty. By around 1555 the St Mary's church expenses had rocketed. Among other things, every time the Queen arrived by barge to confer with the Cardinal, or to convey him in her barge to Greenwich (a fairly frequent occurrence) the parishioners had to pay bell-ringers to ring out chimes of welcome and farewell upon her departure. Fortunately, prominent residents like the Howards footed most of the bill.

UNDER QUEEN ELIZABETH

To the relief of the hard-pressed Vestry, Queen Elizabeth took over in 1559 on the death of Mary, and the expense of church adornment subsided once more. Elizabeth loathed religious extremists and would have no Popery and no Puritanism, either. If the Queen believed in anything, it was the doctrine of Two Bodies - that while the monarch's own body was human in its frailty, at her Coronation she had become possessed of another non-corporeal body, eternal and representing God's will on earth. Accordingly England became Protestant under the Queen. Parish churches must become Protestant and Catholics must attend or be fined for recusancy. No-one was ever entirely convinced about the Howards' conversion, but most local Catholic families assured everyone of their Protestantism and continued to attend services at St Mary's.

Elizabeth understood the importance of her own personal adornment to creating the magical image of the Faerie Queene. She spent a fortune on jewels and finery, although she rarely paid for a meal - she was entertained everywhere she went. The passing of her gaily decorated barge or her arrival ashore were always accompanied by a peal of bells from Lambeth. 'Item for ye ringers when ye queen removed from Whitehall to Greenwich the last of april' and 'item for ringing when ye queen dined at Stockwell when she removed from Greenwich to Richmount' are typical entries in the parish record of the 1580s.

Despite the Armada's defeat in 1588 and the execution of Mary Queen of Scots, the realm did not feel safe from invasion. In 1599 we find (and the misspellings are worse than ever now) 'item paid to the sodyears the 12th 13th and 14th dayes of awguste when the weare trayned in Saynt gorges fellde' and then another payment 'when they were carged *[sic]* in to saint gorges felld upon payn of dethe'. Not everyone supported the Queen's determination to defend the realm; some local people, as we shall see, would have welcomed an invasion.

A BLOODTHIRSTY AGE: JUSTICES OF THE PEACE

Before Henry VIII died in 1547, some of the parish's more taxing duties had been taken over by local Justices. It is worth remembering what ordinary Justices of the Peace could do. Their advisory manual of 1578 explains that common punishments are corporal, pecuniary, and infamous.

Corporal is either 'capital (hanging, burning, boyling, or pressing) or otherwise; cutting off hands or ears, burning or marking hand or face, imprisoning, whipping, stocking, stoning, setting on the pillorie or cucking stool.' Hangings and burnings were common. In Lambeth, they took place at Kennington, at the gallows site now beneath the altar of St Mark's Church.

Pecuniary punishment could be a fine, or it could mean forfeiture of one's office, goods or land. Villainous or 'infamous' punishment meant that 'their oaths shall not be of any credit after', that everything the miscreant owned was forfeit to the Crown, 'and that they be imprisoned and never allowed to approach the court.' This, for instance, was the punishment for perjury.

All these punishments are severe by our lights and the most serious of them seem barbaric. For treason, the punishment was death by partial hanging, followed by castration, disembowelling and quartering.

So we turn to the plot against the Crown that would be implemented, from a base in Lambeth, after the accession of King James I in 1603.

THE CROWN THREATENED

Near midnight on November 4th, 1605, Guy Fawkes was captured in the vaults beneath the House of Lords. He was guarding three dozen barrels of gunpowder with which he intended to blow the King and aristocracy sky-high when they gathered the following day. The gunpowder had previously been stored at Robert Catesby's lodgings at Lambeth, and stealthily transported across the river by boat to a house in Whitehall rented by Catesby's well-connected friend Thomas Percy; thence to the House of Lords.

17. The house on the Lambeth riverside used by Robert Catesby during the Gunpowder Plot.

The Catesby family seat was in Northamptonshire. A 'Mr Cattesbe' gave generously to the cost of ye clocke and ye dyalle at St Mary's Church as early as 1584 so perhaps the family (that is, Catesby's father Sir William) had kept a town house in Lambeth for some time. Once Robert Catesby, Thomas Percy, and Catesby's friend Robert Keyes were implicated, all eyes turned to the house itself. It proved to be a handsome dwelling of classical proportions with a tall arched door on the riverside, from which steps swept down to a point, at high tide, just above the waterline. It was in Upper Fore Street – Fore Street was the riverside road that straggled from Water Lambeth south to Vauxhall.

Thomas Wintour, another of the thirteen conspirators, tells us the role it played. He had brought Guy Fawkes, a mercenary and militant Catholic, to Mr Catesby's Lambeth lodging from Dunkirk in the Spring of 1604. They

> ...came both in one passage to Greenwich, near which place we took a pair of oars, and so came up to London, and came to Mr Catesby whom we found in his lodging....Up came Mr Thomas Percy. The first word he spake (after he came into our company) was Shall we always, Gentlemen, talk and never do anything? Mr Catesby took him aside and had speech about somewhat to be done, so as first we might all take an oath of secrecy, which we resolved within two or three days to do... *Confession of Thomas Wintour, 1605*

Percy, an angry young man, was related to the Duke of Northumberland. Catesby was the main financial backer. This included paying rent for a house Thomas Percy would take in Whitehall, where the gunpowder could be stored and Guy Fawkes retained as his man, 'Johnson'.

Rolling three dozen barrels of gunpowder, not to mention 'a thousand of billets and five hundred of faggots' into a house next door to Parliament might arouse suspicion, however.

> Before this time also it was thought convenient to have a house that might answer to Mr Percy's, where we might make provision of powder and wood for the mine which, being there made ready, should in a night be conveyed by boat to the house by the Parliament because we were loth to foil that with often going in and out. There was none that we could devise so fit as Lambeth where Mr Catesby often lay, and to be keeper thereof, by Mr Catesby's choice, we received into the number Keyes, as a trusty honest man.
> *Confession of Thomas Wintour, 1605*

Lambeth answered perfectly; barrels of gunpowder were delivered to the house in Upper Fore Street. Under cover of darkness, they were then rowed across the inky river in 1604 and again in 1605, a few weeks before the discovery.

Until it was demolished and rebuilt in 1635, Catesby's was locally known as Guy Fawkes' House. The conspirators themselves had long departed this life. Catesby and Percy died fighting on 8th November. Guy Fawkes, despairing and knowing the horrors that lay ahead, made matters worse for himself by his defiance in the presence of the king. He suffered crippling tortures before he and the surviving captives were executed with all the savagery the law could muster.

ARABELLA STUART AT VAUX HALL

King James I was ever watchful for claimants to the throne, and Lady Arabella (correctly Arbella) Stuart was one of them. She was a descendant of Henry VIII's older sister, and like James I himself, she was Scottish. Early in James's reign, his spies discovered a plot, financed by Spain, to remove the king and put her on the throne. She was captured and held under house arrest at Vaux Hall in the custody of Sir Thomas Parrie, who held the house in copyhold from the King. At some point Lady Arabella formed a liaison with William Seymour, whose lineage also gave him a claim to the throne. They were refused permission to marry, and Seymour was held at the Tower of London.

At this late date, Vaux Hall (on the land formerly occupied by Fulk de Breant) must have been a pleasant enough house for a gentlewoman to inhabit. It was 'a handsome tenement' owned by the crown and described not long afterwards as 'a fair dwelling-house strongly built of 19 feet square'. Perhaps Lady Arabella took advantage, during a stroll at dusk in the garden, of its proximity to the river. Anyhow, she escaped on 3rd June 1611, and Seymour fled the Tower. By prior arrangement they both made their way to Calais. He arrived safely but she was seized on English soil and taken to the Tower, where she died four years later at the age of 40. She is buried with other Stuarts in Westminster Abbey.

LAMBETH, THE COURT AND THE INTELLIGENTSIA

Between 1590 and 1700 the northern end of the parish was became increasingly industrialised along the river; the more so after the Great Fire of 1666, for it is said that much of the rubble from the Fire and soil excavated when St Paul's was built was loaded onto barges and dumped near Narrow Wall, where the bulked-out embankment was ideal for timber yards and small industries.

At the same time the Vauxhall and South Lambeth end became – for the first (and so far the last) time in its history – fashionable. Just as Hampstead gained immeasurably from an influx of refugees from central Europe in the mid-twentieth century, so, in the years between Elizabeth's accession and the Commonwealth, did the rural part of Lambeth, with its small incursion of radical Dutchmen, became both modish and sought-after as a hotbed of ideas and advanced scientific thought. This was not simply because of the new immigrants; other wealthy parishioners had royal and city connections. Sir Robert Hatton, of the family of Sir Christopher who had been Elizabeth's Chancellor, had a home in Lambeth and several of his children were baptised at St Mary's. Various Lord Mayors and Sheriffs attended the church. Sir Guilford Slingsbie, Comptroller of the Navy under James I, is frequently mentioned in the parish records.

South Lambeth was charming and fertile and far enough away from Westminster to feel like the countryside (and Pimlico, then called Tothill Fields, was a bog).

SIR NOEL CARON

Sir Noel Caron knew everybody and never made enemies. His talent lay in connecting together people from different walks of life. He was an emissary from Flanders and supporter of the House of Orange, and was already over sixty when he arrived at the court of Queen Elizabeth in 1592 to try and persuade her to claim sovereignty of his country, in defiance of Spanish invaders. She followed her usual wait-and-see policy, but was charmed by this elderly gallant; they were much of an age. And since he was from an occupied country, without an Embassy, she awarded him an estate for his own private use at South Lambeth.

18. A view of Caron's house at Vauxhall, c.1800. Watercolour, artist unknown.

He was delighted with it, and spent ten years building an imposing mansion with two big wings connected by a hall, roughly where the Travis Perkins' warehouse now stands. The convention was to build in the shape of a letter E, as a compliment to the Queen. Above the front door was inscribed '*omne solum est forti patria*' (self-reliance is the strength of the nation). The house was probably built with stone quoins at the corners, in the convention of the time, but mostly out of brick; clay for the yellowish bricks of this area could well have been dug on Caron Park where Claylands Road stands now.

The grounds near the house were laid out as gardens and orchards. The further reaches of the estate were a deer park that stretched all the way to Kennington. This had been hunting country since the heyday of Kennington Palace in the Middle Ages.

By 1607, when King James I gave him a knighthood, the grounds close to Caron House

19. Claylands, a house built on the former clay lands near Caron's home. This illustration, taken from Brayley's History of Surrey *(1841), was made when the house was owned by the Fentiman family, from whom Fentiman Road is named.*

20. Caron's Almshouses c.1800. Watercolour, artist unknown.

were already so well cultivated that Sir Noel was able to send gifts of fruit to friends like Robert Cecil, first Earl of Salisbury, with a note that said how delighted he was to have such a wonderfully fertile estate in which to grow things.

Caron House became the unofficial social centre for visiting Dutch diplomats like Constantin Huyghens, father of Constantin the artist and Christiaan the famous astronomer and mathematician, and London's Dutch and Flemish merchants. There was always a chance of being presented to the King at Lambeth, for James I loved to arrive in his carriage with his young sons Henry and Charles and a caravanserai of courtiers, feast on Dutch cherries from the garden and stroll up and down Sir Noel's picture gallery meeting interesting guests.

Unlike his predecessor Elizabeth, James I had both a family and a young friend. Until about 1614 Robert Carr, the Earl of Somerset, was his favourite. But Somerset married a Howard, and he and his wife were despatched to the Tower as punishment for murder. The King's passion by 1615 was for handsome George Villiers. Villiers, who proved a clever politician, property developer, and cunning all-round manipulator, accompanied King James on many a visit to Lambeth. He was in due course made the Duke of Buckingham; and his connections to Lambeth would include John Tradescant, the famous botanist.

Sir Noel Caron died in 1624 in his nineties, still sharp-witted and by then the official Dutch Ambassador. His Dutch servants and friends had attended St Mary's and subscribed to the parish funds over the years, and Sir Noel himself was much loved and respected locally, having in his lifetime been a generous benefactor to the church and to the poor of the parish. He had seen Lambeth change from a country place to a suburb of London.

When he died he endowed almshouses for 'seven poor but honest women' aged 60 and over. The almshouses were to be built on his own land and financially supported by the occupant of his house.

It seems that as an alien he was unable to dispose of the property he held on lease, so most of it reverted to the Duchy of Cornwall. Caron House was largely demolished by the end of the seventeenth century, but Caron's endowment persisted. In 1853 the original almshouses were pulled down and others reconstructed in Fentiman Road; they are still there today, serving their original purpose.

JOHN TRADESCANT THE ELDER

The Tradescants, father and son, fortified Lambeth's reputation as a resort of the widely travelled and cultivated man of the Renaissance. It is likely that as a young man John Tradescant was a gardener, probably head gardener, to Sir Noel Caron. Certainly in 1607, the year when Sir Noel was knighted, Tradescant felt secure enough financially to get married and start a family. Many years later he was said to have been of Dutch origin himself, although records indicate that he came from a humble family that had lived in Suffolk for centuries. He had only basic education but huge curiosity about the world around him, a natural capacity to observe and learn and a talent for horticulture. (He was first to import the spiderwort *tradescantia* that would sprout relentlessly from macramé baskets in every kitchen in London in the 1970s.)

The earliest known record of his professional life is as head gardener to Robert Cecil's extravagant redevelopment of Hatfield House in 1609. Cecil, the Earl of Salisbury, was about to invest large sums in the grounds, so he would not have commissioned anyone but an expert, and for this reason it is fair to speculate that the Caron gardens at Lambeth are where Tradescant built his reputation. The Earl despatched Tradescant on a glorious buying spree which took him through the plant markets of Holland and Paris. From the Dutch towns he sent back plants tulips, anemones, and other bulbs, walnut and fruit trees. In Paris he met Jean Robin, the great plantsman of the Jardin des Plantes whose name is perpetuated in the robinia tree. Among cartloads of wonders Tradescant brought back orange and pomegranate and oleander, 'one fyg

21. The Tradescant monument in St Mary's churchyard, together with portraits of the two Tradescants copied from Hollar's depictions.

tree in a pot by it Selfe bearying 3 times a yeare', pears, plums, cherries and 'one pot of gilliflowers - cost nothing.'

By 1620 he had worked for the second Earl of Salisbury at Salisbury House in the Strand; and for Lord Wotton at Canterbury, he had travelled to Russia and found mandrake, garlic and wild pomegranates, roses and berries the like of which no-one in England had ever seen.

In 1621 came another connection with Lambeth, for he was allowed to sail on Sir Robert Mansell's great expedition of twenty ships against the Algiers pirates. Arab pirates had for some time been raiding villages in the west of England and Ireland and kidnapping local people for sale as slaves in the markets of North Africa. They must be taught a lesson. Admiral Mansell was not just a sailor. He was, as we shall find, an early and astute capitalist strongly connected to the Vauxhall glass industry; he was a leading investor in the Virginia Company. Tradescant, as Lord Wotton's representative in the weeks at sea, would have known Sir Robert Mansell - it may have been at his prompting that he put money into Virginia himself. His main task was to gather plants and in this he succeeded admirably. He brought back the Algiers apricot and many other exotic trees. The mere fact of getting them back was astonishing; he had to wrap them tenderly against weeks at sea and pack nuts and seeds in barrels of sand. For pressed flowers, he devised a special mixture of glue with isinglass and claret.

To the surprise of English horticulturalists, these plants could grow here. It was as though they had believed that some plants were English, and others Turkish or Algerian; the idea that most, if correctly husbanded, could be raised far from their native habitat, was wondrous in itself. As the papal grip on English thought slackened to insignificance, people dared to wonder, and enquire, and theorise, and experiment, without

22. The Tradescant house in South Lambeth Road adjoined a house later taken by Elias Ashmole.

fear; the minds of men like Tradescant were liberated.

Two years later Tradescant was working for George Villiers, first Duke of Buckingham. This was an age of – not exactly nepotism, not exactly corruption, but certainly an age in which courtiers were expected to exploit their position for financial gain. Villiers, the king's favourite, had risen to be one of the most influential men in the kingdom. He took Tradescant with him to Paris when he and young Prince Charles travelled there to negotiate for the hand of Princess Henrietta Maria de Bourbon. Villiers had obtained several estates in exchange for money and titles, and Tradescant brought back scores of plants to adorn their gardens.

In 1628, George Villiers, Duke of Buckingham was stabbed to death at Portsmouth. Tradescant was suddenly lacking an employer. In the brief interlude before he took up his next, and grandest, project, he took a lease of a house and grounds in Lambeth for his wife and family. The house was a fine three-storeyed building on land that had once belonged to Sir Noel Caron, and is now occupied by numbers 113 to 119 South Lambeth Road. The gardens extended 300 feet from the street and widened out to include what is now Meadow Place. These he stocked with trees and plants he had bought and been given on his travels. At the end of the garden were two acres of orchard, and in time he also bought the leases of a further twenty-one acres of meadow land and several houses in Vauxhall and South Lambeth.

He and his family welcomed visitors to their house. Tradescant was able to escort them around not only his gardens, but his collection of 'curiosities'. A curiosity about curiosities – wondrous artefacts from unknown lands – was the sign of an educated gentleman, someone willing to take a scientific and curatorial interest in the great world; Buckingham himself collected curiosities. Tradescant owned beautiful and strange things of all kinds, from coins and a twelfth-century bestiary to stuffed animals and snakes. According to Dr Ducarel, the great librarian at Lambeth Palace, writing in the 1770s, 'there is reason to think his museum was frequently visited by persons of rank, who became benefactors thereto: among these were King Charles the First (to whom he was gardener), Henrietta Maria his Queen, Archbishop Laud, George Duke of Buckingham, Robert and William Cecil, Earls of Salisbury, and many other persons of distinction.'

In 1625, Prince Henry the older son having predeceased his father, Prince Charles became King Charles I, and would be John Tradescant's employer from 1630. Tradescant became head gardener at Oatlands, near Weybridge, a palace long ago destroyed and now almost forgotten. There he worked with the same enthusiasm as ever. Much to his delight, his life was crowned with academic recognition; he was given a doctorate at Cambridge in 1637. The following year he died, and was buried in Lambeth churchyard.

CIVIL WAR AND LAMBETH HOUSE

By the third decade of the century it seemed to many a jaundiced eye that Parliaments would forever be called into existence largely in order to vote for funds that would enable Royalty to carry on waging war and claiming the spoils for themselves. Charles I was particularly unpopular. He seemed to be both greedy and possibly Papist. Various factions, including the rising merchant class and the militantly Protestant Puritans, had had enough, and decided that the long run of hereditary rulers should be brought to an end before England went the way of Europe, with its overweening monarchs and downtrodden peasantry.

In history books, the Civil War – that is, outright fighting between Parliamentarians and Royalists – takes place between 1642 and 1649. But for Archbishop Laud at Lambeth House, as he called the old Manor House, the revolution began when soldiers broke down the door to the Chapel and desecrated the organ as early as 1624. That was the year when Prince Charles announced his unpopular marriage to the French Catholic Henrietta Maria. When he became King the following year, many of his

23. Archbishop William Laud.

courtiers and ministers of government were crypto-Catholics. Throughout his reign, rebellious soldiers set fire to churches. And while Archbishop Laud was an avowed Protestant, he was authoritarian, powerful and hated as the King's man. Nor was he popular with the Lambeth Vestry, which in 1627 demanded that he contribute towards paving the highway from Lambeth to Newington Butts. He was too mean.

Instead he spent his money on a tower in the grounds of Lambeth House. Laud's Tower was a sturdy edifice to rival the Lollards' Tower and the exquisite additions made by Cardinal Pole. It was completed, according to its inscription which survives, in 1635. But Lambeth House and grounds were in great danger, and Laud must have known it, for he took the precaution of getting the books in the library and some of the treasures removed to Cambridge.

Laud was arrested in 1640, charged with high crimes and misdemeanours, held in the Tower and gradually, over the next four years, brought to trial. In 1642, with battle lines drawn for Civil War, Lambeth House was commandeered. The Lollards' Prison and the small dungeon in Morton's Tower were used to house both Royalist and criminal prisoners. The troops stationed there must have discovered the wine-cellar quite quickly, for they got very drunk, disinterred the embalmed body of Archbishop Parker from its resting-place in the Chapel and threw it into a midden.

In 1643 Laud's personal papers and diary and books were seized. He was finally executed in 1644.

Three years later, with Charles I captured and held at Oatlands, governance in turmoil and the spoils of war being shared among the victorious Parliamentarians, Lambeth House was sold by auction to two men, Matthew Hardy and Captain Thomas Scott. They demolished the mediaeval Great Hall, sold the materials and pocketed the proceeds. (In 1649 Scott, a devious and eloquent fellow and a spy, acquired notoriety as one of the regicides when King Charles went to his death on the scaffold. Eleven years later, with the Restoration, his own head would be displayed upon a pike.)

The Archbishop's dues from the Thames watermen were now payable to Christopher Wormall, Churchwarden. There was a strong economic impetus behind Puritan hatred of Church and Court and all they stood for: the idea that natural justice would be better served by egalitarian Levellers than by this old nepotistic, corrupt order. But it was religion, and its centres of power, that got attacked first.

DR FEATLEY AND ST MARY'S

Dr Featley, from Lancashire, was a rumbustious anti-Papist who had attended James I's minister at the court of France. He was the rector at St Mary's from 1618, early enough to know Sir Noel Caron as well as John Tradescant the Elder. He died during the Revolution under a cloud – not because he was not in some respects quite a calvinistic Protestant, but because he was broad-minded enough to steer a steady course between

24. *Daniel Featley.*

opposing factions. Parliament, when it seized power in 1642, approved Dr Featley sufficiently to appoint him to its Assembly of Divines, but he made the mistake of resigning at the King's behest. The King insisted that Featley remained his Chaplain and could not simultaneously serve Parliament.

Extreme Puritans were grimly pious. The parish records show how the sexes were segregated in church, with women in the stalls and men in the gallery. Any colour or passion, poetry or cheerfulness must go. In 1643, a mob of attackers at Lambeth insisted they would 'cut the rector up small as herbs for the pot' for allowing the Book of Common Prayer to be read in Church – or 'squeeze the Pope out of his belly.' If there was any stained glass left, it did not survive these attacks, and nor did the rector's job.

Dr Featley was hauled before a court for having provided inadequate sustenance for the soldiers. Having been thrown out of his other livings by Parliamentarians, he pleaded that he had been simply too poor. But there was a campaign against him. The House of Commons was told that Dr Featley had 'endeavoured to corrupt his parishioners by his superstitious example of bowing towards the east in his church, and constant bowing in the name of Jesus....' In most respects he appears to have been as much opposed to superstition as anyone at this superstitious time. However, his goods were taken and he was thrown into prison, a sick man; he survived for eighteen months with asthma and dropsy and was released, six weeks before he died, to convalesce in Chelsea. He professed his Protestantism to the end, and was buried at Lambeth Church.

CIVIL WAR FORTS

By the late summer of 1642 the King had fled London to raise a force in the Midlands. London had to be defended from the royalists, and 22 forts set at 2-mile intervals in lines of sight from each other were erected around the outskirts.

One was 'a fort with 4 half bulwarks at the Dog & Duck in St George's Fields.' Over a hundred years later, in 1746, when Cromwell Mortimer, then Secretary of the Royal Society, tramped around London with a map looking for these forts, he was able to scribble on the map that this one was 'still in being'. It was on the site of today's Imperial War Museum – that is, on St George's Fields, used as common land and traditionally lawless, being neither part of the Duchy estate, nor Canterbury lands. It was a suitable spot for a fort because it was over a spring, required in case of siege. Vigilance being thirsty work, the Dog and Duck opened right next door in 1642. The fort's lines of sight led east-north-east to a large fort at Newington, under today's South Bank University; and south-west to Vauxhall.

At Vauxhall was 'a quadrant fort with 4 half bulwarks.' Secretary Mortimer marked it as 'still in being on the right hand as one goes into Vauxhall Gardens' (one would, naturally, have been approaching from Town, i.e., the riverbank). There was a spring too, the Fox Hall spring, just

25. A drawing of the fort erected during the Civil War at Vauxhall, supposedly drawn at the time. It is almost certainly a fake and was probably drawn c.1800. To the right is, perhaps, Vaux Hall manor house and in front of the fort wall is the river Effra.

east of the road to Wandsworth. Without the guidance of present roads or precise distances it is hard to say quite where the fort stood; it was set well back from the river, but offered a clear view up the Thames towards Battersea. At a guess, it was somewhere under the wedge of buildings now bounded by the railway and the Bondway.

There is a drawing (pictured above), made around 1800, which shows this Vauxhall fort from the south, along with a high wall from the fort to the riverbank. There is an archway in the wall wide enough for a cart. This makes sense, for Lambeth Church can be seen in the distance, and Westminster Abbey, and in the foreground Cox's Bridge over the Effra – all in the right places. The accompanying note from Lambeth Archive states that the tall late Tudor house east of the fort is Vauxhall Manor; the implication is that this might be the house once occupied by Anthony Vaux, located just west of Vauxhall Gardens. There is a pub in the foreground, with a sign showing three men in a boat – the Three Mariners (in the wrong place). The Three Mariners had disappeared by 1800 when the drawing was made, and was further north.

The map of outlying forts is a reminder of how little London had developed in a westerly direction by 1642/3. There was a fort at the end of Wardour Street, another in the Tottenham Court Road, and the next one west of Vauxhall lay across the tussocks and bogs of Tothill Fields (Pimlico) at today's junction of the bridge road with Rochester Row.

JOHN TRADESCANT THE YOUNGER

Throughout these turbulent times, there were Tradescants at Lambeth. John the Elder had had a son, born in 1608 at Meopham and educated at King's School Canterbury while his father was working there for Lord Wotton. He very probably worked with his father afterwards, for he was admitted to the Gardeners' Company at the age of 26 and afterwards travelled to Virginia (in which his father had invested). This was an extraordinary endeavour, for the journey alone took six weeks. He returned with American ferns, columbine and jasmine for the plant collection, and early native American skins and weapons which survive to this day.

In 1638, Tradescant the Elder died, and his son took over as head gardener to the King at Oatlands. At thirty he was already a widower, and now he married Hester Pookes. She was cousin to the de Critz family; John de Critz was Serjeant Painter to the King. (Several paintings by him are in the National Portrait Gallery, and his son Thomas's picture of John Tradescant the Younger is there too.)

Despite his service to the King, the younger Tradescant avoided the vengeance of the mob throughout the years leading up to Charles I's execution in 1649. He quietly added to the plant collection at Lambeth, and opened the Ark to the public at sixpence a time – a cost to deter the merely curious. In 1650 the Tradescants were visited at Lambeth by Elias Ashmole and his wife, and as their acquaintance grew cordial they agreed that Ashmole should collaborate with a distinguished friend on cataloguing the contents of the Ark. As the repository of many artefacts unique in England, the collection was a valuable scientific resource.

In 1652 Tradescant, broken-hearted, had to bear the death of his own son, who was buried in the family tomb at St Mary's. Ten years later he himself died in the South Lambeth house, unintentionally leaving his affairs vulnerable to the crafty Ashmole. Hester Tradescant commissioned a tomb at Lambeth *(ill. 21)*. It was strange even at the time, carved in bas-relief with wondrous creatures and scenes from distant lands. Some years afterwards Samuel Pepys, fascinated, made drawings of it; these have survived. The tomb is in the grounds of St Mary's, now the Museum of Garden History. Pevsner's *South London* sneers that it is 'highly reminiscent of *Hypnererotomachia Polifili*,' which must make it worth a visit.

ELIAS ASHMOLE

Ashmole had been born in 1617. He was an assertive, sharp, ambitious lawyer who practised as an attorney in the Court of Common Pleas until 1641, the year before the split between King and Parliament became inevitable. Politically a Royalist, Ashmole made a judicious retreat to the provinces and spent the Civil War keeping his head down as a collector of excise. By 1646, he was a widower, living unnoticed in Oxford. He used the time afforded by his official position to study mathematics and astronomy, genealogy and heraldry. Promotion came: he was appointed Receiver of Excise for Worcester.

In the seventeenth century, science and wishful thinking were still blurred at the edges. If you studied chemistry, you might well seek the philosopher's stone, a way to turn base metal to gold; if you knew about astronomy, you might seek guidance in the stars. Science verged on the supernatural, as evidenced by titles in the field such as *Bate's Mysteries of Nature and Art* of 1634, *Wilkins' Mathematical Magick* and *Porta's Natural Magick*. This kind of thing was dying out, but Ashmole was of the old school. He scarcely drew breath without advising himself of portents from the zodiac. This must have been some comfort when, with King Charles executed and Parliament in the ascendant, he lost his job. Fortunately, the stars foretold that a rich widow was about to come into his life. He married her. She was twenty years older than he was, and he spent the next few years fighting through the courts for funds from her estate. Ashmole, in his gritty lawyer aspect, was determined to win *every time*. He won; he also won when her adult son died, and Ashmole retrieved money from the boy's guardians.

In 1650 (lawsuits simmering in the background) he and his wife came to Lambeth, met John and Hester Tradescant, and befriended them. He arranged to catalogue the collection at the Ark. This was published in 1656 under Tradescant's name. Three years later Tradescant, at the end of a good night out, signed a Deed of Gift. This gave the collection to Ashmole, with the proviso that John and Hester should look after it in their lifetimes. He appears to have regretted this as soon as he was sober, but Ashmole made no move that might alarm him, and played a waiting game.

In 1660 the crown was restored to Charles II and Ashmole was safe to leap from the shadows into a blaze of glory. The following year he was made Windsor Herald and Comptroller of the Excise. He was certainly efficient in the service of his master and doubled its revenue in 20 years. He nonetheless found time to produce publications about his pet subjects, and to add to the valuable library in his rooms in Middle Temple. He also published books on genealogy and history. Convinced that there was no contradiction between science and astrology, he became a founder member of the Royal Society.

In 1662 Tradescant died, leaving a will which was clear in every respect. Ashmole was not mentioned. Hester would have guardianship of the 'Closet of Raryties' and she would choose either Oxford or Cambridge University to inherit the collection upon her own death.

TRADESCANT'S RARYTIES LEAVE LAMBETH

Ashmole pounced. The Deed of Gift made Tradescant's will invalid, he said, so far as it related to the collection and the gardens and orchard.

The case took two years to come to court. On Hester's side were distinguished and intelligent witnesses and old family friends, among them the engraver and mapmaker Wenceslaus Hollar and the painter Cornelius de Neve, who was a kinsman through her De Critz connection. On Ashmole's side were heavyweight lawyers and others from his old-boy network at the Middle Temple, including Sir William Dugdale, who would later become his father-in-law.

Viewed from 350 years later, Hester's case seems strong. Why otherwise would Hollar, the artist from Prague, have supported her? Hollar had been commissioned several times by both Ashmole and Dugdale and had known both of them for years. His former employer, the Earl of Arundel, was the grandson of those Dukes of

26. Elias Ashmole (left) in the robes of the Windsor Herald, and William Dugdale (Norroy King-of-Arms) at the funeral of the Duke of Albemarle, 1670.

Norfolk who had been executed in the reign of Elizabeth and their lands confiscated; through Arundel he had known the John Tradescants well for a quarter of a century – just as he knew Pepys and Evelyn and de Critz and people at Court, and they all knew the Tradescants. And Ashmole.

Everyone knew everyone else. Several were closet Papists who had fled in the Civil War and kept in touch in times of trouble. And yet Hester, who had no influence and to whom nobody owed any favours, obtained Hollar's support.

ASHMOLE WINS

Hester retained custody of the collection for life; after that the Museum and plant collection in the grounds would go, not to a University, but to Ashmole. Perhaps her case had been lost on a legal nicety. Hester was bitter but never vindictive. When the Great Fire roared through the City in 1666 Ashmole, quick off the mark as usual, had his library piled into a boat and sent upriver to Lambeth. Hester took in all the books, and returned them in perfect order six weeks later.

Ashmole was estranged from his rich wife,

and when she died in 1668 he married young Elizabeth Dugdale. At some point in the next decade, they decided to move to Lambeth too. But not just anywhere. They moved into the house adjoining the Tradescants', which had just fallen vacant. Underlying the move was Ashmole's suspicion that Hester had sold some of the artefacts which the court had judged his property.

A woodcut of his house, from a collection dated 1827, shows just how crowded she must have felt. The two houses were not built side by side, but in an L shape, giving Ashmole a perfect view of comings and goings from the garden.

Three years later, Hester was found drowned in her pond. She was buried in consecrated ground two days later.

Ashmole took her house on a lease and extended the garden. He had already begun to have the (Old) Ashmolean Museum built in Oxford and as soon as it was completed he had the whole collection packed up - it took a month - and carried by barge to its new home. The native American artefacts, the pressed flowers, the stuffed dodo and the cherry-stone with 88 faces on one side, the rhinoceros horn and the 'martyrdome of the Bishop of Amphipolis carved in alabaster', all the hundreds of wonders and Raryties, were henceforth to be known as the Collection of Elias Ashmole, a man who had never left the safety of his library to collect anything.

He died in 1692 and the Tradescants' garden was soon overgrown. Dr Ducarel, who lived in their house eighty years later, could find traces, but few of the rare trees and plants were left.

LAMBETH'S NOSTRADAMUS

In the last quarter of the seventeenth century, one Dr Francis Moore was running a school in Back Lane. (Back Lane eventually became Lambeth High Street.)

Besides being a schoolmaster, Dr Moore was also a physician, herbalist, seer and astrologer. In 1697, no doubt with time on his hands, he began to publish an Almanack. *Old Moore's Almanack* is still making predictions. An internet blurb tells us that the 2006 edition 'highlights gardening by the moon, fishing by the moon, winning periods for jockeys and trainers, lighting-up times and high and low water times.' Indispensable.

THE SURVEY OF CROWN LANDS

A vast examination of who owned what, a second Domesday, took place between 1647 and 1658. Parliament was *de facto* ruler and needed money to pay the troops, so it must find out what assets it had.

Land was the obvious source of revenue. William the Conqueror had received almost two thirds of his income from Crown land but this had fallen to less than a third at the time of Elizabeth. Until the time of the Crusades, titles and leases had been awarded by successive sovereigns to loyal supporters like Fulk de Breant in return for assistance in raising defensive forces. Since then, monarchs had grown ever more dependent upon London financiers and upon the consent of Parliament for revenue-raising exercises. Both Plantagenets and Tudors had sold land outright or borrowed against it - no longer simply for a fighting fund, but to maintain their glorious image and to pay for predatory missions abroad. Letters from Mary Tudor show her airily offering exemption from Act of Usury to anyone who would give her a mortgage on property she owned. Elizabeth I had licensed some of her rights, as well as her tangible assets - the right to mine salt, alum or coal, for instance, on some of her estates - thus encouraging a new kind of monopoly, that of the capitalist rather than the guild. However, kings and queens were rarely financially astute. James I sold freehold rather than leasehold and as a result royal revenue was low when Charles I needed it. Charles had to increase rents and this made him even more unpopular than he deserved.

The Survey of Crown Lands found that the books, where they existed, were a shambles. Estates up and down the country had been mismanaged or undervalued or the paperwork was lost. Copyhold could be 'for life' or in lease, but if there were no deeds ... who knew what was going on? In Kennington, Lambeth and Vauxhall, boundary changes and shifts of ownership from Church to Crown and private hands and back again have defeated historians time after time.

But in 1647, with the people's Parliament in the ascendant after five years of civil war, King Charles detained at Oatlands pending his trial, and the King's Church in an anomalous position, it was time to work out exactly what assets could legitimately be liquefied. Parliament kept it simple by confiscating or 'sequestering' the lands and property of the Crown, its royalist supporters, and the bishops just to be going on with. Later on, some of these pieces of land would be sold freehold. 60% of bishops' sequestered lands were given to a small favoured group of Londoners from the City – aldermen, or those citizens of the City who happened to be strongly represented among the Trustees of the Survey. Most of the identified estates were redistributed by 1650. As for Crown property, hundreds of acres of it were awarded to another small group of former servants at royal palaces, or lawyers or physicians or Crown officials: about 350 people. A few provincial clergy or tradesmen were also represented. Despite the big share-out, Canterbury, the richest diocese of all, retained the freehold of most of Lambeth, from today's Waterloo down to Vauxhall.

Duchy of Cornwall lands like Kennington were approvingly noted in the Survey as excellent revenue producers. Having been held in trust for generations of Princes of Wales, they were better documented and managed than Crown lands generally. St George's Fields, which officially belonged to the Bridge House Estates, was free to be nibbled away at the edges by enclosure because Bridge House, an arm of the City Corporation, was a dormant landlord.

Prince's Meadows (the Blackfriars side of Waterloo Bridge today), had returned to the Arundel family, descendants of the Norfolks. Now the Meadows left their hands again. They were let to a William Dover and remained undeveloped. After the Restoration, when he was renegotiating the terms on which he held the land, Dover said that Parliament had over-valued it. He had been glad enough to get his hands on it at the time.

POLLUTION AND LAMBETH

Coal was creeping in. Newcastle sea-coal had been used in industry for centuries, and in late Tudor times it came into domestic use by the London poor because the price of wood was rising beyond their reach. However, most of the Lambeth poor did not have chimneys in their houses and coal rightly got a bad name as choking, smelly stuff that polluted food, deposited soot on your beer and your dress, and made the walls filthy, inside and out. No person with pretensions to gentility would burn it at home.

At the start of the seventeenth century this began to change, under protest. Archbishop Laud, in the 1630s, prosecuted the Westminster brewers for polluting Church property with their smoke and demanded, and got, a financial penalty from them, with which he promised to repair the coal-damaged exterior of old St Paul's. But there was no affordable alternative to coal; charcoal, which was smokeless, and wood were increasingly unavailable in London, not just because forestry was unsustainable but because timber required carriage by road, and the roads were knee-deep in mud most of the year. And with a London population climbing towards the quarter-million, coal deliveries to the Lambeth riverbank now fuelled a booming building supplies industry. Delft tiles were baked here in kilns, lime was slaked for mortar, and glass was made.

Later in the century, Vauxhall glass would be a key English export. Its beginnings are confused but they depended on a good supply of coal, for it is certain that in 1615 Sir Robert Mansell, the Admiral with financial acumen, patented a new way to make glass in coal-fired ovens, and for some time at least, he manufactured it in Vauxhall. In 1635 he obtained the monopoly for providing Newcastle sea-coal to London. The price of coal went down as the price of timber went up; and then, once demand had been created, the price of coal went up too, until Mansell's monopoly was denied by Parliament in 1642.

At the Restoration, John Evelyn wrote *Fumifugium*, an environmental protest, and presented it to Charles II. Black spots he identified were four: the brewhouses in Westminster, 'Kelne (kiln) neer Fox-Hall, Lime-Kelne neer the Falcon (Paris Garden) and Stink of the Easterly Pyle' (the City.) He proposed sending all the dirty trades to the other side of Shooter's Hill. He had not thought through the financial implications of such a radical plan, and nothing happened. By the end of the century coal-dust and soot were beginning to cause serious pollution. The occasional grey fogs which would make London notorious had begun. White was no longer worn. In the early 1700s, textile merchants wrote abroad to warn their suppliers that they couldn't sell white in London, only cream.

THE MARQUIS OF WORCESTER AND VAUX HALL

In the seventeenth century, Vaux Hall (the house and grounds on the riverbank) was known also as Fox Hall or Copt Hall; the freehold was held by the Duchy of Cornwall. Tracing it through history is confusing, as a house just across Fore Street, also on Canterbury land, was occupied in Tudor times by the Vaux family and sometimes called Vaux Hall or Vauxhall Manor.

Vaux Hall and its river stairs and gardens had reverted to the Duchy from the heirs of Sir Thomas Parrie – he who had minded Arabella Stuart there in 1629. Charles I became personally involved with it at that time as it became a small ordnance factory. The King's most important financial backer was the Earl of Somerset, who had inherited the title just one year before. The earl's son, later known as the 2nd Marquis of Worcester, was already employing a Dutch craftsman, Caspar Calthoff, to execute and test his engineering designs at Raglan Castle, the

27. Vaux Hall manor house.

Somerset family seat. King Charles awarded Vaux Hall and its adjoining land, rent-free, to the young man as a base in which to make munitions and test his other inventions. All parties were happy: Parrie the former copyholder because he would be compensated with preferment at court; the King because he would get the most advanced muskets and flintlocks; Worcester because he had a base convenient for coal deliveries to fuel his experiments; and Calthoff because he would be living closer to the news from Holland, currently defending itself against the Spanish. He was a refugee, although circumstantial evidence indicates that he was Catholic and royalist rather than Protestant in his sympathies.

Calthoff is usually recorded as a 'gunmaker' or a 'master mechanic'. At Vaux Hall throughout the 1630s he would work under instruction from Worcester on patent ideas for steam power and waterworks and other ingenious contrivances, besides cannon and other ordnance. The military applications are obvious, but the King - who still controlled licences to mine much of Britain's real estate - was also promised a way to pump water out of flooded mines and off boggy land, to create fountains and pleasure gardens and propel clean water through cities, and generally to move on from the filth, disease and inefficiency which so restrained seventeenth-century industrial progress.

Worcester is often credited as an early inventor of the steam engine, and although his work was interrupted by the Commonwealth he and Calthoff certainly understood the motive power of steam, although they never perfected anything like a railway engine. By 1642 at the latest, with the final break between King and Parliament, he and Calthoff fled, after they had spent over a decade in creative engineering at Vauxhall. Calthoff and his family returned to Dordrecht, where he would shortly resurface in contemporary correspondence and news as lens grinder to the great astronomer Christiaan Huyghens - one of the two Huyghens brothers whose father had been such a friend of Sir Noel Caron at Lambeth. The secrets of lens-making were generally closely guarded; perhaps the Calthoffs had a family connection. Thanks to a telescope made for him at this time, Huyghens would discover Titan, a moon of Saturn, in 1655.

When Civil War erupted in the 1640s, the Marquis of Worcester went into hiding, for he was the financial intermediary between his father and the fugitive King. Parliament sentenced him to death in his absence but he raised forces, fought for the Royalist cause, and was made Generalissimo of English and foreign forces and an Admiral, to boot. But his tenure was always insecure because of his strong Catholicism, and when the King was soundly defeated at the Battle of Naseby and detained at Oatlands, Worcester fled to Paris. There he stayed between 1645 and 1649 while Oliver Cromwell occupied his London home, Worcester House, in the Strand.

Calthoff visited Paris at this time, telling friends he was going to see his brother. He was experimenting, not very successfully, with steam power in Holland as well as working for Huyghens, and Worcester was financially embarrassed. They sat tight, the loyal servant working in Holland and the master mouldering in France, in hope that one day they might return to their old experiments on the banks of the Thames.

In 1652, Worcester could stand no more penury and returned to face Parliamentarian justice. He was sent to the Tower, but Cromwell never intended him to die. With smallpox raging at the Tower in 1654 Worcester was released with a small pension and began to write his *Century of Inventions*, which would be reprinted many times for generations to come.

VAUX HALL UNDER THE COMMONWEALTH

In 1645, Parliament's soldiers led by a courteous Captain Ghest visited Vaux Hall to take an inventory. They must have been there for days. The site, a line of pantiled workshops close to the road and a Long Gallery by the river with the old house and its offices between, and a generous garden, stretched about seventy yards from Gun House Stairs to Vauxhall Stairs. At the Gun

House stairs end (near today's Tinworth Street exit to the Embankment) there were 'great butts' for firearms testing and a locked, inaccessible lodge at the gate.

Ghest and his men arrived by appointment, and meticulously counted forges, bellows, anvils, weights, cranes, files, filing benches, furnaces (seven in the melting house, and one 'to melt silver in' elsewhere), brass, pulleys, vices, iron, muskets, guns, implements for boring guns and a mill for boring, grindstone and trough, 'engines' for waterworks, for tobacco cutting, water lifting, hammers and tongs, sledgehammers, wheels, racks, drills, cannon, casts, scores of ingenious locks; and a joinery, stabling for six horses, many outbuildings and 'private rooms' like kitchen, lodgings, and garrets. Some of the private rooms were occupied by a John Bishop, 'Engineer and Overseer of all the Instruments of Warre', who now must pay rent for the first time but undertook to do so, and to repair the long wall beside the road.

The soldiers saw 'in the first Modell Room two stories high, one leaden waterwork, seven great wheels made for perpetuall mocion, little copper waterwork, wooden model for an iron mill to grind corne, four water fountains ... modell of a coach made of purpose to let loose the horses, if they should prove wild'. There was a second 2-storey 'Modell Room' and 'one Modell of a boat to go of itself against the stream and tide' and other inventions ... All this in an age when even educated men surveyed such marvels with an awe verging on the superstitious.

At the old house was a wash-house with a furnace and cistern, a pump, a dresser, press and racks; a buttery, another kitchen, a cellar, hall, study, withdrawing room, chambers and closets; a round lead cistern in a garret; a pump in the yard; a 'stone cistern in first court'; and a big garden. Everything throughout was in good order and well-maintained, although all the windows were broken in both house and workshops. There had probably been trouble from a mob in 1642.

There was a curious oasis amid the evidence of industry: 'One faire roome called the King's Dining Roome under the said two modell rooms with two chimneys in the same at either end, one with chimney pieces of black and white marble and curious fretworke over head, there are not anie materialls in that roome...'

They were shown over the 'sope and copper foundry', the workshops, Vaux Hall and the Forge by one William Joulden, who had been chief workman to Calthoff and was still living there with his family and working for William Lambert, a gun founder. Joulden was as nice as pie to Captain Ghest who duly included, with his inventory, a plea that Joulden be allowed to stay as a rent-paying tenant, since without his assistance they would not have been able to find, or describe, half this stuff.

Finally Joulden revealed the Long Gallery, beside the river. It was forty yards long, brick-built and must have been intended as a kind of showroom. But it had never been finished and stood, windowless and lacking ridge tiles, sheltering some possessions Calthoff had left behind. Captain Ghest took charge of it and undertook to have it made weatherproof.

In 1647 the King, under house arrest at Oatlands, was induced to assign Vaux Hall to William Lambert and his family (possibly a relation of Cromwell's second-in-command John Lambert). Lambert was called a 'founder', a foundryman or arms manufacturer. After the King's execution in 1649, the authorities were undecided whether to sell the place or not, but it was among the 'Mansion Houses' specifically exempted from sale by the Commonwealth in an Act of 16 July, 1649 along with others including Scotland Yard, Somerset House, Hampton Court, and the Old Artillery Ground.

In 1652 Vaux Hall was put up for sale anyway. A war with the Dutch had just begun and the government needed every penny it could scrape together. In March 1652 the House of Commons Journal, Volume 7, records that it had been:

> ...ordered, that the Trustees at Worcester-House be authorized and required to make Sale of the house called Vaux-Hall, with the appurtenances (at Ten Years Purchase, according to the Value set by the Survey) to John Trenchard, Esquire; he

laying down Ready Money for same, and having undertaken to set up a Manufacture there for Advantage of the Commonwealth.'

THE RESTORATION: LAMBETH TAKES SHAPE

The merry dance whirled right about. After the Restoration of Charles II in 1660, the Crown demanded return of property 'alienated' and sold off by Parliament under the 1646 Act of Sequestration. Samuel Pepys, who spent many a happy hour in Lambeth, reported in his diary the dismay of his friend Mr Pargiter, who had to forfeit everything. Trenchard, as we shall see, was in the same position.

Gleefully retrieving all they could, a different group of favourites began to make a profit. Ladies at the court of Charles II were allowed to plead for grants of 'concealed property' they had traced, at their own expense, as having once belonged to the Crown. (That was the kind of mess the records were in.) Astute use of such advantages earned many courtiers a tidy income from estate agency, rent and licence arrears going back many years, and sale of goods. And the King made haste to dispose of Crown land north of the river. In the ensuing decades London's ducal estates, with their leafy squares and grand terraces, would be laid out in the West End.

In Lambeth, however, very little land changed hands permanently. Most freeholds remained with the Duchy, Christ Church Canterbury and (in St George's Fields) Bridge House Estates, which belonged to the Corporation of London. The Duchy assigned long leases on most of Kennington to Sir Robert Clayton, a City merchant, whose family would retain them until the property reverted in the nineteenth century.

Bridge House Estates was at this time inactive in St George's Fields. The land was treated as common land and would have been extremely expensive to drain.

The incumbent Archbishop of Canterbury in 1673 was almost as reluctant as his predecessors to contribute towards the common good. He grudgingly forked out £50 towards paving the road from Lambeth to Newington Butts (the one that Laud had refused to contribute to fifty years earlier), but made it clear that this was a one-off payment and the Church would not be responsible for repairs. On Canterbury land, which comprised most of the Lambeth riverside south of the Palace, successive Church authorities were reluctant either to invest in the property or to forego short-term rentals in favour of long leases to developers, and the same attitude prevailed at the Vestry.

The Duchy of Cornwall would commence development later, but a patch of land shaded by trees, just a hundred yards from Vauxhall Stairs across Fore Street, was let as a pleasure garden. It must surely have opened after the Restoration, although there may have been a garden there before the Civil War began. Pepys, in 1662, already knew the Old Spring Garden well, but it had been superseded by the New. It was possible to take a pleasant afternoon stroll in either of them while avoiding putting your hand in your pocket:

> ...Thence home, and with my wife and the two maids, and the boy, took boat and to Foxhall, where I had not been a great while. To the Old Spring Garden, and there walked long, and the wenches gathered pinks. Here we staid, and seeing that we could not have anything to eat, but very dear, and with long stay, we went forth again without any notice taken of us, and so we might have done if we had had anything. Thence to the New one, where I never was before, which much exceeds the other; and here we also walked, and the boy crept through the hedge and gathered abundance of roses, and, after a long walk, passed out of doors as we did in the other place, and here we had cakes and powdered beef and ale, and so home again by water with much pleasure. This day, being the King's birth-day, was very solemnly observed...
>
> *Thursday 29 May 1662*

The river on the Lambeth side remained poorly embanked, poorly drained and fit rather for wharves and factories than for dwelling-houses of consequence. These, in any case, would have required bridges across the river. Proposals for bridges were opposed by the watermen; by Canterbury, whose administrators were content to accept an income from the horse ferry; and by

28. *New Spring Garden, an engraving of 1741 by M. Ramano.*

the Corporation of London which received tolls at London Bridge. The Thames remained as the Romans had left it, bridged in one place only, for another ninety years.

CHARLES II AND VAUX HALL

Among those who had been awarded property under the Protectorate, some claimed they had meant to pay for it all along but had waited for the royal family's return. Others offered to buy a lease. John Trenchard did not last long at Vaux Hall. Having bought it in 1652, he had to forfeit it to the Marquis of Worcester upon the Restoration. (Trenchard may have been a gunmaker. There was a pamphleteer John Trenchard who is quoted to this day by the American gun lobby in defence of the Second Amendment and a vast militia, rather than a standing army; he was active around 1705, and probably of the same Dorset family.)

The Marquis of Worcester re-installed Calthoff and his family in Vaux Hall. They were triumphant. Worcester submitted proposals for a 'college for artisans' at Vauxhall; it is in the papers of the Royal Society. But he and Calthoff were old men. Also, there was a young rival. While they had spent twenty years as fugitives Samuel Morland, an equally imaginative inventor and spy, had been a diligent clerk in the circles surrounding Oliver Cromwell. Then he reinvented himself.

> 'And once, upon an invitation, his Lordship (Worcester) dined with Sir Samuel (Morland) at his house; and though his entertainment was exquisite, the greatest pleasure was to observe his devices; for every thing showed art and mechanism, as 1. A fountain 2. A cistern in his garret supplying all parts of the house. 3. His coach was most particular. 4. A portable engine, moved by watch-work; it had a fire-place and grate, cost £30. He took it with him in his own coach, and, at inns, he was his own cook. '

The description is from a 1661 memoir by Lord North, who also knew Robert Boyle, the Marquis of Worcester, Evelyn and Pepys, all men standing on the edge of a new scientific age. Worcester, like Morland, like Pepys, indeed like everyone whose paranoia was well-founded, was interested in ciphers and codes as well. Rigorous observation, experiment and proof were new, mysterious and exciting. Worcester describes in his *Century of Inventions* a fountain he had made rise to a height of forty feet. These 'waterworks' about which he and Morland and others were so passionate were ignored as 'impossibilities' by most educated men; yet if they worked, they would have practical use in fire-fighting and in conveying unpolluted drinking water.

Morland had an advantage over Calthoff and Worcester in asking the King for patronage for his inventions - he had saved Charles II's life. Overhearing his masters plotting to assassinate the would-be King during the Protectorate, he had secretly communicated the danger to Charles. At the Restoration he got a knighthood, and a pardon although he had been a Commonwealth man, and in 1661 he was rewarded with a warrant granting him 'the sole making of an Engine invented by him for raising water in mines or pits, draining marshes, or supplying buildings with water.' Morland was also an enthusiastic inventor of calculating machines.

Worcester in 1663 was still pleading with Charles II and Parliament to continue the patronage begun by Charles I. He had already spent much of his own money on inventions 'practicable with my directions by the unparalleled workman both for trust and skill, Caspar Kaltoff's hand, who hath been these five and thirty years as in a school under me employed.' But the application of science lagged behind the ingenuity and skill of the few far-sighted enough to pursue it, and the new King had a different agenda.

Calthoff died *c.*1663 and left a widow, Martha, three daughters and a son, all of them young and two of the girls unmarried. They remained at Vaux Hall with the King's consent, the son having been awarded the lease after the father. Their oldest daughter had been fortunate enough to marry without a dowry. Her husband, Peter Jacobson, was a sugar-baker from a London Dutch family, but his business was razed to the ground during the Great Fire of 1666. 'Engines' for raising water from the Thames had been invented and promoted often enough to the King, but when they could have proved their worth they were not available to douse the Fire.

The Jacobsons, their livelihood burned out, moved in with Mrs Calthoff's family at Vaux Hall and Peter Jacobson spent £700, then an enormous sum, on converting the property to carry on his old business. By the time this was complete the following year, the Marquis of Worcester had died and Caspar's only son Jacob was abroad - said to be 'held up by the Emperor of Russia.' So in consideration of the amount Peter Jacobson had disbursed, the King granted him a lease on:

> 'All that part of our Mansion House called Vauxhall or Ffoxhall, part of the Manor of Kennington, in the County of Surrey, extending in length next the River Thames 186 feet, or thereabout, and in width 22 feet, or thereabout; and all that other part of the same Mansion House adjoining the premises, and from thence extending towards the S.E. 47 feet, and in width N.W. 33 feet, or thereabout, and in other parts 24 feet, or thereabout; together with all that area or place adjoining and fenced in, extending in length 14 feet, or thereabout, and in width to the W. end 40 feet, and to the S. end 47 feet, or thereabout, together with free ingress and egress in and through the steps and doors existing at the N. end of the aforesaid house, and through and over the area there, called the Court-yard, appertaining to the aforesaid House, and all that Stable lately built upon part of the said place or area last mentioned, consisting in length 28 feet, or thereabout, and in width 17 feet, or thereabout; also that shed 26 by 10 feet premises in or near the Parish of Lambeth, and now in the tenure or occupation of Peter Jacobson.
>
> This Lease granted in consideration of the expense incurred in repairing and amending the buildings for and during his natural life, at a Rental of only £5.'

The whole huge tranche of land must have retained many of the outbuildings from its time as a munitions factory and experimental steam-power workshop. It seems that someone (Joulden?) knew how to keep the famous Water-Commanding Engine going after the death of Calthoff and Worcester in the 1660s, for it is said to have worked from 1663 for the next six years. Huyghens saw it, and so did many others including, in 1669, Cosimo de Medici, the haughty young sixth Duke of Tuscany.

Martha died in 1672, and Peter Jacobson's property was passed on to Gertrude Jacobson, a grandchild. The only man of the family was another son-in-law, Claude Denis. At the end of 1674 he sold the rights in Vaux Hall to Sir Samuel Morland, who had obtained not a loan but 'a grant' of £400 for the purpose, presumably from the King.

John Aubrey, who visited, said Morland added a mirror-lined room and that the garden (which was extensive) now held 'fountains very pleasant to behold' and was 'much visited by strangers.' It must have been decisively separated from the former sugar-bakery and soot-laden engineering works on the rest of the site.

It is possible that Morland's discreet tenancy of this riverside house, so convenient for Whitehall, proved useful to the King. Denne wrote primly of Vaux Hall 'The King seemed to have reserved this messuage for a villa of pleasure; and to this, and not to an insignificant alehouse, he probably was wont, in his water-tours, to resort with his ladies.'

This is supported by some slight evidence from the French Ambassador. Between 1675 and 1677, when Charles II was hounded by determined women, particularly his current mistress Louise de Kéroualle and his wife Catherine of Braganza, he conducted an affair with Hortense, Comtesse de Mazarin. For a royal mistress, Hortense was unusually discreet and modest in her demands. She would accept no hints from the French Ambassador, Courtin, that she might use her affair to the advantage of her own King Louis. She refused to admit that she and Charles had formed a *liaison* and they managed to give Courtin's spies the slip. On 25th June, 1676, the Ambassador wrote home in frustration that the couple made frequent excursions on the Thames and that the King disappeared from his rooms in Whitehall every night, not returning until 3am.

So there may just be a clue, here, to the purpose to which Charles put Vaux Hall. The Reverend Denne was certain that a chair from the house, 'richly ornamented', and allegedly used by the King, years afterwards found its way to the Three Mariners pub on Fore Street, where it was kept as a talking-point.

SAMUEL PEPYS AT LAMBETH

Lambeth Ale was famous - later in the century the royal household of William and Mary placed a regular order - and The Three Mariners is mentioned with approval in Pepys' Diary:

> 'I go to Whitehall, and there with Captains Rolf and Ferrers we went to Lambeth to drink our morning draft, where at the Three Mariners, a place noted for their ale, we went and staid awhile very merry, and so away. And wanting a boat, we found Captain Bun going down the river, and so we went into his boat, having a lady with him, and he landed them at Westminster and me at the Bridge.'
> *12 June 1661*

Graham Gibberd, in *On Lambeth Marsh,* has made a study of the sites of Pepys's favourite pubs in Lambeth. The Three Mariners was on the riverbank side of Fore Street, opposite where Salamanca Street today emerges at the Embankment. Because Bazalgette's Embankment incised the bank at this point, the site is now underwater. Evidently you can't keep a good pub down, for it has risen from the waves as The English Maid, a pub on a boat. (On the sandbank behind The English Maid, at low tide, is a wide flagstone slipway; it is easy to imagine a pub beside it.)

Pepys often cut across London Bridge from his home in Seething Lane, walked across the open fields of Lambeth and took a boat from Stangate to work at Whitehall. Among the low weatherboarded houses on the marsh he found a pub called the Halfway House, so called because it was half-way between London Bridge and Stangate. There is still a pub there, too: the Stage Door, in Webber Street behind the Old Vic.

Sometimes he would meet one of his conquests on the Whitehall side and take her across the river to Stangate for a drink:

29. Samuel Pepys.

> '...and away to Westminster Hall, and there sight of Mrs Lane, and plotted with her to go over to the old house in Lambeth Marsh, and there eat and drank, and had my pleasure of her twice, she being the strangest woman in talk of love to her husband sometimes, and sometimes again she do not care for him, and yet willing enough to allow me a liberty of doing what I would with her. So spending 5s or 6s upon her, I could do what I would, and after an hour's stay and more, back again and set her ashore again.' *25 July 1664*

Graham Gibberd identifies the 'old house' referred to at the junction of Lower Marsh and the Westminster Bridge Road, on the corner further from the river, as Bishop Bonner's House *(ill. 30)*.

When Pepys was in a more intellectual mood the following year, he visited Lambeth House – which would soon become known as Lambeth Palace – to see the recent reconstruction of the Great Hall. The new Archbishop was Juxon, who in January 1649 as Bishop of London had attended Charles I on the scaffold. At the Restoration, Juxon retrieved the books from the library that Laud had prudently deposited at Cambridge, and built the Great Hall we see parallel to the river today. Pepys was in two minds about Juxon's decision to reconstruct a facsimile of the Hall destroyed under the Commonwealth, rather than erect something new in the modern style.

ALTERNATIVE ENTERTAINMENT

People of all classes were as likely to attend an execution as an ale-house. Executions of felons from both Southwark and Lambeth took place at the south end of Kennington Common, at a spot alongside the ancient highway (Kennington Park Road) upon which now stands the altar of St Mark's Church. In mediaeval times this lonely spot must have been convenient for immediate lynching after an attempted highway robbery.

An eye-witness's report of a burning and double hanging there on Wednesday, 24 April 1678, has been preserved. It was printed as a dire warning to the godless.

The first victim was Sarah Elston. She was from Fishmonger's Alley, Southwark, and married to a hatter. They 'had been married several years; but lived with much Discord and frequent Wrangling; of which some now would partly excuse the woman, and allege the man as the principal Cause of their Differences by his ill husbandry, cross carriage, ill company, and other provocations, not here to be mentioned.' But in September of the previous year, 'a Quarrel arising between them, and he having beat her very severely, she with a pair of Sizzars gave him a wound on the left part of his Breast; whereof, without speaking one Word, he died.' She was sentenced at the Spring Quarter Sessions to be burned at the stake.

She pleaded for two weeks in which to prepare herself for death. Stay of execution being granted, she was visited by 'Ministers, and other good sober understanding Christians' and listened, repented, and bewailed the 'Ill Course of her former life'. However the day arrived, and 'a Stake being set up, she was conveyed thither on a Hurdle, being clothed all in White, with a vast multitude of People attending her'. There were prayers, there were apologies, and according to the anonymous author Sarah exhorted all wives to 'remember that their Husband is their Head, and that the Apostle requires them to be obedient to them in every thing, and this is not only to the kind and indulgent, but even the peevish and forward ought to have the same observance.'

A likely story. The fire was kindled, and 'giving two or three lamentable Shrieks, she was deprived both of Voice and Life, and so burnt to Ashes according to the Sentence.'

Next that day were two men who had robbed 'a Gentleman' near Putney of £20 eleven months before; they had waited almost a year for trial. Gabriel Dean was formerly a pipe-maker, and John Masters a 'person well educated, but falling into poverty, [who] having been in prison for debt, and under other crosses, was seduced to ill courses.' Both were strung up on the gibbet.

CLOUDS OF SMOKE ON THE HORIZON

Since the late Middle Ages, wealthy English people had used imported glassware and looking-glasses and window-glass. Great buildings like the Chapel at Lambeth, and rich parish churches like St Mary's, had stained glass, generally made on site in a glass-house set up for two or three years and later dismantled. But during the seventeenth century, glass vessels, scientific instruments and spectacles, and windows became affordable by the emergent middle classes.

English glass for routine use as vessels could be made anywhere, since the main requirements were sand and potash, clay for the pots to heat it in and wood to keep the furnaces going. As early as the 1560s, the first Huguenot glassmakers came to London, bringing new expertise in the making of crown glass for windows. The problem for glassmakers was the shortage of wood to fire the furnaces, because coal gave an unreliable temperature and, in any case, tainted the glass. At last, in 1610 Sir William Slingsby (an elder brother of that Sir Guilford Slingsbie, James I's Comptroller of the Navy, who was such a diligent attender at Lambeth Church) obtained a patent for a way to use coal. His method did not work terribly well. Sir Edward Zouche and others, including the King's glazier, took out a patent for a better system. They had established a glass factory in Vauxhall, close to river transport, by 1613. This may, even at this early date, have been on the 9-acre site occupied by the famous later Vauxhall glass factory. It was across Fore Street from Vaux Hall between today's Glasshouse Street and Tinworth Street. Like Vaux Hall it was held copyhold from the Crown by Sir Thomas Parrie.

Two years later Zouche and other wealthy men were joined in business by Sir Robert Mansell, the Admiral who had taken Tradescant along on the Algerian expedition. Very quickly, Mansell – who had wide business interests – bought out the others and put the patent into his own name. But within a few years he had closed down the loss-making glassworks at Lambeth, probably to the relief of neighbours affected by the clouds of coal smoke. (It was a brief respite before a Captain Scott – a predecessor of Worcester and Calthoff – began making ordnance on the Vaux Hall site.)

Mansell appears to have moved the glass business to Newcastle, where he, and in his absence at sea his astute wife Lady Elizabeth Mansell, made a great success of it. They imported Italian workers and manufactured looking-glasses to a standard never before achieved in England. The Newcastle factory closed in 1642 when the workers fled before the Scots invasion, and reopened later.

After the Restoration, Mansell died, but glassmaking was about to return to Lambeth. George Villiers, second Duke of Buckingham, was as vivid, outrageous and charming a character as his father had been. Unfortunately he lacked sticking power. His passions rarely endured and his fortunes waxed and waned. He invested in the glass industry at Greenwich and from 1663 onwards, in Vauxhall; three years later he left suddenly to fight the Dutch; he fell out of political favour, and lost his patent for looking glass made in the Venetian way, and he lost it because it was said that the Venetian technique had been known for years at Vauxhall, and Zouche and Mansell had made Venetian looking-glass there as early as 1620. Be that as it may, Buckingham knew when he was beaten, and assigned the factory to his manager, a man called John Dawson, who had been apprenticed to Venetian glassmakers at Vauxhall and was wise enough to keep a trade secret.

Towards the end of the century a building advertised as the Duke of Buckingham's '*Old* Glass House' was being used as a showroom. This was probably the Little Glass House; there was a Little one and a Great one on the Vauxhall site, and a couple of workmen's cottages and a substantial house for Dawson and his family, as well as factory equipment, furnaces and a mill. The famous English glassmaker George Ravenscroft, for the last decade of his life, worked with Dawson there. When John Evelyn visited in 1676 he was mightily impressed by all he saw, particularly the looking glasses 'far larger and better than any that came from Venice' and 'huge vases....clear, ponderous and thick as crystal'.

Dawson had managed to obtain capital from a distinguished London merchant, John Bowles, and other businessmen with interests in glasshouses in Southwark. Glasshouses were all over the place (a small one sprang up on Sir Samuel Morland's land when he left it), but Vauxhall was big, internationally known, and the only one making looking-glass and plate glass for coaches. This site was not ideal. Even the biggest sheets must be placed on boards and carried perilously across Fore Street, like an invalid on a stretcher, to Glasshouse Stairs for transport to customers.

It was well known that the workers of Vauxhall were brought over from the continent and worked for high salaries, paid whether or not they had work. This was significant, for in the 1690s – to finance war against the French – William of Orange's government imposed a 90% tax on glass. Pleas of hardship availed the artisan glassmakers nothing. All over London, they went out of business. It is perhaps not coincidental that one of the Commissioners who rejected their pleas was John Bowles, the wealthy businessman whose own large-scale glass houses in Vauxhall and Ratcliff and Southwark were able to survive despite the tax. Vauxhall Glass would go on to even greater fame in the coming century.

WALKING TO EXECUTION

A map of 1681 shows barge-houses 'built upon by Royaltie' at the south end of the manor garden at Vaux Hall – the north side of Vauxhall Stairs.

Today, huge yellow amphibious vehicles rush down a ramp at Vauxhall Stairs, and plummet laden to the waterline with squealing tourists. But in 1685, a State Barge would set off from here on a grim journey. Charles II had just died and his younger brother James, Duke of York, was now James II. Protestants were appalled, because James was a devout Catholic. A good number rallied to the Duke of Monmouth, a bastard son of Charles II, but were defeated almost at once. Monmouth was seized by the King's men at Ringwood in Hampshire and brought under heavy guard to the royal barge houses at Vauxhall. There the handsome prisoner embarked upon his last sombre trip downriver to Whitehall Stairs, ferocious denunciation, and beheading.

Lambeth in the 18th Century

In the first half of the eighteenth century London, a city of over half a million people north of the river, seemed to many observers morally, as well as physically, polluted. In London you could climb socially, by re-inventing yourself, or descend, unknown and unremarked, into penury and death in dependence on gambling and gin. Gin had been encouraged by William of Orange in restraint of French imports and encouragement of English corn, and now that silly, pious Queen Anne was on the throne, its consumption was out of control. What with the poor succumbing to ignorance and hard liquor, and the rich to self-obsession and gambling, London society was falling apart.

Culturally, all this was remote from Lambeth, which was still a village by comparison. Behind its bustling waterfront, and its ribbon development along the main roads, it mostly remained, for at least thirty years after the century began, a formless rural sprawl.

A COUNTRY PLACE

In Lambeth, there was an awful lot of sky. If you were able to climb to a high point - like the turret of Mr Tradescant's old house, for instance, or the roof of long-dead Bishop Bonner's Tudor mansion on Lambeth Marsh - Westminster Abbey stood huge across the river and Westminster Hall seemed nearly as big. On a clear day the City's dozens of church spires gleamed in the distance like swords piercing the blue sky.

On the Surrey side there was nothing so imposing as Lambeth Church, with the Palace beside it, except high-shouldered St Mary Overie down in Southwark, which soared out of a sea of houses. There were houses along main roads like Kennington Lane and Lambeth Marsh, Fore Street and Broad Walk (the western edge of Paris Garden). Otherwise Lambeth was mostly green, with windmills. Wind and water, horses and

30. House on Lambeth Marsh traditionally said to be Bishop Bonner's house. Watercolour c.1825, artist unknown.

men were the regular sources of energy, and windmills were used for grinding starch and mustard as well as corn. Close to Norfolk House was a mill used at one time for grinding drugs. A firm of millwrights was established on the South Bank, and there was even a Dutch sawmill there, close to the water - a remarkable innovation during the Commonwealth, which Oliver Cromwell personally came to view. It was the only London sawmill for many years, for after the Restoration, angry woodworkers destroyed later attempts to erect them.

South and east on the great plain you could see the hills of Streatham and Sydenham and Blackheath. The river's north bank gradually rose towards Islington and Hampstead. At night there were twinkling stars - there was no street lighting to detract from their brilliance. If John Evelyn was right about the pollution of forty years before, then soot-laden smog was already drifting over the City; but you wouldn't know from pictures. You wouldn't know what was going on in Lambeth either. Artists naturally

31. Windmills at Lambeth, c.1750.

32. An 18th-century view of the drug mill in Mill Street, now Juxon Street. It was the property of the Apothecaries' Company and was used for grinding drugs up to 1867. The mill was demolished to make way for the London & South Western Railway and housing.

picked clear days for their views of London, often drawn from a vantage point south of the river. The tacit assumption was that Lambeth held nothing to marvel at, so they turned their backs on it and illustrated the wonders of the metropolis as tourists have always done.

Around the mid-century, with more industry in Lambeth and a new bridge, young men back from the Grand Tour brought a fashion for antiquarianism and encouraged curiosity about Lambeth Palace. This was part of old London, and there wasn't much of that left since the Fire. It was mediaeval: it had cloisters under its library and a gallery built by Cardinal Pole and a cluster of ancient buildings beside the chapel. The guardroom still contained muskets, blunderbusses and pikes (in 1780 a platoon of soldiers would be briefly posted there in case of attack by the Gordon Rioters). The place was an odd anachronism; the dole was still given out at the gate, and the crypt, where Anne Boleyn had negotiated the manner of her execution, was slowly silting up to waist height with earth swept in during successive floods. In 1753 a story went about that a tortoise which had lived in the Archbishop's garden for 120 years, no less, had accidentally met its end thanks to a careless gardener.

King George III owned a number of views of Lambeth Palace from Millbank, showing the horse-ferry and stairs, the tree-lined Bishop's Walk along the riverside, and barge houses where St Thomas's now stands. Canaletto, who lived in England for ten years at the mid-century and saw London with a fresh eye, painted an unconventional view across the Thames from Richmond House in Whitehall. The opposite shore was by then a jumble of red-roofed riverside cottages amid trees, with St Paul's massively prominent in the distance. The same view today would show the South Bank arts complex and Waterloo Bridge.

THE LAST YEARS OF CALM

In Parliament as early as 1671 a Mr Waller ('a poet') had said 'In Paris there are many bridges – in Venice, hundreds – but we are still obstructing public things. The King cannot hunt, but he must cross the water!' In the matter of crossing the Thames, London Bridge, or the ferries, were still the only way. A bridge at Putney had been suggested, and 'if from Putney, why not from Lambeth?'

There were the usual protests. Westminster rentals would go up, the City would suffer, the Thames would silt up, and so on. The watermen's rates had not increased since 1559! Their plight was surely worthy of consideration ... Bridges were opposed by successive Archbishops, who objected to losing revenue from the watermen; by the watermen themselves; and by the City Corporation which enjoyed the tolls of London Bridge. And perhaps Londoners until the 1720s were 'still obstructing public things' because City funds were attracted to more exotic opportunities, like the East India Company. A bridge across the Thames was dull and problematic, so it remained unbuilt. Only after the South Sea Bubble burst in the 1720s would serious money be released for infrastructural projects like Westminster Bridge, so reassuringly tangible and visible.

33. The boatyards of Searle and Goderey at Lambeth, by Thomas Rowlandson.

34. A barge either being repaired or made at Searle's boatyeard at Lambeth in 1830.

So between 1700 and 1750, Lambeth and the watermen quietly got on with business as usual. Wharves lined the riverbank at Narrow Wall (today's South Bank) and the royal barge was built just north of Stangate. Contemporary pictures show the river crowded with sailboats, wherries (large rowing boats) carrying passengers to and fro, and horses in the traces of ornate coaches, serenely floating on wide rafts, heading for the horse ferry stairs. The watermen must have had tremendous skill. They had never made much money; their fares were fixed and publicly posted, and after 1696 they had to wear badges to show that they were licensed by the City Corporation, and could operate their river taxi services only from permitted points. On the Surrey side these now extended to Lambeth and Vauxhall. Watermen worked hard and skilfully in all weathers, providing unsubsidised public transport to all, and passed their knowledge of the river from generation to generation. However, the watermen knew their trade would be doomed if the river was bridged once more.

VAUXHALL GARDENS

After William and Mary came to the throne in 1689, the middle classes and the tradesmen's families prospered. They had a higher disposable income than ever before to spend on their own social life. They wore imported silks and satins, they drove about in coaches, and they wanted to be entertained away from the smelly alleyways of the city. The pub garden, in all its variants, flourished. The promenade and picnic also offered opportunities for flirtation, especially if there was evening entertainment - not the cruel sports of the old Bear Garden, but romantic playlets or amusing songs. Food, drink and music in Vauxhall Gardens grew to new heights of popularity in the years before 1750, when Lambeth was still rural.

The Gardens stood where Spring Gardens stand today, roughly from Goding Street to St Oswald's Place. New Spring Gardens was their original name. This makes no sense since the only Vauxhall spring we know of was near the Wandsworth Road, but these undoubtedly were the idyllic gardens that Pepys knew. The Gardens increasingly improved and developed; and they would play an important part in the development of music, circus and music hall. In the early days there was a capacious 'old house' through which people entered from the west (river) side. It may have been the Tudor mansion of Anthony Vaux, the brewer.

'The quality' made the place fashionable, and they included early Hanoverian Georges - not that royal patronage was any guarantee of respectability. At night the Gardens twinkled with a thousand lanterns whose light served only to deepen the darkness round about. From the start it was impossible to keep tarts of both sexes and varying degrees of professionalism from descending upon such a vast outdoor business opportunity. Jonathan Tyers took over in 1728 with a thirty-year lease and smartened up Vauxhall's reputation, but besides the card-rooms and concert room and lantern-lit paths, there remained dark walks, shady nooks, grottoes and quiet trysting places at every turn.

On ground-plans of Vauxhall the wooded

35. *Dining at Vauxhall in 1755.*

36. *An admission ticket to Vauxhall Gardens made out 124 years to the day since Pepys' diary entry.*

arbours look like tidy rectangular flowerbeds, but contemporary pictures show that it was flat, and much more tree-shaded than the plans indicate. We know that improvements over the years brought a Rotunda, supper tables in alcoves around a crescent adorned with oil paintings by Francis Hayman, fountains and sculptures. The painting studio on the north side of the Gardens would have interested Canaletto, who had begun his career as a painter of scenery. His own painting of Vauxhall's Grand Walk (1751) – recently rescued from sale abroad (and now on view at Compton Verney) – hints at something the size and scope of Battersea Park. It wasn't nearly as big as that. It was only twelve acres, but 'I flew rather than ran up the walk, hoping to secure my safety by returning to the lights and company we had so foolishly left' gasps Fanny Burney's heroine Evelina as late as 1778. In the dark, she had been mistaken for a prostitute. Canaletto painted the place in daylight, when it seemed respectable. But at night, landscaping skills that exploited trees, shrubs and moonlight, abundant drink and inadequate food (you could read the paper through the sliced ham, they said), and – as a sure-fire release to inhibition – the popularity of *domino*, or the mask, often resulted in the kind of accidental disorientation and loss of virtue for which Vauxhall was famous. And in the early days when ladies wore paniered skirts, Louis heels, towering wigs, white lead, rouge and patches and flirted in the language of the fan, the barely lit walks were a gift to transvestites.

When George I arrived in London in 1714, a court musician from Hanover was already here. This was George Frederick Handel. His first composition for the King was the *Water Music*, played during an evening party on the Thames in 1717. He was famous for 'outdoor music' and from about 1732, Jonathan Tyers commissioned him to write for Vauxhall, where the Prince and Princess of Wales were frequent visitors. His latest concertos became part of the repertoire.

37. The Chinese Pavilions and boxes at Vauxhall Gardens.

Handel was a convivial fellow, one of the anti-Walpole set of young artists and musicians who frequently met at Slaughter's Coffee House in London, and he happened to know a talented young sculptor from France, who would also make his professional career in England. In 1738 Francis Roubiliac sculpted a figure of Handel as Apollo, sitting in his nightgown and cap plucking at the strings of a lyre while a fat cherub idled at his feet. This affectionate image was exhibited in Vauxhall Gardens until the 1780s, and it made Roubiliac's name. It is now in the Victoria and Albert Museum.

The crowds at Vauxhall loved Handel and in April 1749 the *Music for the Royal Fireworks* was given its first public airing there – a rehearsal for its playing in Green Park the following week to celebrate the Treaty of Aix-la-Chapelle - by an orchestra of over a hundred. Twelve thousand visitors listened and were delighted.

Tyers also befriended William Hogarth, a young artist. Hogarth, a Londoner, had married in 1729 and with his wife briefly took summer lodgings in South Lambeth. Tyers agreed to exhibit pictures of Henry VIII and Anne Boleyn which Hogarth had made a few years earlier, and in 1736 Hayman copied Hogarth's *The Four Times of the Day*, four satirical illustrations of contemporary life, to adorn the crescent of supper-tables in the Gardens. *The Four Times* initiated the anecdotal-series style later followed in the *Harlot's Progress, Rake's Progress* and *Marriage à la Mode.* Hayman's version was painted in oils, while Hogarth made engravings of *The Four Times of the Day* for sale as prints. The only works we know Hogarth designed especially for the Gardens were silver season tickets. He got a gold one that allowed him free entry to Vauxhall for life, with 'a coachload' of friends.

Hogarth, such a narrative artist, illustrated London life of his time in every aspect: courts, brothels, Southwark Fair – yet of Vauxhall, mentioned by contemporary writers for a hundred and fifty years, there is almost nothing in his work. Just one poignant sketch from life at

38. Vauxhall Gardens depicted by Thomas Rowlandson, 1784. Mrs Weichsel, a popular singer, is entertaining the visitors. In the group at the left are Dr Johnson, Oliver Goldsmith, Boswell and Mrs Thrale. On the right, the Prince of Wales whispers into the ear of his mistress, the actresss 'Perdita' Robinson.

the Gardens is dubiously attributed to him. It depicts Tyers' exhausted book-keeper, Thomas Smith, slumped asleep in a chair at four in the morning, having done the books at the end of a long night. An open ledger shows 'Receipts on a Gala Night, Vauxhall.'

What with Handel's music, Hogarth's pictures, Monsieur Roubiliac's famous sculpture, some fine baritones and sopranos on stage and the nightingales in the trees, it was obvious that crowds were not pouring into Vauxhall Gardens simply for paper-thin ham and expensive booze. Sex, yes; but an aesthetic, or even a spectacular, experience also lured them in off the Thames wherries. The attractions were all too successful. Alighting from a tiny boat was none too easy when there were shoals of them bobbing around the Stairs; ladies burdened by voluminous skirts must clamber from one to another in their tiny, buckled satin shoes with Louis heels. And when Westminster Bridge opened in 1750, the press of coaches was so great that the journey down to Vauxhall could take an hour and a half; and as one visitor reported 'We then alighted, and after scrambling under bellies of horses, through wheels, and over posts and rails, we reached the gardens where there were already many thousand persons.'

There was even a parking lot, marked *Coach Park* on Faden's map of 1785; could it be the earliest ever? It is a private car and lorry park to this day – Szerelmey's yard, off Kennington Lane.

The Gardens, always having to go one better than Ranelagh, came to rely on spectacle: fireworks, balloon ascents and eventually – at the start of the nineteenth century – more ambitious entertainment indoors. But that came later. In the meantime, Jonathan Tyers achieved the difficult feat of maintaining his Gardens at the height of fashion for over thirty years. The lower, older floors of St Peter's Vicarage on Kennington Lane are said to be where later managers of the Gardens lived. In 1767 Tyers died and his two sons Tom, a barrister, and Jonathan took over. Mr Barrett, who became the Gardens' proprietor at the end of the century, was a son-in law of this younger Jonathan.

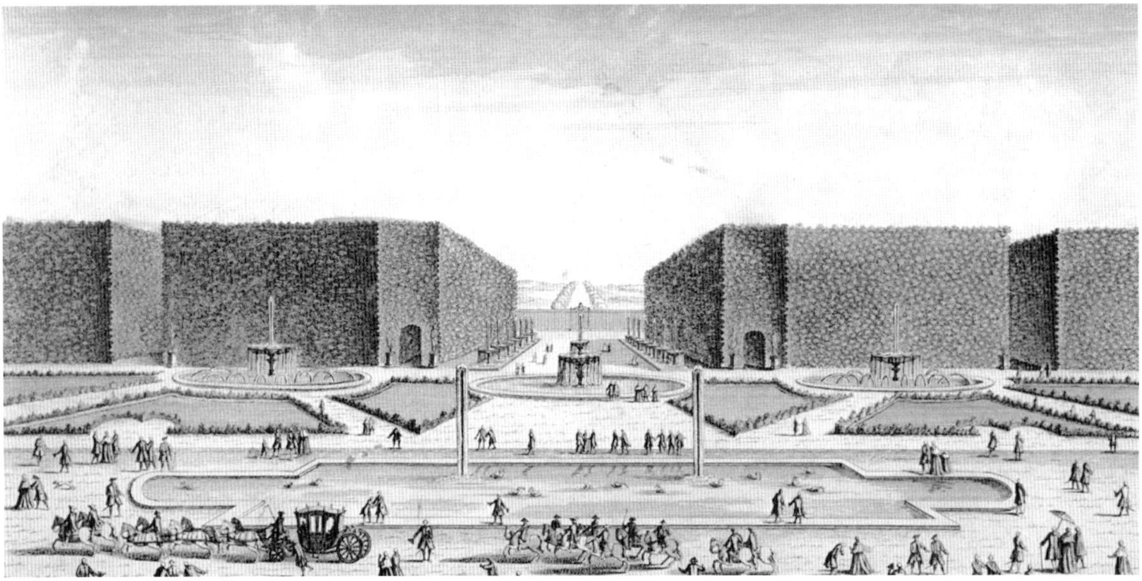

39. A view of Vauxhall Gardens c.1750. Coloured engraving, artist unknown.

THE ROYAL BOTANICAL GARDENS

William Curtis, a chubby fellow with a florid complexion, was a botanist of prescience. He roamed the wet fields around London noting what was soon to disappear – willows of all kinds; hops; warty agaric, the starry agaric, the striped boletus and the sinking morel; the solid puffball and the black mucor and the fingered clavaria; black nobbed liverwort, warty liverwort, fern jungermannia and scaly jungermannia, wild germander, water horehound, stinking gladwyn, frog's lettuce, devil's bit, dogberry, parsley-piert, water-violets…

He set up the Royal Botanical Gardens and ran them in Lambeth Marsh, roughly where Waterloo Station now stands, from 1779 for ten years. Curtis, a nice man whose education as a Quaker had impressed him deeply, intended his Gardens as a place of instruction, for the six thousand plants were labelled in Latin and English and there was a small private library. His subscribers were promised 'a check to the baneful and enervating effects of luxury and dissipation'. They paid a guinea a year for unlimited access,

40. William Curtis, publ. 1802. Stipple engraving by William Evans.

41. *Curtis's London Botanic Gardens, by James Sowerby (1757-1822).*

with a guest, to the gardens and the library; for two guineas they might also select a root or some seeds, to add to their own plant collection.

Curtis was hugely enthusiastic and curious about ways to classify, use and conserve the natural world. As the Latin botanical code familiar to us was still being argued over, his plants were displayed in categories such as medicinal, culinary (he was particularly keen on seakale), or poisonous. He wanted farmers to breed seeds that would produce better crops in greater abundance. Having begun life as an apothecary in Gracechurch Street and attended lectures at St Thomas's on Bankside, he was interested in the curative qualities of plants. And he added geology and entomology to his interests; entomology being particularly timely, as Lambeth's trees in the 1780s (as in the 1980s) were stripped bare by brown-tailed moths. Curtis's *History of the Brown-Tailed Moth* may not be on every naturalist's bookshelf, but his botanical studies left a lasting legacy. He was influential in getting the Latin code introduced; and he founded the exquisitely illustrated *Botanical Magazine* in 1787. (It continues today as *Kew Magazine*.) He employed a series of superb artists and colourists, most of whom had to leave him because he couldn't pay them enough. James Sowerby, the Lambeth painter, was one of those. Sydenham Taste Edwards, whose name is included because it is unforgettable, stayed with him to the end.

Curtis had been brought up at Alton, in Hampshire, less than five miles from Selborne and the family of Gilbert White, whose *Natural History of Selborne* became famous; and in Lambeth, he was friendly with White's two brothers, Thomas and Ben. Thomas was Curtis's partner at one time, and Ben, a London bookseller who published books on natural history, had part of the old Tradescant property on South Lambeth Road. His brother Gilbert visited him there, and in his correspondence liked to compare the climate in Lambeth with that in Selborne. Few of Tradescant's specimens were still alive then. If the fate of Curtis's venture is anything to go by, perhaps the increasingly smog-laden air had something to do with that.

At first Lambeth had seemed perfect for a Botanical Garden. 'The situation being low, renders it peculiarly favourable to the growth of aquatic and bog plants, and all such as love a moist bottom, an inestimable advantage in dry summers' Curtis enthused. But over his eight years in Lambeth the gardens were subjected to more and more industrial pollution. Ironworkers and heavy industry were moving in. The plants suffered. And so did the visitors, because roads hereabouts were disgracefully muddy in winter. Finally, in 1789 when his landlord raised the rent, he moved the entire enterprise to Brompton, opposite the hospital on the Fulham Road. There he set up a new garden and announced, with relief, that he 'had the pleasure of finding it encouraged by the patronage of many of the nobility and other personages, celebrated no less by their rank in life than by their laudable endeavours to promote the public welfare.'

LAMBETH'S OTHER GARDENS

Vauxhall Gardens are of course the best known, but there were several pleasure gardens in Lambeth before Westminster Bridge was built and even more afterwards. Walter Besant, in nostalgic mood at the end of the nineteenth century, said that they 'lay like a string of pearls around South London'. They were a strange hybrid, a response to the demand for entertainment, informal social contact and fresh air, fed by a supply of expert gardeners, show folk and entrepreneurs, and they lay along a continuum between the uncouth exhibitions of the fifteenth century and the music hall of the nineteenth. The Temple of Apollo has long been replaced by Webber Street, the Flora Tea Gardens is somewhere under a block of flats, Belvedere Gardens gave its name to a road, Cumberland Gardens lies beneath MI6 and there are many others now buried under concrete and tarmac. Here are four of the best known:

Cuper's Gardens was so called because during the Commonwealth, part of Prince's Meadows was let to Boydel Cuper, a well-known figure locally – he was Collector for the Poor at St Mary Lambeth in 1650 and had been gardener to the Earl of Arundel. At one time Cuper's Gardens extended all the way from the riverbank under today's Imax Cinema and St John's Church.

A small bridge over the mouth of a stream stood close to the river; perhaps Cuper renewed or repaired it at his own expense, because it came to be known as Cuper's Bridge and the river stairs as Cuper's Stairs. From 1678 his son opened the place as tea-gardens. Ferries brought day trippers from the City and the Strand, which had become an important shopping street.

Maps show that Cuper's Gardens contained some nicely planted walks, and a picture from

42. Cuper's Gardens, c.1760.

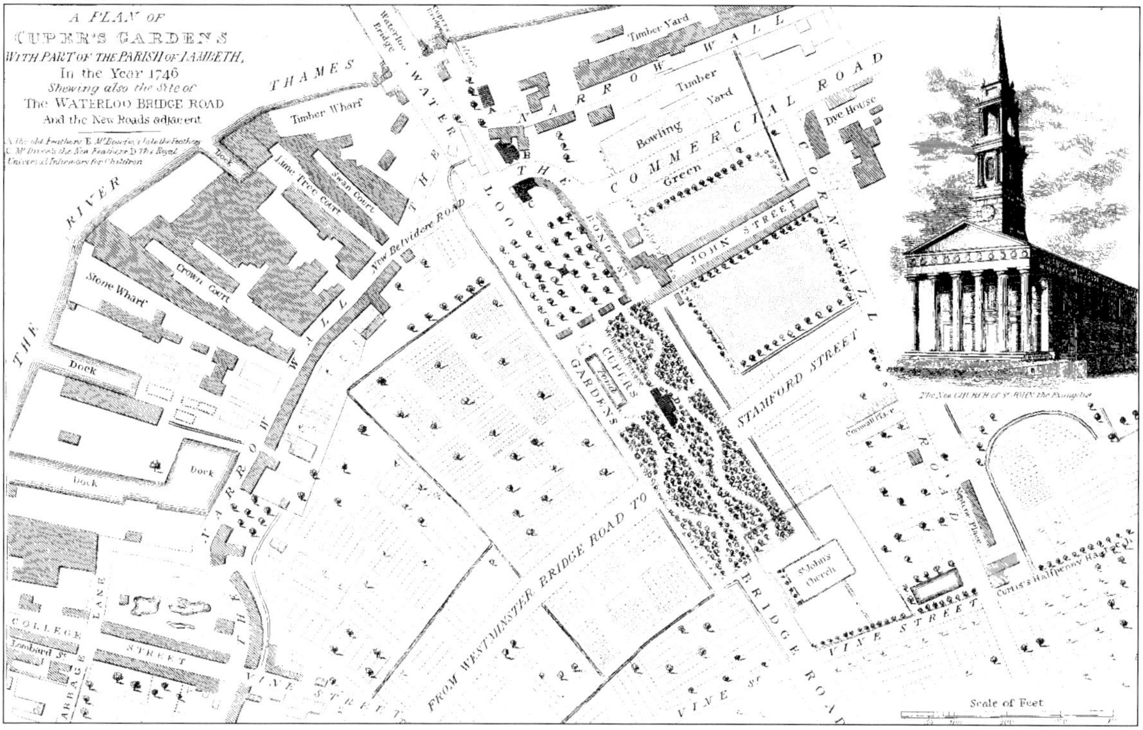

43, Map showing the extent and location of Cuper's Gardens with subsequent roads shown.

44. A building in Cuper's Gardens.

the Lambeth Archive shows a gazebo, a wooden quay and some sturdy cottages close to the river. Towards the end of its life, in 1750 when the edges were being nibbled away by lettings, there remained a riverside tavern, and the usual firework displays, arbours, musical entertainment and so on. All this seems entirely decorous, although they were popularly known as Cupid's Gardens, which may explain their suppression as 'a nuisance' in 1753.

Lambeth Wells was in Three Coney Walk, which is now Lambeth Walk, near the sharp turn into the Lambeth Road. There were two springs, and you could buy bottled water and take it away; this trade probably helped finance the pleasure garden on the site. From the *London Gazette*, 30 April 1696:

> 'Lambeth Purging Waters in Langton Gardens, Lambeth Fields, near the Three Coneys, will be opened tomorrow. The place is extremely pleasant and fitted for the entertainment of persons of all Qualities. On Tuesdays, Wednesdays and Fridays the Musick will be continued until four after noon, and the other days until seven. To prevent mistakes, on the top of the house which covers the Well is a Golden Ball.'

It seems St Thomas's Hospital, then in the Borough, ordered Lambeth Wells water for its patients. Ladies and gentlemen took the waters in the morning and strolled in the gardens in the afternoon. Lambeth Wells continued until the 1750s, when competition from St George's Spaw finished it off. The main building became a Methodist Chapel and then an alehouse. What became of the Golden Ball is unknown.

St George's Spaw (spa) was next to the Dog and Duck, in St George's Fields. In the sixteenth century Gerard had written 'of water-violets I have not found such plenty in any one place as the water ditches adjoining St George his Fielde near London' and before Westminster Bridge encouraged the trampling hoi-polloi, it was still a charming place in summer. The fields remained largely undrained and impassable in winter, although they had been dry enough in September 1666 to be turned into a tent city for refugees from the Great Fire.

The aperient waters of the Spaw were sold from 1695, and fully exploited from 1731. You could pay a penny for a bottle or fourpence for a gallon. By the 1750s there was a Long Room with music and all the delights the public had come to expect of pleasure gardens. Dr Johnson, in a letter to Mrs Thrale on 10 July, 1771, advised her to take the waters there.

The Spaw became less important than the Dog and Duck on the same property, probably through the commercial acumen of Mrs Hedger, the proprietor from the 1770s. She served late breakfasts on Sunday, a sure-fire winner even now. Mrs Hedger's son was still running the pub towards the end of the century, and the pleasure gardens beside it, when Mr Barratt – a magistrate – ensured that it lost its licence. At the time Barratt was running Vauxhall Gardens, its major competitor. Hedger made a deal with a London vintner who would come and sell his own wines on the premises, thus technically circumventing the law. On Sundays the swimming pool and bowling green, the live music, good wine and large meal served in the middle of the afternoon, ensured the Dog and Duck's continuing success with City gentlemen and their mistresses.

Eventually, Hedger decided to redevelop the land and make more profit for less trouble. The Bridge House Estates objected but he said this was common land and he could do what he liked. The lawsuit went on for years. Finally a compromise was reached. Hedger would take a 21-year lease but he made a solemn undertaking not to develop. If he did, he would have to pay a penalty of £500.

Hedger signed, paid the £500 fine and put up a row of houses. He made £7,000 a year out of his tenants until his death, and the Hedger family organised matters so that on the day before his 21-year lease was up, the houses had been demolished and the materials sold. After that, Bridge House Estates offered no leases shorter than 65 years.

THE ROYAL CIRCUS

The memoirs of Joseph De Castro, an old actor-singer and early member of an acting dynasty, explain better than anything the colourful Lambeth hinterland in which actors scrambled for a living between pleasure garden, pub, circus and theatre and eventually, music hall. According to the illustration in the front of his book De Castro was a rubicund, indeed bibulous-looking gent; but his career on the boards lasted over forty years, and his memoirs were sponsored by scores of distinguished luminaries including Kemble, Kean, the Duke of York and Lady Caroline Lamb.

He was the unlikely offspring of the Rabbi at Bevis Marks, London's original Sephardic synagogue. His memoir is in many ways a tribute to Philip Astley, the most enterprising of South London showmen; but Astley was not his first employer.

To understand why circus - and eventually the music hall - became so popular, it's necessary to know the social and legal situation. Stage performers in the eighteenth century lived in constant danger of prosecution. Royalty and the Church had been forced to concede political power, religion no longer framed sophisticated opinion, and authority was challenged daily in the public print. Humour struck like a dagger. Government was easily undermined by satire and quick to put a stop to it. From 1737 licensing laws enforced by the office of the Lord Chamberlain permitted only two theatres in London, at Drury Lane and at Covent Garden, to put on full-length dramas.

The outdoor pleasure gardens were a washout in winter, but people must be entertained. Burletta - burlesque - got round the rules to some extent. Actors could perform monologues (but not in rhyme), short one-act plays or songs. For the rest, producers must pad out their shows with harlequinades, wonders, equestrian displays and clowns, or risk the combined wrath of the licensed theatres and the magistrates, and imprisonment.

Those actors who were not hired at the so-called Winter Theatres must get taken on where they could. De Castro, who did a nice line in impersonation and could hold a tune, got his big break in 1782 at the Royal Circus, which together with the Equestrian Coffee House, was across St George's Fields from the Dog and Duck. This was near the junction (now St George's Circus) where the new Blackfriars Road and the new Westminster Bridge Road cut across flower-filled meadows and joined up en route to the old roads towards Kent and Portsmouth. It was all rural and attractive; cows grazed here and there was a circular Lactarium, with real milkmaids (so uplifting to the romantic spirit) selling butter and cream only a few hundred yards from the Royal Circus.

45. Joseph De Castro.

Being beyond the bounds of Southwark and Lambeth, the Fields were also used for public meetings of an incendiary nature. Lord George Gordon's six-thousand-strong anti-Catholic rabble set off from there in 1780 to make a violent protest against Catholic Emancipation, and there were frequent trade meetings - De Castro saw the London hatters on the Fields in 1783, demanding higher wages.

46. Extract from John Rocque's map of London, c.1746, showing the main part of Lambeth.

In 1782 it was Charles Dibdin, the dramatist and composer then managing the Royal Circus, who hired De Castro, for an evening of 'Exhibitions of Horsemanship and Dancing by Young Ladies' and 'A new Pantomime in two parts called the *Vicissitudes of Harlequin* ... in which will be introduced the favourite *Balloon Song* by Mr Decastro'. There were 'dresses and decorations by Signor Lupino' (an early theatrical in that Lambeth dynasty) and 'fireworks by Signor Rossi .... "*Vivant Rex et Regina!*"'

De Castro's *Balloon Song*, written by a Mr Pigott ('then well known on the turf') took off. So when Dibdin walked out a year later, and De Castro disloyally stayed to play another season, Dibdin was livid and when he returned in 1784 he sacked everyone, including De Castro, who had worked for the proprietor in his absence. By this time De Castro had made a lot of friends. One of them was Old Grimaldi, father of the clown, who lived near Stangate, and about whom he had a favourite story:

> In the year 1780, during the riots in London, it was a common practice to write with chalk on the street-doors and shutters of the houses 'No popery.' Grimaldi seeing it went into the streets, and says 'Vat is all dis about?' – when he was informed that he must write on the outside of his house 'No Popery;' upon which he immediately goes in the front...and writes up 'No religion at all here' which was so good-naturedly read by the rioters, that he and his premises were passed unmolested.

Old Grimaldi, an acrobatic dancer, appears to have bullied his son into clowning, yet he had a whimsical eccentricity about him: he once decorated his Lambeth garden with hundreds of silk flowers in winter.

After many vicissitudes the Royal Circus closed around 1790. Its proprietor, the man with whom Dibdin had squabbled, whose name was Hughes, got an opportunity to take his troupe of horses and riders to perform before the Empress Catherine at St Petersburg. She was so enthralled that she had a special amphitheatre built for them, and when Hughes was called home to deal with issues surrounding Lady West's claim for ground rent on Royal Circus, he sold the horses to the Empress.

On his return he let out the derelict Royal Circus as a holding pen for imported sheep, goats and mules. Lady West (she of West Square) pursued him for ground rent and didn't get it, so she repossessed. Hughes, left with a homeless flock of four-footed liabilities, became an animal trainer to the big theatres. The Royal Circus eventually re-opened, under new management, at the turn of the century. It became the Surrey Theatre, and would achieve fame as a Music-Hall.

ASTLEY'S AMPHITHEATRE

In 1784 when Dibdin put him out of a job at the Royal Circus, De Castro looked towards Astley's rival outfit.

Philip Astley had retired as a cavalry sergeant-major around 1768, when he was still only 26. His great asset was the magnificent regimental horse presented to him, it is said, by General Elliott as a reward for exceptional valour in battle. He rented a field at Halfpenny Hatch, near the Hatch House Tavern where you paid a halfpenny toll to ride along the old path to Bermondsey. (It was called Curtis's Hatch later, when it was part of William Curtis's land.) The Hatch House Tavern stood on the corner of Whittlesea Street and Cornwall Road – there is a pub there still – and Astley's field was under today's Roupell Street. Astley put on open-air shows of daredevil riding. Within a few years of working in Lambeth and travelling about with his show, he had earned enough to take a plot in a better position. It was between Westminster Bridge Approach and Stangate behind the barge houses, and undeveloped. (The nurses' wing of St Thomas's is there now.) He bought it from an old pheasant-keeper.

The shows at Astley's Amphitheatre included trained monkeys, dogs and a pig, tumblers and rope-dancers and 'the favourite pantomime called the *Vauxhall Jubilee*, with the Temple and Temple Walks superbly illuminated.' It was successful from the start, and Astley worked hard, taking his troupe to Dublin and Paris

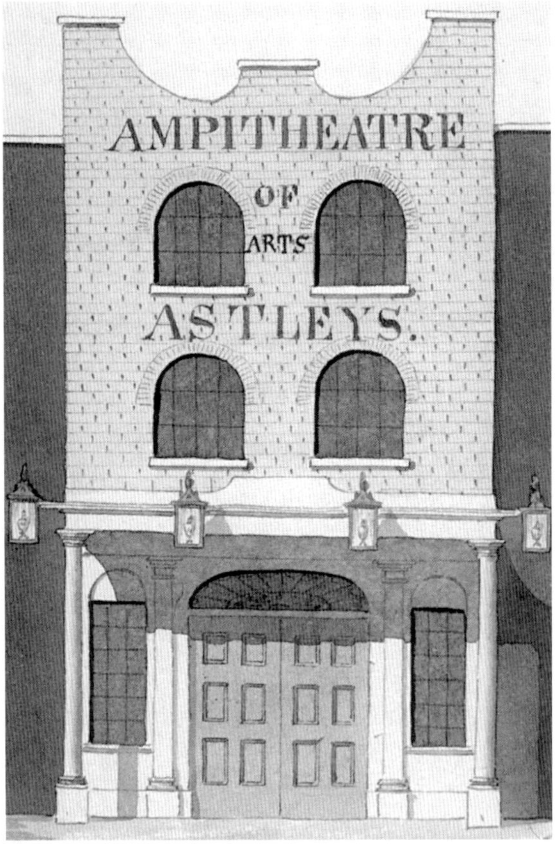

47. Astley's Amphitheatre c. 1790. Watercolour, artist unknown.

when the London season was over.

De Castro could not have worked for him in 1783 anyway, since Astley had been briefly imprisoned for promoting an illegal performance. He got out of jail when the Lord Chamberlain belatedly realised that he had imprisoned his own daughters' riding-master. But the following year, De Castro heard that Astley was back in town and paying well for burlesque singers. He bought dinner for Mr Fox, later Astley's stage manager, at Wheelwright's Tea Gardens (unofficially 'the Gig Shop') in Mount Row, Lambeth (on Faden's 1785 map, close to Carlisle Lane). Mr Fox dropped the required word and De Castro was invited to visit Astley at his house 'near the box-office,' where he lived with his housekeeper Mary Connelly. De Castro got the job, and it was the start of a long friendship.

Astley was soon attracting other acts away from the Royal Circus. His troupe performed at Versailles for Marie Antoinette and Louis XVI. He set up an Amphitheatre in Paris, and took some houses nearby. He did his best to steer clear of political involvement. Over in the Fields, at the Royal Circus in 1789, the Year of Revolution, a show called *The Destruction of the Bastille* got two actors hauled off to the Bridewell; Astley wisely stuck to *The Twelve Labours of Hercules*. However, during the Revolution his Paris houses were commandeered for barracks and it was years before he finally received the back rent he claimed from the French government. He also ran an Amphitheatre in Dublin, but parted with it after the Union in 1800.

The Amphitheatre at Westminster Bridge was burned down in 1794 and again in 1803. This time it was rebuilt in great style. The interior, in the shape of a horseshoe, was designed by Mr Grieve of the Covent Garden Theatre and made by Mr George Searle, the boatbuilder of Stangate, who had built the City State Barge. Searle also made the front drop, which was so admired that audiences called for it to be lowered specially for a good long look.

A great attraction in the first few seasons, besides the usual costume battles and other spectaculars, was the zebra. With every playbill, Astley advertised the bewildered creature for sale at 400 guineas. He and his wife, also a professional rider ('Mrs Astley's performance in the part of Zulima was deservedly admired') had raised their son John to ride in public, and although it is doubtful that he ever rode the zebra, Master John Astley was a hit with the crowds. In due course he took over the lease of the new theatre from his father. He also set up another London theatre, the Olympic, where the Aldwych now stands.

The family were supporters of local trade. The annual Astley's Wherry Competition – a race of two heats around a boat moored off Cumberland Gardens at Vauxhall, and around a beacon at Hungerford, culminating in the presentation of a wherry in the Amphitheatre – was usually won by a pair of strong young watermen. Philip

48. The arena of Astley's Amphitheatre, from a print published in 1815.

Astley in retirement developed property. He had built a smart house to live in. It was called Hercules Hall after his money-spinning *Twelve Labours* and stood on the triangle at the north corner of Hercules Road. Kennington Road, a mere track before Westminster Bridge was built, was now lined with fine terraces, and Astley copied them in Hercules Road. In the end he owned the entire triangular site as far as Cosser Street.

He died in 1814 at his house in the Rue du Faubourg St Honoré. His son John also died, much too young, seven years later, in the same house, in the same bed. They were buried in Père Lachaise.

ROADS AND BRIDGES

In the first half of the eighteenth century there were regular coach services through Lambeth to and from London Bridge and the ports of the south and south-west coasts. The main artery was the old Roman road now Kennington Park Road. There were no coaching inns – those were in the Borough. A couple of sizeable ponds lay close to the old road, and there were pubs nearby so that drovers could refresh themselves while their cattle drank. One was on St George's Fields by the Dog and Duck, and another was near Kennington Green; in the next century, the pub on this site would become famous as The Horns.

Post roads – in Lambeth this meant Kennington Park Road – were repaired, but otherwise, the haphazard economic infrastructure left many roads untended. Nearly all the secondary roads

49. *Kip's view of Lambeth Palace in 1697, showing the horse ferry.*

had been in use since the Middle Ages and were used to get to and from the river or St George's Fields or Kennington Common. Lambeth Marsh still ran to Stangate, the boundary roads of the old Paris Garden curved back to St George's Fields from Bankside, Kennington Lane passed the dilapidated barn that was all that remained of Kennington Palace, Lambeth Butts was still there, Lambeth Road ran to the horse ferry from St George's Fields, and a track from Cuper's Gardens led to Kennington Park Road.

Along the main routes, horse-drawn carts were used for moving goods: drinking water which increasingly was supplied in barrels, building materials, fuel, and food and drink. Hackney carriages existed, but not south of the river, and most people found it more convenient and comfortable to travel along the Thames as Pepys had done. The wealthy kept their own spectacular barges; many are shown in Canaletto's view of the Thames which looks positively Venetian. For all sorts of reasons, having to do with the water supply, the need for access to a dry road, and the need to work, the highest densities of population were still around Lambeth Marsh and the gate of Lambeth Palace and along the Wall.

There were some turnpike trusts, but before 1730 almost all of them were outside London. Later on, when the bridges were built, toll booths were set along their approach roads and carts and carriages paid to get across. Getting these bridges built at all was a wearisome, dispiriting struggle that lasted two centuries. There exists a drawing from the 1720s by Henry Hulsbergh headed 'Vauxhall Bridge: new design for a bridge over the River Thames near Lambeth.' It was to be a cart-width wide, with lodges at each end and seven arches. Its height would rise from seven to one hundred feet above the river, and it would rest on pontoons, with alcoves for pedestrian shelter. Hulsbergh's design was commissioned by William Pulteney, Earl of Bath, and intended for the Lambeth Bridge site; but any bridge remained contentious, because of the combined wrath of the watermen, the Church and especially the City.

So Westminster Bridge, which opened in 1750,

50. The southern end of the new Westminster Bridge in 1751, with Lambeth Palace in the distance.

represented defeat for successive generations of protestors. It acknowledged Westminster's importance, but it was Lambeth that was most visibly changed by it.

The bridge in fact presented a challenge, because nobody knew how to build a solid structure in the sucking gravel and fast-flowing waters of the Thames. Old London Bridge had nineteen arches with swirling rapids around its piers, so nothing like that would do. A French architect called Labelye was hired and after a false start, got it nearly right. Sadly his stone bridge was just too heavy for London's gritty mud, and eventually shifted. In Victoria's reign it was replaced with an iron structure. The tall sheltered alcoves so considerately placed at intervals along the original bridge were described as a threat to public morality. In 1769, Blackfriars Bridge opened. The riverfront between the two new bridges was already lined with houses and wharves. Narrow Street - a lane, with pleasant houses facing the river - followed the shoreline but no longer ran through open fields and alongside a high embankment; it was met at right angles by a number of cart-wide lanes. Broad Wall, a.k.a. Broad Street (earlier, Angel Street) marked the western edge of Paris Garden and emerged at Barge House Stairs (near today's Oxo Tower).

Cobbled and well-lit, the new bridges were both useful and delightful to use: an immediate success. The approach roads were built as high and dry as they could be before tarmacadam; Westminster Bridge Road was built on chalk foundations over the Marsh. This, and the Blackfriars Road, led from the bridges to the new St George's Circus, and from St George's Circus to Newington Butts (the Elephant and Castle) where they met the City to Portsmouth route.

Lambeth, once so sleepy, became a transport hub. Nothing would ever be the same again.

At this time revolution was in the air, and Circuses permitted the militia a clear line of sight from which to shoot down the rebellious hoi-polloi. London, unlike Paris, has never adapted well to this defensive-hub theory, as St George's Circus demonstrates. There is nothing there of the Place de la Concorde's clear intent

51. The Obelisk at St George's Circus, with the School for the Indigent Blind to the left and what was then Bethlem Hospital (now the Imperial War Museum) in the background to the right.

52. The first Lambeth Bridge, built on the line of the old horse ferry.

53. *William Blake, by John Linnell.*

to dominate. The elegant Portland stone Obelisk is dedicated to an otherwise forgotten Lord Mayor and the spoke-roads curl away dispiritedly after a few hundred yards. .

Around 1770 the Lambeth Road, shown on maps as Church Street, leads boldly from the Archbishop's Palace to the Dog and Duck; this too would ultimately join the others at St George's Circus. Lambeth Bridge itself was not built until 1854, after roughly 150 years at the planning stage.

WILLIAM BLAKE

William Blake, the poet, painter and engraver, was in his thirties when he moved to Lambeth from Soho in 1793 with his wife Catherine, and his sojourn here was the most productive and prosperous time of his life. He is often thought of as a strange and lonely visionary. He was of course a visionary, but a sociable one, with a thriving trade at this time, and many friends who appreciated his genius. Blake and Catherine, who assisted him in his work, lived at 13 Hercules Buidings. This was Philip Astley's development on the east side of the Hercules Road near the Lambeth end. The Blakes lived in a pleasant three-storey house with a basement and a garden in which Blake planted a vine. There they entertained, among others, John Flaxman, the sculptor, who lived nearby and had done a lot of work for Mrs Coade at her Artificial Stone Manufactory on the river *(see p. 87)*.

We retain a nostalgic image of a place long after we know it's not like that at all any more. Lambeth for a Londoner of Blake's generation was still, in the mind's eye, an Eden of flower-filled meadows and healthy dairymaids. Yet *Songs of Innocence and Experience* was published here, and Blake, who struggled between his fervent belief in a supreme being and the apparent triumph of evil over good, could not ignore the intrusion of industry into the Lambeth idyll. The Blakes found themselves living in an environment increasingly polluted by distant hammering and grinding, air heavy with smoke and grit, and filthy drinking water.

At this time, with the industrial revolution in full gear to fight the Napoleonic Wars, demand for arms brought heavy industry and an inrush of unskilled labour to Lambeth. On every side ironworks, stoneworks, potteries and printworks were becoming mechanised. Kilns and mills and chimneys rose into the sky and claypits and brickfields scarred the flowery meadows. Further north in Lambeth beside the river stood the shot tower *(ill. 54)*, a colossal thing, a hundred and fifty feet high. Inside it, gobbets of molten iron were dropped from a great height and formed cannonballs to fire at the French.

Lambeth traditionally had been home to skilled agricultural workers, craftsmen and boatmen, leavened with a scattering of artists, performers and scientists, Huguenots and Jews, Italians and Dutchmen: occasionally bohemian and not always prosperous, but essentially cultured and decent. Clear-eyed, Blake saw a great grey swell of distress and ugliness approaching. The

54. The shot tower at Lambeth, near to William Blake's home. This operated from 1789 to 1937.

pressure of population and wartime privations were making country life miserable for thousands from the English and Irish countryside, and they trailed into town to seek their fortune. With them came dysfunction, poverty and crisis that had to be dealt with. While country vestries sent people back to where they came from, Lambeth was where the human tide stopped; where the drains were non-existent, the water sources filthy and the buildings overcrowded. There was public drunkenness; drink was cheap and pubs were numerous, especially around Astley's, and people spent as little time as they could in their one shared room.

There were outbreaks of cholera, there were fights and abandoned children, there was cruelty to animals. There was child labour; little sweeps climbed the chimneys, little thieves picked pockets, and little children were employed pushing clay into the moulds at the Coade stone factory. Some of the girls were taken in at the Female Asylum around the corner from Hercules Road and taught to obey orders and to work.

55. Blake's house in Hercules Road.

Preachers bellowed at credulous bystanders on Kennington Common and St George's Fields. On every side sprang up missions and charity hospitals, ragged schools and chapels, and disaffection between the Irish incomers and the English.

Lambeth became less a retreat and more a hell of social upheaval and industrial grime. Blake himself was not rich, but he lived in a solid brick house and enjoyed the convenience of a clean, pleasant life, funded by his craft. Hercules Buildings must sometimes have seemed like an island of privilege in a sea of misery.

In 1800 he and Catherine left for Sussex near the sea. The three years they spent there brought no immediate professional success for William but he felt inspired to write *Jerusalem*. The 'green and pleasant land' part was all Sussex; the 'dark satanic mills' were his enduring impression of Lambeth.

THE LYING-IN HOSPITAL

In 1760, there was no maternity hospital in Lambeth. St Thomas's was overwhelmed, and anyway in the Borough. A City merchant called Thomas Guy had endowed Guy's, in the grounds of St Thomas's, in 1725, but it was for the incurably ill. The Magdalen Hospital for Penitent Prostitutes had existed close to Blackfriars Road for as long as anyone could remember, but the neighbours would raise eyebrows if you volunteered to go there. Also these places were too far from Lambeth Marsh. The stream of immigrants and vagrants was never-ending and rates of peri-natal mortality were high for both mothers and babies. Pregnancy was particularly life-threatening in Lambeth, ill served by anyone except 'wise women', apothecaries, and barber-surgeons. The diet of poor people put them at risk. Rickets, caused by a lack of the vitamin D obtainable from milk and butter, reduced pelvic width and poor girls and their babies often died in childbirth. Poverty, stumbling science and a social care system reliant on charity and the parish made this inevitable. Land was being dug up for housing and dairy cows were scarcer; so milk, which in hot weather kept for no time at all, had to be transported long distances on bad roads. Demand in Lambeth far exceeded supply so the stuff was watered down and might be tubercular anyway. Butter was too expensive for most people. Drinking water, unless you lived in a house with its own well, must be bought or obtained from public pumps, and the public supply was often polluted. It was less safe than small beer, the usual drink. Fruit and vegetables were not considered a necessary part of the diet and if grown on foul land they could cause outbreaks of dysentery. Meat was expensive. The subsistence diet, even for children, was beer and bread. Overcrowding around Lambeth Marsh meant whole pauper families living in one room.

56. The first Lying-in Hospital in Westminster Bridge Road, pictured here c. 1800.

57. Milk deliveries by hand cart, seen here outside Rowling's Dairy at the corner of St Alban's Street and China Walk. The dairy was founded in 1815.

A kind philanthropist came to the rescue of those poor women who were expecting babies in such conditions. His was an inadequate attempt, but there was nothing else and it was a brave start that led to lasting good. Dr John Leake was a 'man-midwife'. His medical training wasn't great, but then no doctor got well-trained in the eighteenth century. Hunter, the great surgeon, was working across the river at St George's, but he was unique. All a young man needed to proclaim himself a doctor was a basic comprehension of anatomy and some Latin and Greek. Leake had some practical experience in the use of forceps and other instruments already in use, but his real strength was his personality. He was determined and well connected, and got hold of land on the road approaching Westminster Bridge and raised subscriptions to build a hospital on it 'for the relief of those child-bearing women who are the wives of poor industrious Tradesmen or distressed housekeepers, and who either from unavoidable misfortunes or the expenses of maintaining large families are reduced to real want. Also for the reception and immediate relief of indigent soldiers' and sailors' wives, the former in particular being very numerous in and about the City of Westminster'. There were a lot of wars in the eighteenth century, in Europe and Canada and America, from which soldiers and sailors

58. The General Lying-in Hospital in York Road in 1950.

came back to poverty – along with their wives and children.

From the moment of its opening in 1767, the controversial thing about the Lying-In Hospital (for it was later reconstructed as the dignified building, recently restored to life as part of Tommy's, that we see today on York Road) was its liberal policies. Leake was lax about swaddling, but that wasn't the main problem. What so outraged the Lambeth Vestry was the women. Some of them had *no husband*. Usually, hospitals demanded a marriage certificate from women who arrived to give birth, but staff at the Lying-In Hospital wouldn't bother to ask. The Vestry were furious at being landed with pauper mothers, their children born in the parish and therefore entitled to a place in the workhouse or some outdoor relief. They expected vociferous support from Sir Joseph Mawbey, the High Sheriff of Surrey, in a confrontation with Dr Leake, but he mysteriously absented himself. Mawbey was also President of St Thomas's on Bankside, and probably was happy that Leake's establishment was taking away some unwelcome patients from his own hospital.

When the Lying-In Hospital started, there was no understanding of infection or of the importance of good food, and money was in short supply. There were outbreaks of disease. Yet women were grateful for the care they received, and over the years, the peri-natal mortality rate slowly improved with advances in medical understanding.

SCHOOLS

There were schools in Lambeth in the seventeenth century when it was still rural and the established Church taught all that a young man was required to know. At the end of the eighteenth century, there were still some private schools; there was one in Carlisle House, just a step from William Blake's house, and a Freemasons' School for Girls in Westminster Bridge Road. But Lambeth was fast losing its reputation as a place to send middle-class children.

At the same time wealthy City industrialists recognised the inhumane conditions in which poor children were reared, and were trying to do something about it.

Such enlightened thinkers opined that feral

59. The Freemasons' Charity School in 1801. Drawn by S. Rawle.

children, should they live, were inevitably destined for crime and immorality. But if they could learn to read and write, to be punctual, hard-working and disciplined, and to fear God, they would become a resource for employers and at peace with themselves.

A boys' school in Lambeth was already a model of its kind. It had begun in 1706, forty years later than it should have done. In 1660 one Alexander Jones, who had bought some Bishop's Lands during the Commonwealth, informed the Vestry that they would be used for a Free School, and that he would make an endowment of £24 per annum for the benefit of 24 poor scholars. When he died in 1661, the endowment was made but his property, including a house in Blowbladder Street, was restored to the Crown. Blowbladder School, thankfully, never came into existence, but a Mr Lawrence, one of Mr Jones's trustees, made alternative land available. Since Mr Lawrence's bequest allowed for various relations to live in his property for their lifetimes, it was forty years or more before the Lawrence bequest could be activated. The school when it finally opened was the Lawrence Charity School, in Dog House Fields (later called Lambeth Green but now under the railway; roughly the site of the CP Hart showroom in the vaults between Hercules Road and Carlisle Lane).

In Lambeth there was already a school for eight poor boys endowed in the previous century by Thomas Rich. Latin and Greek were supposed to be taught in order that the Bible might be read, and the ignorant thus transformed into useful members of society. But a classical education had not been necessary since King James' Bible, in English, became widely available, and Dr Denne, the Rector at St Mary's later, dropped Latin and Greek at the Rich school. He believed that the transformative power of religion, if it had any, needed supplementing with practice, and he introduced a more utilitarian regime. The boys learned to read in the morning, and in the afternoon they spun and wove their own clothes, just as they did in workhouses. The emphasis was on hard work and discipline, reducing the strain on the pockets of benefactors and providing a better-educated workforce for Lambeth industry. More boys could be taken into the school, more could attain basic literacy and all boys who behaved well and worked hard could hope to be apprenticed.

In the 1750s the Rich school was failing and the Lawrence Charity school was doing well, so they merged at Lambeth Green as the Boys' Charity School. In 1808, a new building was provided. The Coade Stone boy in an alcove outside may have been modelled by Flaxman.

There was a Coade Stone girl too. In 1706, Archbishop Tenison had instituted a school for twelve girls of poor families in Lambeth High Street. By 1787 this had become the Girls' Charity School, with 24 pupils, and the trustees pleaded for subscriptions so that they might take in more.

> 'The great extent of this parish, the late rapid increase of buildings and inhabitants in it, the number of its poor, and the vicinity of the metropolis, furnish incontrovertible arguments in favour of a plan, which has for its object the Education of Children, the daughters of indigent families ... to rescue them ... and to form them to habits of religion, virtue, and industry; and by thus uniting the interest of the community with the happiness of individuals, has an almost irresistible claim to our support....'

Five years later in 1792 there were 36 pupils, almost all of whom could hope to get a good character and go into service. Like the boys, they were taught from the age of eight or nine to work, and were generally out in the world by thirteen or fourteen.

> Mrs Reed, at the School House, High Street, Lambeth, will see to it that needlework sent to her will be executed on the following terms:

A coarse napkin	*One penny*
A fine napkin	*Tuppence*
A pair of coarse sheets	*Ninepence*
A pair of fine sheets	*One and sixpence*

...And so on. They also made shifts and shirts. We often forget, admiring the exquisite ladies and gentlemen in portraits by Gainsborough and Reynolds, that every inch of their petticoats and bodices and fine lace cuffs was stitched by patient hands, usually the patient hands of children. A lifetime of drudgery was the lot of nearly all girls and women and many gave up and went on the streets. The benefactors of schools like these were determined to make the girls into faithful servants – fidelity was everything. At the girls' charity school, they promised that if a girl remained in her situation for three years in the first five after leaving, she could qualify for two guineas from the Treasurer.

MRS COADE'S STONE

Coade stone, which like most local industries contributed both pride and pollution to Lambeth, is still to be seen in towns all over England, especially in London. It was made for roughly seventy years between 1770 and 1840 in a works that was established by Miss Eleanor Coade at King's Arms Stairs on the south bank.

With the deference then accorded to age and seniority, she was called Mrs Coade, but she never married. Eleanor and her sister Elizabeth came from a prosperous family of wool-trade dissenters at Lyme in Dorset, with family connections to the Barings, and to Bristol, and rather tenuous links to the Cornish china-clay industry. They arrived in London in the mid-century with their parents and settled in Hoxton. In 1769 their father went bankrupt and soon afterwards he died.

Eleanor was then 36, a Baptist, friendly with many Dissenters and running her own linen-drapery. She and her mother and Elizabeth knew, possibly through their chapel, one Daniel Pincot, a one-time wax modeller for Josiah Wedgwood who had a showroom for artificial stone architectural ornament in Covent Garden. Pincot directed them to his factory site south of the river. Artificial stone had been made at King's Arms Stairs since the 1720s; in 1722 a man called Holt had patented a way to make it out of glass, lead and clay. He even published a book about it, claiming that the Pyramids had been made out of something very similar. Batty Langley, the early design-and-build merchant, apparently wheedled the secret out of Holt's workmen and

60. Eleanor Coade's stone works at Narrow Wall, Lambeth, c.1800. Watercolour, artist unknown.

61. Ornamental works displayed outside the Coade factory c.1800.

began a factory in Southwark, but he did not do well. At Lambeth, Holt continued to manufacture arches, pedestals, copings, grottoes and so on until 1757.

In 1767, Pincot, with his own much better artificial stone recipe, appears to have taken over Holt's site. Perhaps he was looking for an investor in Eleanor Coade. If so he got more than he bargained for.

The business he showed her was on Pedlar's Acre. Where College Street joined Narrow Street, there stood King's Arms Stairs and Martineau's Brewery. (It's all under the Festival Hall and Jubilee Gardens now). You could sink wells around there if you wanted fresh water. The first factory was behind the brewery, looking like a farmhouse set in a small stoneyard. The Widow Coade and her two daughters took it and lived in it and Eleanor set about building the business.

Elizabeth died young. But it had always been Eleanor who had the scientific understanding, the artistic vision and the commercial acumen. She branded their product Coade Stone and for the first two years, employed Pincot as manager. Then she took on John Bacon, who had finished his apprenticeship to a potter at Lambeth a decade previously and whose job for the rest of his life would be to sculpt the artificial stone and design pieces for sale. They kept quiet about exactly how it was made, but the secret was in the name: it was called *lithodipyra,* meaning twice-fired stone. Clay that had already been hard-baked into stoneware was ground up into a grog, mixed with more clay and a few other minerals, rolled and pushed into plaster moulds and then fired again at very high temperatures. This is a crude explanation of a subtle process, but essentially accurate. The inclusion of grog prevented shrinkage of the malleable clay. The result was not stone, but ceramic, and as such

62. The Lion Brewery at Lambeth, drawn by Thomas Allom and published in 1841. The Coade stone lion on the roof of the building was later placed at the Lambeth end of Westminster Bridge, near to the former County Hall.

must be fired with immense skill if it was to endure.

Perhaps Eleanor had an eye for architectural fashion, or perhaps she was simply good at reading a balance sheet. Either way she had recognised an opportunity whose time had come. Robert Adam, Sir John Soane, John Nash, Samuel and James Wyatt and every other notable contemporary architect used Coade stone ornamentation. From 1774, it was undoubtedly the most practical option, for timber ornament was disallowed under a new Building Act and Coade was cheaper than stone. Only time would tell whether the Coade stone would endure and at first there was some doubt; but the dubious were persuaded by its fashionable appeal. And Bacon's modelling was so sharp and so sensitive and the Coade catalogue so extensive that reservations were put aside, all the more quickly when both he and Eleanor were awarded medals by the Royal Society of Arts. When Bacon obtained the King's patronage, nothing stood in their way.

There exists a copy of the Coade catalogue, etched by Blake, published for private circulation between 1778 and 1780. Here are pages of classical statuary and architectural detail in abundance. The bodies of the life-size Neptunes and Zeuses are contorted by exertion and emotion. If you wanted a face of snake-haired Medusa to place on the keystone above a fanlight, she would be horrifying; a Minerva would be supremely wise. For the fountain below your terrace you could commission Diana the Huntress, or a girl water-carrier supporting an urn on her head, artfully exposing a breast as her toga falls – or a pair of naked warriors – or a bevy of cherubs. Or a couple of modestly draped ladies bearing lamp brackets, or a fireplace with candle holders sprouting from the head of a Sphinx. There is movement and liveliness in all of it, although the faces of the animals are humanoid.

A lion, head thrust belligerently forward, one paw on a stone ball, wears the manic stare of Margaret Thatcher.

By 1800 Eleanor was a wealthy woman. The old farmhouse was long gone, replaced by something more elegant, and the Coade factory, with its big kilns and chimneys and stone mill, would soon extend its site to Westminster Bridge, where the showroom stood on Coade Row, opposite Astley's Amphitheatre. All over London – especially in Bloomsbury and the smart new houses of Kennington – whole streets of terraced houses were adorned with Coade stone urns and columns and capitals and classical motifs. Acanthus leaves, dentils, egg and dart mouldings on panels, cornices, bas-reliefs and vermiculated stonework decorated noble houses in grand squares. Allegorical figures represented science, music, farming, fishery, and art. The stuff was everywhere, but it was not mass produced. Skill of a high order was evident.

When Bacon died in 1799, Eleanor, who was in her sixties, took on John Sealy, a cousin who was already working with her, as partner. They employed well-known sculptors and a workforce of about twenty men, with some children for the repetitious work.

Sealy died in 1813. He is buried at Lambeth where, sadly, his tomb is a rare example of mis-fired Coade stone; bits have scaled away. Upon his death Eleanor made William Croggon, another relation, her manager. When she died aged 89 in 1822, with a contract for work on Buckingham House just beginning, Croggon had not been made a partner, so litigation ensued for many years while he conducted business as usual. He went bankrupt in 1833, largely due, it seems, to bills unpaid by the Duke of York. He died in 1835. The Coade stone lion (now at Westminster Bridge approach) that originally surmounted the Lion Brewery next to the bridge was made around 1837; but no more Coade stone appeared after 1843.

Coade stone adorns Hammerwood Park, Philadelphia, and the entrance to the zoo at Rio de Janeiro, which is a replica of the Brentford Gate at Syon House. You can find it in Montego Bay, Jamaica, at St Paul, Boston, Massachusetts; in Sydney New South Wales; and in storage in Montreal, as the original of Nelson's Column, thirty years older than the London one. Most of us are more likely to admire it on the houses around Bedford Square or Kennington Green.

The bed of the horse mill used at the Coade factory was reverently set into a grassy bank in front of the Royal Festival Hall when it opened in 1951, and there it remained as a little-regarded curiosity for over fifty years. Since the recent (2006) refurbishment of the frontage, it has disappeared.

LAMBETH POTTERY

Coade stone was, technically, pottery, and both Bacon and Pincot had been trained in that trade. Dissenting and Dutch traditions were strong in the industry, which had existed, in a small way, in Lambeth since the late sixteenth century if not earlier. South of the river was the perfect location for potters, who required among other things a good water source, good river transport, and ideally, humid cellars in which to season the clay. Damp, riverine Lambeth, so close to a big market, was ideal.

There isn't a lot of early Lambeth ware that survives but the earliest examples date from around 1600, and experts say they show Dutch and Italian influence. The pieces are utilitarian, but undeniably beautiful – typically tactile, fat jugs and wine jars with inscriptions such as CLARET or RHENISH, and drug pots. After William and Mary came to England the pictorial blue and white Delft superseded all that.

Early in the eighteenth century small potteries were well established in Vauxhall and Pedlar's Acre. One near Lambeth Palace was in Norfolk House, the mansion confiscated from the Duke's family after his execution. Descendants of the original potter ran it until 1763, when the old building was pulled down. Carlisle House, the former home of the Bishop of Carlisle, was also occupied by a pottery between 1700 and 1745.

In Back Lane (Lambeth High Street behind Norfolk House) there was another small pottery that kept going until it was absorbed by Doulton's

63. The potteries at Lambeth c.1793.

in the nineteenth century. At Vauxhall there was a pottery at Glasshouse Stairs, another at Gun House Stairs, and yet another at Bridgefoot.

Lambeth Delftware was useful rather than fashionable. Lambeth kitchen tiles, drug pots, kitchen plates and wine-bottles were sold widely and often to the catering trade – you would see it in pubs and coffee houses. Designs were flowers, tableaux from the Old Testament or *chinoiserie*, on a greenish-tinted white ground. Batty Langley, writing in 1748, implied that the 'white potters' at Lambeth produced tiles inferior to the Dutch. They looked all right, but were not so precisely measured, which for a builder could be infuriating.

Well-known local firms were Chilwell, Griffiths, Stiff and Stephen Green, and they tended to inter-marry and to exchange workers. Lambeth Delft retained its reputation as serviceable stuff, though creamware (being less fragile than Delft) was coming in by the end of the century and some of the Lambeth potters were influenced by work produced at Fulham. But everything would change when the Napoleonic Wars ended and the first Mr Doulton arrived.

THE GLASSHOUSE

At the end of the seventeenth century, the old glass factory at Vauxhall had passed to a syndicate. John Dawson, the manager who owed his prosperity to the Duke of Buckingham, died in 1712 leaving to a daughter an annuity from 'the Little Glass House' and to a son, The Three Mariners pub. After various investors had taken a hand in Vauxhall Glass the factory passed back to the descendants of John Bowles, the London merchant who had been prominent in the first syndicate. Its reputation grew as it overwhelmed even the Venetians in exports, and its profits provided the family with a good living for decades around the mid-century. Phineas Bowles, son of John the merchant investor, had

64. The Falcon glass works at Holland Street, near Blackfriars Road, published in 1842. By Thomas Allom.

eleven extant children and he and his wife were able to raise them at Loughborough House, a mansion set in 234 acres of parkland less than two miles from the factory, between Camberwell and Brixton.

The last member of the Bowles family to be actively involved with the glassworks refused to invest in the new, cheaper French methods of casting glass. Either he was Luddite about it, or simply ready to retire, but the famous Vauxhall glass houses closed in 1785. A vinegar distillery was later established on the site by (Sir) Robert Burnett.

SIR JOSEPH MAWBEY

In the eighteenth century there were numerous small gin distilleries and one or two larger ones in Lambeth. Setting up a gin distillery required big capital but once it was in operation, it provided work to copper founders, plumbers, bricklayers, coopers and coalmen, millers and bargemen, farmers and sugar importers, among others. After the mid-century, the laws were changed and high taxes put gin beyond the pocket of the labouring classes – and, more importantly, the Army, who must be sober – but the trade settled down, rather than going into a terminal decline.

Joseph Pratt had grown wealthy from a gin distillery in Vauxhall and offered Joseph Mawbey, his young nephew from Leicestershire, the opportunity to study at Lambeth and enter holy orders. This Joseph Mawbey did, but at the

65. A cartoon by James Gillray in 1788, depicting Sir Joseph Mawbey (centre) playing cards. The cartoon is called 'A pig in a poke. Whist, whist'.

age of 17, thanks to the illness of another Pratt nephew, he was precipitated into the family business. He took to it, and years later when his uncle died, he inherited it. He became Member of Parliament for Southwark, served as Magistrate and High Sheriff of Surrey and was made a baronet. In some circles he was a figure of fun; he was called by Walpole 'vain, noisy and foolish' and lampooned by Gillray.

In the 1790s, with gin heavily taxed but not so cheap as to threaten public order, the Vauxhall distillery was still vast. Mawbey, wary that over-consumption and drunkenness could lead to another crackdown, concentrated on exporting his product and maximising profit. A contemporary observer reported that two thousand hogs were 'kept grunting on the grains' outside his factory, for later sale to the Navy as food.

Sir Joseph Mawbey married a Pratt cousin, became very wealthy indeed and bought building leases in Vauxhall and Kennington. When he died in 1806 *The Times* reported a sale of his:

> '... freehold and copyhold estates, consisting chiefly of well-secured ground-rents, including Messrs Fassett and Burnett's Distillery at Vauxhall, with the reversion of the premises after 1899, four adjoining dwellings, let at will, a spacious Dwelling House let to the trustees of Licensed Victuallers, and the ground rents of four houses in Kennington Lane and Mawbey's Pond ... ground rents from Parson's brewhouse and houses in Saville Row, Pear Tree Acre, Pratt street, Carlisle Lane, Park Place and Church Street, Lambeth; sundry houses and an inclosure of pasture land at Mawbey Place, South Lambeth.'

THE VINEGAR MAN

Mark Beaufoy's family had come over with the Conqueror, and his branch of it were Quakers from Evesham, in Worcestershire; like Lambeth a fertile, fruit-growing area with good river transport. His father died young, and in 1734 aged sixteen he was sent as apprentice to a distiller in Bristol. His articles of indenture reminded him that 'Taverns he shall not frequent, at Dice he shall not play, Fornication he shall not commit, Matrimony he shall not commit....' One day he would have to make his fortune; and London beckoned. A friend wrote to him from the capital:

> 'London is the world in miniature, here are all degrees of human Life from the King to the weather-wise Cobbler, Archbishops Bishops priests Deacons Poets Painters Politicians Philosophers Fools Fops Fiddlers Whores Rogues and Pickpockets (both noble and ignoble) are here in abundance - but among all the different clases, Whores and Lawyers seem to be the most numerous, their occupations are something akin, they stand in the Corners of the streets or run about like Beasts of Prey, seeking whom they may devour - Whores of all Ranks from dirty Peg to the Duchess - really they are the finest Women in Town - the moment you receive this, Dear Beaufoy, pray that I enter not into Temptation or run into any kind of Danger.'

He couldn't wait to get there. When his apprenticeship was over and matrimony permissible, he married, in 1743, Elizabeth Hanbury ('one eye and a large fortune' one malicious contemporary informed another - her father was the prominent Bristol Quaker Capel Hanbury and she was related to the Ambassador at St Petersburg). They moved at once to London and took possession of a house on the shore, formerly part of Cuper's Gardens. This was still a pleasure garden, although much declined.

Mark Beaufoy had spotted its potential. Here were outbuildings with their own landing stage where barley malt could be offloaded and vinegar barrels shipped out. He called this Vinegar Yard, set up a distillery, and set about getting contracts to supply malt vinegar, a useful cleaning fluid. It was in demand for swabbing the decks of

66. Mark Beaufoy, by Richard Josey, after Thomas Gainsborough. Published 1877.

ships. His letter of 1756 to His Majesty's Commissioners of the Navy reads:

> Gentlemen....I take the liberty to lay before you 4 samples of Vinegar....

- and he provides some useful information about its acidity and manufacture before continuing:

> ...I hope Gentlemen for your Preference on Account of having in the last Warr broake the Combination of Vinegar makers (till then invincible) by taking the Contract for Vinegar Myself, which I discharged to the satisfaction of the Victualling Board, the consequence whereof is a Saving to ye Crown of £1,500 per Ann on a Warr Consumption of this Article.
>
> (*signed*)
> The Vinegar Yard, Cuper's Gardens

In the eighteenth century, tens of thousands of barrels of Beaufoy's Vinegar would be hoisted off Thames barges down at Greenwich and swung aboard for the high seas.

67. Beaufoy's vinegar factory in the late 18th century.

Cuper's Gardens at last closed down. Jesus College, Oxford, which owned the freehold, stripped the lead from the roof of those of its buildings which were unoccupied and left them to rot, upon which the derelict shelters in an untended wilderness attracted prostitutes, criminals and vagrants. Mark Beaufoy wrote to the Principal of Jesus College that the place was 'now the emblem of ye Haggard, the seat of Desolation, and the Disgrace of our Neighbourhood.' In 1763 he took over a bigger slice of the site, including more buildings which he demolished and re-used to extend his distillery, and his product range. It is said that he had resolved to make vinegar, rather than spirits, after being horrified by Hogarth's *Gin Lane*. Quakers were not opposed to alcohol, just to gin; Truman, Hanbury and Buxton were Quaker brewers, and indeed *Gin Lane* shows beer, in opposition to spirits, as a healthful drink. Beaufoy obtained a liquor licence and imported dried fruit to make British Wines – 'sweets' they were then called. There were plenty in the family who could tell him how to do it and provide a ready market, too; the Capels and the Hanburys on his wife's side were wine and brandy merchants. What with the wine, and the Navy contracts for the vinegar, he amassed a vast fortune out of what a contemporary tour guide called 'this ocean of sweets and sours' that poured forth from south of the river.

The Beaufoys were well connected, well liked and honourable. The Society of Friends encouraged trade and Mark's correspondence is peppered with family news of the Hanburys and friendships with other well-known brewing and banking families. Quakers had to stick together, since the Test Acts protected the established Church and discriminated against them. Dissenters were officially prohibited from holding public office. Mark Beaufoy stood without success as Member of Parliament for Evesham. He and his wife lived simply, and were kindly and encouraging parents to their seven children. Two of their three sons Henry, John Hanbury, and Mark, were particularly talented.

Henry, the oldest, born in 1750, was prodigiously bright, charming and handsome. He was educated as a Dissenter and was his father's pride and joy until, as a young man, he behaved like a hero in a Gothic novel: he fell in love with a pretty heiress, Elizabeth Jenks - a Ward of her uncle, Plowden Slaney - and they eloped. Elizabeth was not a Quaker, and Mr Beaufoy would not relent. However Henry, with abject contrition and considerable charm, managed to overcome his father's reservations quite soon, and Elizabeth was welcomed into the family.

Henry was a partner in the firm but never an active one; instead he became Member of Parliament for Minehead, and later for Great Yarmouth, and secretary to Pitt the Younger and a considerable public figure and activist for repeal of the Test Acts. He died aged only 45 in 1795. Gainsborough had to leave his portrait, a companion to that of Elizabeth, unfinished.

The middle son, John Hanbury Beaufoy, came home from the Grand Tour and managed the vinegar distillery in Cuper's Gardens, spending his spare time in country pursuits at his estate in Dorset. He married, in St Margaret's Westminster, Agnes Payne from Barbados. He managed the business astutely and it supported the entire family in style. When in 1812 the Strand Bridge Company purchased the Cuper's Gardens site for the construction of their new bridge (later to be called Waterloo Bridge) John Hanbury Beaufoy moved the distillery to South Lambeth.

The youngest Beaufoy boy, born in 1764, grew up to be Colonel Mark Beaufoy. He was at least as brilliant as Henry, and like him, married against his father's wishes. His bride was his beautiful cousin Margaretta Beaufoy. In 1784 they ran away to Gretna Green and thence to Neuchâtel, where they had two children, Henriette (Harriet) and Henry. Mark and Margaretta did not fit into Swiss provincial society, which they regarded with much amusement while quietly doing what they pleased, which was indulging their scientific curiosity. Margaretta was a mathematician, Mark an amateur astronomer and physicist, and they lived contentedly off Mark's revenue from Vinegar Yard.

In 1787, six days after the first climb of Mont Blanc by Saussure, they arrived at Chamonix determined that Mark could do it too. They brought along a nursemaid for the children so that Margaretta, in her ankle-length skirts, could accompany her husband and their porters on the uphill hike (there were no footpaths then) for the first few days. For the final challenge Mark wore just one loose layer of white linen - jacket and trousers - against the sunshine, while half a dozen local men lugged supplies including a rope, hatchets and a ladder for crossing crevasses. He made it to the top, where he made observations and took measurements while the porters lay down and fell asleep. He was the first Englishman to climb Mont Blanc.

In 1787 they returned to London, and had more children and lived at Hackney Wick, conveniently near the Dissenting Academy where the little ones could be educated. Mark, a colonel by virtue of his post with the Tower Hamlets Militia, devoted his time to experiments at Greenland Docks, Rotherhithe. He was working out how best ships could manoeuvre through water - an interest sparked when, as a schoolboy, he had observed how vessels behaved at Lambeth. He was a founder of the Society for the Improvement of Naval Architecture.

Margaretta died suddenly in 1800. Widowed, Colonel Mark Beaufoy went on to write papers on ballistics, to build an Observatory near Harrow Weald, and to become a governor of Harrow School. In the next century the family firm at South Lambeth would pass to his descendants.

Great machinery of Empire

Everything didn't change overnight in 1800. Thomas Milne's Land Use map of that date shows the Lambeth riverbank built up, and houses crowded along the main roads, but the spaces in between are still meadow and market gardens. The wealthy have settled in fine houses along the Kennington Road, a route properly established since the construction of Westminster Bridge. Away from smoky riverbank industry and close to clean water-sources, Kennington Road curves around the site of the old drovers' pond by the Horns to join Kennington Park Road. Lambeth Road bisects St George's Fields to meet the Blackfriars Road at the Obelisk.

Victory at Waterloo, and the end of the Napoleonic Wars in 1815, truly ushered in the nineteenth century. For Lambeth the great change came when the civil engineer John Rennie completed the pale granite Strand Bridge, opened by the Prince Regent in 1817 and renamed after the battle. Rennie knew the site well; for nineteen years, from 1791 to 1810, his workshops had been at Jamaica Wharf, off Upper Ground.

At Vauxhall, construction began on Vauxhall Bridge and a new road straight to Camberwell, skirting a circular market garden just before St Mark's Church. Sir Robert Clayton, a brilliant eighteenth-century financier who had long ago leased from the Duchy of Cornwall much of the land crossed by the new road, was let down by his heirs; they sub-let unwisely and the family lost most of their holdings by 1834.

Prince's Meadows, on the South Bank between Blackfriars and Waterloo Bridge, belonged to the Duchy, but was on long lease to the Lett brothers, Thomas and John. They had timber yards there and now began to sub-lease their land for development. What had been a formless huddle of lanes behind Narrow Wall was up for development. *The Times* reported on 17 September 1824:

68. Vauxhall Bridge c.1850, viewed from Cumberland Gardens. A lithograph, artist unknown.

69. *The opening of Waterloo Bridge in 1817.*

> The south bank of the Thames, near Waterloo bridge, will shortly be cleared of no less than 50 old houses, which are now pulling down. The narrow dirty passage along the bank to Pedlar's Acre and Westminster Bridge called Narrow Wall will be opened by the removal of the above obstructions and rendered more commodious to passengers. It is at present called Belvedere Road.

Labour was plentiful, and a map of 1824 shows that most of Lambeth's cultivated land, including the north part of St George's Fields, most of Vauxhall and parts of Kennington as far south as the Oval, had by then been built over to house the workers. Draining the area for building had at last become financially worth while. The population of London, which had risen to two million at the turn of the century, was soaring. An agricultural depression after the long wars ended in 1815, allied with massive unemployment among returning soldiers and sailors, meant that people poured into the city on foot or in carts or even, if they could afford it, by coach. Many settled south of the river. If they found accommodation at all, it was cheaper and perhaps, being relatively rural, more familiar. And they could work in local industries, for there was no cheap public transport away from the river, and ordinary people expected to work within walking distance of home.

BETHLEM HOSPITAL

When in 1815 the Royal Bethlem Hospital for the Insane – Bedlam – was installed where the old Dog and Duck had been, at St George's Fields, the site of Mr Hedger's gleefully exploitative ventures and a thousand bad-tempered political rallies was at last tamed. The duckpond, which Cromwell's soldiers had overlooked from their fort and where Hedger, at the pub, had served wine without a licence, was tidied up and made perfectly round. Trees were planted in smart lines and gravel walks were laid; a long wall separated the new hospital from carriages and riders along the road.

This was the latest incarnation of a hospital already nearly 600 years old. Bedlam had been founded as a priory in 1247 when a mediaeval Alderman of the City bequeathed some land off Bishopsgate to the church of St Mary's of Bethlehem, in Palestine. Like other priories it offered hospitality to travellers, and in the course of the next hundred years or so became known as

70. Bethlem Hospital in the 1890s.

a hospital - a place of refuge and cure for the infirm. From at least 1403, it specialised in the mentally infirm of both sexes. Its buildings were demolished and rebuilt over the years on the original spot (now covered by Liverpool Street station).

From 1547 Bethlem Hospital was taken over by the City of London. After the Great Fire they moved it to imposing, if draughty, purpose-built accommodation in Moorfields. Here, in the next century, were the fashionable visitors and wretched chained inmates depicted by Hogarth; members of the public were permitted to come in until 1770.

Architecturally magnificent though the new Bedlam was, it had been carelessly built over the old City ditch, and after a hundred years was becoming unfit for habitation. Outside, in what is now Finsbury Circus, a pond filled up; inside, the floors sank and bounced. The inmates had to be moved - and the City at last found a use for St George's Fields.

The Lambeth building, for 200 patients, opened in August 1815, and essentially took the form of the Moorfields one, but without ornament. There was a long frontage of 580 feet, with a forbidding portico, the Royal Arms in Coade stone, and a rather subdued dome. Four galleried floors dominated the interior. Improvements on the old model included a visitors' room, day rooms and coal fires on each floor. Each patient had his or her own room with bedding. Violent patients seem to have been confined in the basement gallery. Straw bedding was used there. It was where incontinent patients ('those who have little regard for cleanliness') were made to stay. On the top floor were the incurables.

Behind the main building stood two independent blocks for 'criminal lunatics'; Bethlem had for many years accommodated the violent insane. The inmates of these two buildings, some occasionally manacled, were controlled by the Home Office until they were moved to Broadmooor in 1864.

Patients worked. The women looked after laundry and sewing, the men hauled water. One man, in the Criminal buildings, kept tame birds and small animals. He spent over forty years in

Bedlam after an attempt on the life of George III in 1800.

Between 1830 and 1850 the architect Sydney Smirke remodelled the hospital, and added the pepperpot dome we see today on the Imperial War Museum. The road was moved away from the frontage and the present-day lawns added. Over the years, treatment came more and more to concentrate on recovery. As patients improved they were entertained by small aviaries of songbirds indoors, by pets, and by communal areas indoors and out. Days were regulated into working time and free time. The idea was to prevent boredom and keep the inmates occupied.

Another failed regicide was sent to the criminal wing of the hospital in 1840. Edward Oxford had been 18 when he took a pot shot at Queen Victoria, and after the first few years of imprisonment he decided to make the best of it. At Bedlam he taught himself French, German and Italian, took up the violin and became good at chess. He also learned wood-graining and house-painting. When Broadmoor opened he

71. Richard Dadd, Bethlem's most famous patient, painting a scene from Midsummer Night's Dream *c.1856.*

was sent there, but not for long; three years later, in 1867, he was released, on condition that he emigrate to Australia. He was only too pleased to comply, and twenty years later published a book there called *Lights and Shadows of Melbourne Life* under his new name of John Freeman.

The best-known criminal patient of all, Richard Dadd, really had committed murder. When delusional he had killed his father. He was 27 then, had trained under Turner at the Royal Academy Schools, and was a tragic figure of recognised talent as an artist. He continued to paint at Lambeth for twenty years and at Broadmoor until his death in 1886.

From 1857, every parish had to provide for its own mentally infirm patients. Bedlam gradually became a private clinic for those who could afford it, and most of Lambeth's demented must henceforth end their days in a workhouse or a County Asylum.

BEAUFOY'S NEW VINEGAR FACTORY

Early in the nineteenth century the Strand Bridge Committee began negotiations to buy up Cuper's Gardens, where the bridge would meet the south bank. Several local firms moved away, and Beaufoys' was among them.

John Hanbury Beaufoy set up a fine new vinegar factory with a clock tower behind Caron House off the South Lambeth Road. His illegitimate son had been killed at the Battle of Talavera in 1809; maybe this is why, in 1812, he was relieved to retire early from commerce and London life. He gave control of the business to his nephew, Colonel Mark's son, Henry Benjamin Hanbury Beaufoy (known in the family as HBHB.)

HBHB, like his father, was an adventurous man possessed of scientific curiosity. Shortly before taking over at South Lambeth, he had made a balloon trip from Hackney to Colchester; and he was elected a Fellow of the Linnaean Society at an early age. His domestic arrangements scandalised the family, for he lived with a Miss Eliza Taylor, 'at one time a columbine at Astley's.'

Indifferent to their opinion, HBHB and Miss

Taylor cohabited contentedly at South Lambeth for over thirty years. He managed the business, gave generously towards local education and collected books in peace. According to a later Beaufoy 'quite late in life he married her, and his family paid her the compliment of calling on her at once.' The family were formidable. HBHB had six brothers and sisters. A brother, Captain Mark, fought at Waterloo, and one of his sisters married a Mr Thornhill, of the South London family closely related to the Kembles and Mrs Siddons, the actress.

When HBHB died, four years after Eliza, in 1851, the South Lambeth vinegar factory was inherited by his youngest brother Captain George, who had been a Fellow of the Astronomical Society since 1828. In 1864 he died, and since the heir was a minor, the business was managed by George's widow Anne for ten years. In 1874, as soon as he came of age, Mark Hanbury Beaufoy became owner and manager; he was MP for Kennington in the 1890s. His eldest son, Henry Mark, was the last Beaufoy to manage the South Lambeth vinegar distillery. He was killed in an air raid in 1941.

THE ROUPELLS, PROPERTY DEVELOPERS

The Roupells had come to England from Holland with the court of William of Orange. One side of the family had prospered in London while the others, the John Roupells, struggled to keep up.

In the late eighteenth century the most recent John Roupell, often described as a scrap metal merchant, would be listed as a neighbour of the Beaufoys, inland of them in Cuper's Gardens. This Mr Roupell was determined to restore the family fortunes, and his opportunity arose when Lambeth's working population began to soar.

He had set up a lead smelting factory in Cross Street (now Meymott Street), on the Lambeth side of Blackfriars Bridge Road. In a small house alongside it he and his wife Catherine lived with their only son, Richard Palmer Roupell. The richer John Roupell became, the tighter he got with money, and for years they lived in cramped accommodation next to the factory, which belched out arsenic-laden fumes. The son had an unsatisfactory relationship with his father, although they shared a preoccupation with business and with ploughing profits back into land acquisition.

Before 1800 John Roupell, who already owned several houses near his factory, bought the land around Halfpenny Hatch which had been briefly owned by William Curtis, the botanist, and his family. For a while it remained undeveloped as he bought and rented out houses in Prince's Square (Cleaver Square), behind a grand Kennington mansion owned by his rich Roupell cousin. Between 1810 and 1819, probably due in part to his son's urging, he acquired a large part of the Thurlow Estate on and around Brixton Hill, which was rolling, wooded countryside then; when he developed it in the 1820s it would become Roupell Park.

As for the old Curtis land next to Cuper's Gardens, by 1824 John Roupell had knocked down a windmill that stood on it and was building a sizeable grid of terraced cottages which he rented out to working people. In 1829 one of them burned down in the course of construction; John Roupell was blamed for the accident because he had driven his workmen to cut corners in order to bring the job in on time. He was not insured. He drove on regardless and in 1839 there were 82 houses in the estate, which centred on Roupell Street. He named other streets Catherine, Richard and John, after his wife, his son and himself; those were changed later.

John died in 1835, and his wife in 1839. They were buried at St John's Church, then newly built. Their tombstone says they were 'of Roupell Street'.

They departed this life never knowing that their hard-working middle-aged bachelor son, Richard Palmer Roupell, already had three children. Since the end of the Napoleonic Wars, Richard Palmer Roupell had been spending Sundays in a modest villa in Pitt Street, Peckham, with a woman called Sarah Crane. John Roupell, a man of decided views and scant generosity of spirit, would have cut him out of his will had he known, because Sarah was only a carpenter's daughter. So it was not until his mother's will was proven that Richard, aged 58, married Sarah – pregnant again at 43 – and began to build a fine house on Brixton Hill, where he extended Roupell Park to 55 acres. Aspen House was a conventional double-fronted, forbiddingly tall and angular stucco house (many like it remain along Brixton Road) with steps up to the front door. Richard Roupell, their fourth child and only legitimate son, was born there in 1840.

Richard Palmer Roupell now bought more land; he owned a pottery that stood in Fore Street from 1841, never sold anything that brought in rent, and acquired large country estates around London, all cleverly purchased just before the railways came.

He shared another trait with his father: his attitude to children. Richard Palmer Roupell was unforgiving, and careful with his own money, and had never lived with his illegitimate children so barely knew them. His first, rebellious son John left for the Cape as soon as he became an adult and died there in 1861, having made no mark.

His second son, William, would break the family mould with a resounding crash. He was apprenticed to an attorney, but must scrimp to get by since his father would allow him only a pound a week. Scrimping was not William's style, yet he had no 'expectations'. As he was illegitimate, he had no legal claim on the family property. In 1853 when he was 22 he forged his father's signature on a document giving him possession of some land, and borrowed money against it. Thereafter he forged that signature as later generations would sign credit card slips, without thought of the morrow. His new affluence seems to have gone unnoticed at home.

In 1856 Richard Palmer Roupell died at Aspen House and William opened the strong-box by the bed. The three large family estates – at Kingston, Great Warley in Essex and Roupell Park, Brixton Hill – had been left to 16-year-old Richard, the legitimate heir. This would not do at all; as William alone knew, Roupell Park at least was already mortgaged. So he quickly burned the will and forged a new one, dated ten days before his father's death, which left everything to his mother and made him the executor.

Thereafter all he had to do was obtain his mother's consent to carry out transactions, among them the disposal of the Fore Street land to Doultons for their drainpipe factory. Well funded, William Roupell was nominated Liberal candidate for Lambeth by his friend Frederick Doulton. He delivered rousing speeches (*ROUPELL AND NO INCOME TAX* blazed the placards) to packed audiences of property-owning voters at the Surrey Music Hall and the Royal Victoria (the Old Vic). His nomination was criticised because he was young, inexperienced, and rich; the election was darkly reported to have 'revived corruption and dissipation'; but razzamatazz is irresistible. The £6,000 William spent on back-handers, 100 public-houses specially opened, flags, bunting, equestrian displays to delight the crowd, a fur-lined greatcoat for public appearances and a battle-bus carriage drawn by four grey horses, gave satisfaction to one and all. He won by a mile and became Liberal MP for Lambeth.

There were cries of consternation and dark hints. An anonymous pamphlet was published, price 3d. Lambeth, it said, was now laughed at as a rotten borough, as

> '...an able, energetic and honest representative, who had served the constituency and the Liberal interests of the country well, was almost hooted from the hustings, while a mere novice, of whom not one in a hundred of the electors had the slightest previous knowledge, was elected by an overwhelming majority in his stead. It is evident, Sir, that there are some evil influences at work in society, of whom proper account has not yet been taken.'

The *Morning Advertiser* had published a toadying piece about Roupell's great wealth but nobody knew where it came from. Dismay in other quarters was so great that an enquiry was held. Roupell emerged unscathed.

He was already a member of Lambeth Vestry and after the election he set up a corps of the

Surrey Rifles Volunteers in Kennington. This began in 1860 with a public meeting at The Horns and continued under the dynamic leadership of William himself, with his generous funding. He bought new uniforms and equipment for the men. He was genuinely popular with many people, partly because he lived locally – though few of his friends and supporters can have known that his early years had been spent in humble circumstances in Peckham.

The end came in 1862. Pressed for money, he burned some forged documents and fled to Spain. His young brother, Richard, brought him back. He faced a series of trials. It seemed that no sooner had he admitted fraud and forgery in one case than another instance was raised against him, so although at the outset the contrite and foolish fellow had been sentenced to transportation, the eventual penalty was a 14-year stretch spent mostly in Portland prison on the Isle of Wight. He returned to London to live with his mother in 1876. Over the next quarter-century most of the protagonists in this story died and much of the property, including Aspen House, was sold off.

William Roupell lived on as the only notable relic of the John Roupell family and a pillar of the community. 300 mourners attended his funeral at West Norwood cemetery in 1909.

CLOWES THE PRINTERS

William Clowes was a hard worker with good family connections. He began bookbinding and printing in Villiers Street, off the Strand, in 1803. A few years later he opened a printworks in nearby Northumberland Court, and prospered thanks to excellent work and prestigious contracts with the Army and Admiralty and learned societies.

But books were printed by hand press, which made them expensive. Clowes knew that advanced technology, already at work at *The Times,* could be exploited by book printers to

72. Clowes' type foundry in 1842.

bring down prices. In 1824 he installed a steam press at Northumberland Court to churn out pages at a previously unheard-of speed. The machinery made so much noise that his landlord and next door neighbour, the Duke of Northumberland, complained bitterly. The Duke was rarely at Northumberland House (a massive pile which occupied the Whitehall-Strand corner) but he and his staff united in court to complain of wells drained by Clowes' steam-press's well, of falling soot and plaster and a deafening racket. It was a confrontation between old aristocracy and new industry; aristocracy was supported by, among others, one of the Duke's postilions, who on entering Town had pipe-clayed his breeches until they were snowy, hung them up overnight and found them soot-blackened in the morning. Clowes' brief, for industry, retorted that if we were talking soot, Clowes had one chimney and Northumberland House had 80.

Industry won. Defeated, in 1825 the Duke paid Clowes to go away and take his equipment with him.

He went, naturally, to Lambeth, to a factory site previously leased from the Lett brothers by the designer-makers of the steam press, Messrs Applegarth and Cowper. (Applegarth and Cowper were brothers-in-law, and Mr Cowper lived on Kennington Road). Clowes took a spot between Upper Ground and Stamford Street in Duke (now Duchy) Street. It was an excellent location, set conveniently between Blackfriars and Waterloo bridges, next to the river along which great bales of paper could be transported. There was plenty of room and wells could be dug. Clowes and three of his four sons installed state-of-the-art technology from Applegarth and Cowper, and the speed and efficiency of their work brought in big contracts.

The move got off to a shaky start. Printed books were a luxury, and in the 1820s slump, publishers were going bankrupt. Seven of Clowes' customers failed in a week, but he kept going. In book and periodical publishing, his lifeline was his friendship with Charles Knight, who founded the Society for the Diffusion of Useful Knowledge, and was determined to diffuse *useful* knowledge rather than mawkish religious nonsense to working people. For him Clowes printed *The British Almanac* as an antidote to Old Moore, and many other cheap and successful booklets and directories that tapped into a new hunger for secular understanding.

By 1840 William Clowes & Sons in Duke Street was the largest printworks in the world, employing 600 people at 20 Applegarth Cowper machines, 23 hand presses and 5 hydraulic presses. They printed the Mulready envelopes (forerunners to postage stamps) under Post Office guard; they had a type foundry on the premises and six composing rooms of which the longest measured 250 feet from end to end. As for the great steam presses, to see one operated by Clowes' men was a highlight of the Great Exhibition in Hyde Park in 1851. By that time the firm was being run by two of Clowes' sons. And of course it produced the Catalogue to the exhibition.

In 1856 Queen Victoria's two eldest sons, the Prince of Wales and Prince Alfred, with their suite, toured the Duke Street establishment. It became quite fashionable for upper-class young men to take factory tours, to remind future leaders of the might of industry. The firm printed the Law Reports; it printed numerous Bills and Petitions for and against the Railways; it produced Dickens' unfinished *Mystery of Edwin Drood*. It printed *Hymns Ancient and Modern*. From Duke Street, Victorian England expressed itself to the world.

Clowes and his sons were unusually progressive employers. They respected the artisans who worked for them and encouraged unions and arbitration procedures, fostering a tradition of unionised printing that remained unbowed until the 1980s. Four and even five generations of local families worked for Clowes.

The firm flourished in Lambeth until the Second World War. The Clowes family largely financed the original London College of Printing in 1921 when it took over a former school building in Stamford Street (which later became the London Nautical School).

The Clowes works was destroyed by heavy bombing in 1941. Clowes descendants were already long-established printers at Beccles, in Suffolk, so the two parts of the firm amalgamated and manufacturing ended in London. As William Clowes, the firm flourishes today.

STEPHEN'S INK

From 1834 Stephens' Ink was made behind the Clowes factory on the Stamford Street side.

Henry Stephens - born in 1796 - trained at Guy's at the same time as John Keats; they were among four students who shared a house on St Thomas's Street, and it is marked by a blue plaque which commemorates both of them. After his training he moved to Hertfordshire where, as a talented surgeon he devised a method of operating on hernia (in the days before chloroform) that worked better than any that had gone before. His work gained the respect of the king's surgeon Sir Astley Cooper, who insisted that he return to London.

He took lodgings at 54 Stamford Street, close to the Rotunda, where he discovered his latent entrepreneurial streak. Fascinated by chemistry, and never content with the ink he must write with, he experimented with some success on a new formula and soon found himself giving away samples. Demand grew, and he decided to make the ink in quantity in the cellar, and sell it. According to his daughter's memoir, his Uncle Josiah told him not to be so foolish.

"You're not a businessman, Henry; don't do anything of the sort. If you can find someone to give you £50 for the receipt, take it."

His professional friends said "You will lose caste if you go into a business; the Royal College of Surgeons will surely turn you out of the society."

Stephens must have been an unconventional, as well as a talented man, because he was not afraid of being 'in trade' and carried on.

Ink was made from all sorts of things. The best writing ink came from fermented oak gall, a fungus, to which other substances (molasses, sulphuric acid, soot, charcoal from bones, iron filings, sulphuric acid and/or other additives) were put according to the durability or blackness of the ink required. Stephens' Blue-Black Writing Fluid was 'a carbonaceous black writing fluid, which will accomplish the so long-desired and apparently hopeless task of rendering the manuscript as durable and as indelible as the printed record'. It flowed well, didn't smear or blot or clog, and demand was tremendous. Also its introduction was coincident with the first (not yet entirely efficient) mass-produced fountain pens.

73. Henry Stephens the elder.

Production moved to the stables and yard across Stamford Street where Stephens kept his horse and carriage. There he employed a foreman and some men to do the bottling, although as demand grew three firms of stoneware bottle-makers together, including Doulton's, couldn't supply the containers fast enough. Once bottling was sorted, Stephens obtained agents in Paris and New York and began making wood stains as well; these were used on the doors and panels at the Great Exhibition, and 'the Queen and Prince (Albert) came often, early in the mornings, to see how everything was going on.'

He and his second wife lived in York Road for five or six years before taking refuge from Lambeth's noise and dirt in Finchley – a country village then. His second son, Henry 'Inky' Stephens, moved the factory to Finchley, where the Stephens Collection is open to the public.

MAUDSLAY'S IRONWORKS AND ENGINEERING

From 1810, Maudslays of Westminster Bridge Road supplied the heavy machinery that would power the British Empire. Having been largely famous for its marine engineering, the firm thrived on railway contracts after the 1840s, making hauling engines and locomotives and pumps. From Lambeth emerged rolling mills and other machinery for the Royal Mint, and mints in places as far apart as Calcutta, Bogota, China, Calcutta, and Constantinople. Machinery was made for the French government's tobacco factory, for printing calico and packing meat cubes, and for dozens of purposes never before imagined. Maudslays made a beam engine for Chelsea Waterworks and a time-ball for the Cape of Good Hope and another for Sydney, NSW. The screw propellers and paddle wheels of scores of ships were proudly imprinted with the firm's name from Valparaiso to St Petersburg. Closer to home, Maudslay's produced the ingenious shield which Brunel's workmen used in tunnelling under the Thames.

The firm hadn't begun in Lambeth. Henry Maudslay was a model achiever of the Victorian age; a self-made genius, a hero described by Samuel Smiles in *Self-Help*. He had been born in Woolwich in 1771, and had trained as a blacksmith at the Arsenal from the age of twelve. Later he had become works manager to the ingenious ironsmith and inventor Joseph Bramah. He is said to have influenced the design of Bramah's patent lock and hydraulic press.

When Bramah refused to raise his pay, Maudslay set up by himself in Wells Street. In

74. Henry Maudslay, a lithograph by Charles Motte in 1827.

1800, Marc Isambard Brunel (later builder of the first Thames tunnel, and father of Isambard Kingdom) commissioned him to supply innovative block-making equipment for HM Dockyard at Portsmouth. He was 'widely known as a mechanic of great skill and ingenuity' at a time when new machine tools were in growing demand; his original screw-cutting lathe is in the Science Museum. Minutely accurate work was required for astronomical instruments and the Government made him a special grant of £1,000 to improve the technology. He took out many patents for machine tools required for different industries and invented the micrometer (also in the Science Museum).

He moved briefly to Margaret Street, bigger premises where he hired a draughtsman, Joseph Field, from Portsmouth docks. In 1810, once more out of space but now an established business of high repute, they moved to their final and most successful site off the Westminster Bridge Road. Here as Henry Maudslay & Co, Engineers, they employed talented young engineer-inventors including Samuel Seaward, who with his brother would become a famous

75. The Maudslay Engineering Works in Westminster Bridge Road.

76. A shop crane manufactured by Maudslay.

marine engineer, James Nasmyth, inventor of the steam hammer, Joseph Whitworth who patented the screw thread, and David Napier, who would found the Lambeth family firm famous, in the next century, for aero engines.

Around 1830 Maudslay, at least two of his sons and Joseph Field became Maudslay, Sons & Field, specialising in mills and steam engines – one of which can be seen today in the Brunel Museum at Rotherhithe. Maudslay's works continued to produce world-beating machine tools that would cut screws, threads, chamfers, mortices and bores consistently; until his time, industrial machinery had been made by hand, with consequent inaccuracy. Heavy machinery was tested to Henry's own standards of perfection. At Lambeth, the firm made the engine for a river steamer in 1815 and many subsequent naval engines, notably that of the first steam vessel commissioned by the Royal Navy (*HMS Lightning* in 1823). In the 1820s Maudslay turned his attention to astronomy. He was only 60 when, most unexpectedly in 1831, he caught a chill on a Channel crossing and died.

At its height Maudslays' works occupied most of the block between Frazier Street and Westminster Bridge Road, near Lambeth North

77. Formerly an apprentice with Maudslay, David Napier set up his own business here in York Road.

station, as well as a smaller site behind Christ Church. But from the 1860s Lambeth was too cramped for the kind of work it must produce, and too prone to flooding, and marine projects

78. View from the Thames of Fowler's Ironworks, with the shot tower in the background to the left.

were carried out from a new site at Greenwich. The founding families were involved in the business, but at the turn of the century had lost control. Reginald Maudslay, a descendant in the family tradition of engineering talent, set up the Standard Motor Company at the turn of the century but had the sense to do so in Coventry where there was room for expansion.

In 1899, the Maudslay works on opposite sides of the Westminster Bridge Road closed because of financial collapse. In the bankruptcy sale that followed, Maudslay's bought back much of their own equipment and continued to work from Greenwich until the company shut down in the early 1930s.

DOULTON'S POTTERY

London potters, like engineers and brewers and distillers, knew each other and the work of each other's firms; so when a young man called John Doulton finished his apprenticeship in Fulham around 1812 he looked to one of the many potteries in Lambeth for his next position. He was taken on at a pot-house in Vauxhall Walk. It was almost opposite one of the northern entrances to the Gardens, and there Dorset clay was bashed, watered and trodden before being stored in the damp to become usable clay. Doulton became an expert thrower of pots.

He lived frugally and saved in hope of an opportunity, which arose in 1815. The firm was owned by Mrs Jones, a partner's widow, and Mr Watts. Upon his majority Jones Junior was supposed to take a one third share, but in 1815, having been discovered in a crime, he fled to South America. Doulton took the one third share.

79. John Doulton.

He and Watts prospered in the post-War boom, but a slump followed. They fended off competition by doggedly seeking out contracts for earthenware bottles for ink, blacking and beer, ointment pots and jars for anchovy paste, stoneware barrels and flasks blazoned with demands for Reform. Pots in the 1820s often carried a message, as tee-shirts do today.

Doulton was the creative master and salesman and Watts did the books and tended the growing number of kilns. A patient blind horse, taken on to operate a horse-mill in 1818, beat the clay.

In 1826 the firm moved to Lambeth High Street, then a a narrow, cobbled lane, where in the course of the nineteenth century it would expand on both sides of the road, absorbing several existing potteries as well as houses, gardens and a school and adding new kilns and workrooms. The old dock at the junction of Black Prince Road and Fore Street was used for offloading clay and shipping out big commissions by river.

Henry Doulton, John's second son, was apprenticed in the factory from 1835. Doulton's was now making tea-sets and tankards as well,

80. Doulton's first factory at Lambeth. From a watercolour by Thomas Wakeman, c.1840.

81. *The massive Doulton works on the Albert Embankment, pictured in* The Builder, *2 August 1879.*

and was becoming a significant local employer. Throwing a pot was more difficult then than it later became, for steam power had not yet been applied to the business and the potter had to kick his own wheel around; steam was an innovation for which Henry Doulton was responsible. In 1840 the firm acquired a huge new kiln in which terracotta sculpture could be fired.

That year, these technical innovations enabled 21-year-old Henry to make a 300 gallon Ali Baba Jar – the biggest in the world! – which stood at the works entrance to Doulton's, then a double-fronted factory with a yard opening onto the High Street.

The mid-century brought a faster, more efficient, more sanitary world of railways, massive drainage schemes and the electric telegraph. Doultons, following the money and heavily investing in new machinery and labour, exploited every one of these innovations. Henry opined: 'If there is stagnation, decay soon follows and finally dissolution...You must be ready to put yourself out of business in order to stay in business.'

From the 1850s to 1880, most of Doulton's profits came from London's long-overdue investment in drainage. A great friend of Henry's, Edward de Crecy, was on the Metropolitan Board of Works, which helped; and in the 1850s Mr Bazalgette, who conducted tests on pipework before recommending the award of contracts, became Chief Engineer to the Metropolitan Commission of Sewers. Many of the drainpipes still in daily use in London were made by Doulton's. (Watts' name was dropped after his death in 1853 and later still, the firm and its wares were known as Lambeth Pottery and Royal Doulton). Here in Lambeth was the world's first factory for making salt-glazed vitrified pipes and conduits; it produced architectural items too, like chimneypots. It supplied insulators for the electric telegraph and for early telephone exchanges; it made wash basins, hooded baths, chemical vessels and closets and sanitary ware.

A photograph taken from the old iron Lambeth Bridge before 1860 shows the Ship Tavern on the waterfront, and H DOULTON DRAINPIPE WHARF alongside *(ill. 106)*. The huge terracotta Doulton's factory of which a small part remains today was not built until after the Embankment was constructed in the 1870s. It consisted of high manufacturing blocks and a tall chimney, and dominated the riverside between Vauxhall and Lambeth Palace. Queen Victoria, the Tsar of Russia, the Sultan of Turkey, the Maharajah of Baroda and the King of Siam were among the dignitaries who came to marvel at the work inside. By 1890 there were 70 kilns.

In 1873 old John Doulton died, aged 80. A portrait painted in the year of his death *(ill. 79)* shows a handsome 80-year-old with a snowy comb-over, his beard worn beneath the chin in the fashion popular in the 1830s and recently revived by radical Islamists. From 1880, art pottery was also made by Doulton's at Burslem. The move to Staffordshire was gradual, as was decline at Lambeth. By the early 1950s most of the factory had been demolished.

DOULTON AND THE LAMBETH SCHOOL OF ART

The original Lambeth School of Art was in Black Prince Road. It had been founded in 1854 by a former curate at St Mary's who was on his way to becoming Dean Gregory of St Paul's. The Principal, John Sparkes, worked hard to persuade Henry Doulton that his students had a role to play in his industry. Henry was an enthusiast for the arts, but he had already attempted a revival of Lambeth Delft without commercial success, and didn't want to try the aesthetic approach again.

At last, in 1860, he gave in and allowed George

82. Laying the foundation stone of the Lambeth School of Art in 1860.

Tinworth to use a small part of a workroom for modelling. Tinworth's family, like the Doultons, were Dissenters who worshipped in the York Road Chapel. Tinworth worked for his father, a wheelwright and drunk (a renegade who didn't attend Chapel) during the day and attended classes at the School of Art in the evenings.

The other workers were at first derisive of this bible-reading young teetotaller and gave him a board on top of a barrel to work on and a rejected chimneypot for a seat. He quietly got on with his first job, which was to design water filters for domestic use. Since the Great Exhibition there had been an aesthetic shift from economy and proportion to decoration. The most utilitarian object must be beautified, and Ruskin saw some of Tinworth's work and introduced it to his friends.

Henry Doulton spotted that the hour of 'art' pottery had come: the aspirational middle classes would buy it. They wanted even the humblest of homeware to be decorated, or glazed, or modelled and mass production could be applied to this new departure.

Art-school notions proved technically challenging. Tinworth began by decorating pots in blue and brown, but the blue was usually lost in firing. This was corrected in time for the Paris Exhibition of 1867 where his work was much admired, and orders came in. Henry resolved to prepare seriously for the next major international exhibition in 1871. He set up a small art department, consisting of Tinworth and two more students from the School, a brother and sister called Arthur and Hannah Barlow. This time they had a runaway success despite technical disasters behind the scenes. Pollution, variations in temperature and grit in the kilns could ruin a week of modelling and incising. Most of these problems were solved with the help of Sir Arthur Church, a specialist in the chemistry of ceramics, and by 1873 they had worked out how to make a blue salt-glaze called Doulton Blue which was shown in the Vienna Exhibition.

Tinworth and the Barlows were joined in the art studio in 1872 by Frank Butler, another School student, who was deaf and almost dumb. Many more followed, including two other Barlow siblings and so many women workers that they were given their own accommodation. By 1885 there were 250 artists in Doulton's art pottery department, all but ten of whom had come from Lambeth School of Art.

Self-expression was encouraged; the work of most is recognisably their own, and signed with their own mark. Techniques and effects changed constantly but many of the artists, including Butler and Tinworth, spent their working lives at Doulton's. After the First World War, clutter was no longer fashionable.

The stoneware frogs for the cast iron seats on the Embankment were made by Tinworth; so was stoneware for the fountain in Kennington Park. Some fine late terracotta from the factory can be seen at the old hospital, now a King's College extension, just north of the Imax cinema at Waterloo, and the exuberant frieze around Harrod's Food Hall is Doulton work. Exhibition pieces were shown at the Chicago World's Fair. There is a collection of Lambeth art pottery on show in Sydney, more in the Smithsonian, and most of all in the V & A. Much of the modelling and painting took place in the Black Prince Road block of dedicated studios that were never demolished, and are now used as offices.

The School of Art produced numerous well-known painters and illustrators who never worked at the pottery at all. Arthur Rackham, Glyn Philpot, WC Symons, WS Frith and Eric Kennington were among them. John Sparkes himself later became Principal of the Royal College of Art.

RELIGION STILL AROUND

The Church of England celebrated victory over Napoleon, and the flood of incomers to Lambeth, by building four new churches south of the river. They would be dedicated to Saints Matthew, Mark, Luke and John the Evangelist. St Mark's would be on the old gallows corner soon to be directly accessible from Vauxhall Bridge, and St John the Evangelist would be on Cuper's Gardens.

83. St Mark's Church, Kennington.

84. St John's Church, Waterloo Road, in 1827.

The elegant new St John's Church and its burial ground were consecrated and dedicated in 1824 by the Bishop of Winchester (the church was in the diocese of Winchester, since it was in Winchester's parish of St Mary Lambeth.) The bishop was assisted by the rector, the Reverend Dr George D'Oyley. The congregation were reminded 'Be ye not unequally yoked together with unbelievers' and that Jesus had exhorted the populace to 'Make not my Father's House an House of Merchandise'.

That was where the threat seemed to lie. Although both unbelief and commerce were doing rather well, neither menaced the new churches. These remained the location of christenings, marriages and funerals for the complacent classes. But even the Church of England was aware that all was not well with the workers. Churchmen wrung their hands and supported such organisations as the Association for the Relief of the Manufacturing and Labouring Poor, which attempted to achieve change without social upheaval. The Reverend Dr D'Oyley later helped to found King's College. He hoped it would counteract the whiff of secularism about University College.

Poor incomers tended to favour Catholicism or, more often, the robust Nonconformist style of Wesley or Charles Spurgeon . On Waterloo Road were the New Jerusalem Chapel and the Zion Temple, and new places of worship – Methodist, Baptist and so on – continued to spring up throughout the century, on Lambeth Marsh and other busy streets; Spurgeon raised enough money to build the Metropolitan Tabernacle at Newington.

St Mary's, the fourteenth-century parish church, would be largely torn down and rebuilt by the Diocese of Winchester in 1851. Successive Bishops of Carlisle, who had long ago let out the land they got at the Reformation, were nineteenth-century landlords to Carlisle Rents and the White Horse pub. Canterbury still owned the ten acres of garden behind Lambeth House, along with the old way down to the Thames, the riverside run of barge-builders' cottages and watermen's dwellings on Bishop's Walk, and the land from Westminster Bridgefoot to the Marsh occupied by Astley's and the Canterbury Arms.

Lambeth House itself was a charming muddle, very much the old manor house it had been in mediaeval times, with impressive additions, and brickwork sadly eroded by pollution from the potteries. To an incumbent archbishop in the vibrant, go-ahead, 1820s, it seemed unfit; and maybe, despite a sixteenth-century overhaul of the drains, it was; but he was much criticised for pulling the place down.

Blore, his architect, demolished the huddle of mediaeval dwelling houses and built a grand mock-Tudor north front. He knocked down the mediaeval cloisters and Cardinal Pole's gallery and moved the contents of the Library (which included the last will and testament of Dick Whittington, Katherine of Aragon's divorce papers and an eye-witness account of the death of Queen Elizabeth, besides the Lambeth Bible and other priceless books and illuminated manuscripts) into the Great Hall.

He rebuilt the Guardroom so that nothing remained of its fourteenth-century origins except the roof. He didn't touch the crypt where Anne Boleyn had pleaded with Cranmer. It was disregarded, its oldest parts already in use as a wine cellar and lumber room, though seriously damp and silting up with river mud every time the river spilled over its banks.

86. The chapel at Lambeth Palace, c.1810. Watercolour, artist unknown.

85. The library at Lambeth Palace.

The Marseilles dessert fig, quietly thriving since being planted in a sunny spot by Cardinal Pole, was allowed to remain. When Blore finished, in 1834, Lambeth House had become Lambeth Palace. As for the dole – no longer bread, but money – which had been distributed at the south gate for nearly six hundred years, it was finally stopped in 1842.

NEW IDEAS

Socialist ideas of workers' rights, and the egalitarian new preachers, and later, the self-help creed of Samuel Smiles, were in the air. People wanted social justice; they were no longer content to remain in their station; they wanted to *get on*. Speakers stood up to expound new ideas. Certain places, like the Rotunda at the Blackfriars Bridge end of Stamford Street, or Kennington Common, seemed to be inhabited by a spirit of dissent.

87. Rowland Hill, of whom Sheridan said, 'His ideas come red hot from the heart'.

A radical preacher, Rowland Hill, the son of a baronet who got religion in his youth and used his education and his money to spread the word of the Lord in his own 'earnest, eccentric and eloquent' manner, had opened the New Surry [*sic*] Chapel (later the Rotunda) close to Blackfriars Bridge in 1783. It was a brick-built two-storeyed octagon with windows in tall blind arches and a fine round lantern on top; there was an echo of the Paris Garden bear-pit about it (and it was pretty much on the same site). Inside, it was a perfect demagogue's auditorium, with galleries all round, and on the ground floor, unbanked seats from which listeners looked up at a tall pulpit. After his death it became, briefly, the Surrey Institution, with the Lever Collection which included wonders from Captain Cook's journeys to Botany Bay. Since controversy attracted more people than stuffed animals did, it became the Rotunda. William Cobbett spoke there in 1830. He was no young firebrand then, but a radical institution.

In 1848, agitation for Chartist reform reached its height under the leadership of Feargus O'Connor, and a major protest march from

88. Surrey Chapel in Blackfriars Road.

89. The Chartist meeting on Kennington Common in 1848.

Kennington Common was advertised for April 10th, following a previous meeting in March. *The Times* responded to O'Connor by whipping up a moral panic. Before the March gathering, it had reported that in view of 'disgraceful disturbances' a week before at Trafalgar Square, the meeting at Kennington would be met by 4000 police and a further hundred men, armed with swords and firearms, on horseback. Magistrates would open local courts from 9am and 20,000 Special Constables had already been sworn in 'for Middlesex alone.' Broken granite, recently laid for road repairs near Kennington Common, was removed. Extra guards were placed on Buckingham Palace and the Bank and 'the gunsmiths of London have....agreed to unscrew the barrels of all fire-arms in their possession so that in the event of a seizure being made by the rabble the weapons will be perfectly useless'. If the crowd had not dispersed by 6pm, the police would clear it.

Unsurprisingly, the March meeting went off peacefully. The Chartists were asking for household suffrage, the secret ballot, equal representation, short parliaments and the abolition of the property qualification for parliamentary candidates – not for tumbrils to roll. And they asked nicely. The April meeting and protest march from Kennington were to end with the presentation of a petition.

Before the event, *The Times* condemned the plans as seditious, revolutionary, and inspired by foreigners:

> 'The most powerful armies of the world have been beaten by the sudden assault of a few ill-armed workmen and boys. Paris, Vienna, Berlin, Rome, Naples, Palermo, Turin, Milan, Venice, Munich, and a score or two lesser capitals, are now under the dictation of the populace.'

Terrified readers were promised that 'a hundred thousand men will gather, armed with stout bludgeons'. The railways would bring enormous delegations. The 'mob' was baying at the doors of Westminster. Arms including firearms and cutlasses were sent from the Tower of London to seats of power – the Mansion House, the Admiralty, the banks and the docks.

This frenzy, whipped up by O'Connor's own statements to the press, played precisely into the hands of those who opposed him. Not only did he fail to appear at the meeting (his decline into insanity was making him unstable), but the crowd was maybe 'only' 20,000 and the petition, for which he had claimed 5.7 million signatures, proved to contain under two million, some of them fake; a remarkable number, but his bluster and overstatement had made a fiasco of the 'monster meeting'. The result was a damp squib.

> 'The spectacle [of this relative calm] will not be lost on those nations which are yet in the vortex of change. They will know where to look for the stability they long for ...'

reported *The Times* smugly, looking at Kennington and finding evidence of 'a peaceful, prudent, and loyal metropolis', although graciously conceding that the Chartists' point of view was not unreasonable. Today the Chartist gathering on Kennington Common is principally recalled because one of the first news photographs was taken there – apparently from the roof of The Horns.

TAMING THE PEOPLE

The authorities – that is, the Watch, the magistrates and later the police force – dealt with threats to public order differently according to their cause. Individuals were prosecuted for alcohol-related disorder but little was done to control the breweries and distilleries which in the 1820s were investing in glittering gin palaces. In the New Cut, part of the long street market that straggled from Lambeth Walk via the Marsh, an observer reported 'I suppose there are £25,000 being spent in building gin-shops. I should think they must cost seven or eight thousand each house.'

Politically motivated disorder met with more fundamental reform – not in response to public demand, but in order to make action against the state less physically likely. In 1800 Kennington contained St George's Fields and Kennington Common, two unfenced, unsupervised places where crowds had been gathering to hear political and religious speakers for hundreds of years. St George's Fields had not, technically, been common land since the Middle Ages, and now it was visibly enclosed with the arrival of Bethlem Hospital in 1815. Kennington Common didn't last long after the Chartist rally. Within a few years it was railed off, designed and re-invented as Kennington Park. (Young Booth, who would soon found the Salvation Army, was working at a pawnshop across the road at the time; no doubt he approved.) When the Great Exhibition was dismantled from Hyde Park, Prince Albert's Model Dwelling for Artisans was brought along and re-erected in Kennington Park as inspiration for property developers. The little house (designed for two families) is there still, overlooking neat flower-beds and tarmac paths on one side, and Richard Seifert's redeveloped office block on the other.

While fresh air and exercise were much approved, Vauxhall Gardens, Cumberland Gardens next to Vauxhall Bridge, and other relics of the raffish eighteenth century were not. Vauxhall Gardens in particular was complained about as a public nuisance, and was finally closed down in the 1850s. Terraced housing was built there. Brunswick House and gardens *(ill. 142)*, once occupied by Joseph Pratt the distiller, endured a deafening innovation: the railways.

REVOLUTION

Lurking behind every aspect of this chapter so far is the transport revolution that transformed Lambeth.

In 1800, there were bridges only at Blackfriars and Westminster. Carters and coachmen paid tolls to cross them and stagecoaches paid in bulk to use the major turnpike roads. Large heavy loads must be carried long distances by barge along the river.

With new bridges at Lambeth, Waterloo and Vauxhall, gaslight and the gradual spread of cobbled streets throughout the district, wheeled traffic increased, but many of the old limitations remained. The railways changed that from 1838.

90. *Prince Albert's Model Houses when built for the Great Exhibition in Kensington in 1851. Moved to the new Kennington Park after the Exhibition closed, they are now known as Prince Consort Lodge.*

The London & Southampton Railway terminated at Nine Elms and later, the line was extended to Waterloo. Food and fuel could be imported from the countryside; raw materials could be offloaded from the river and onto trains; people were astonished to find they could travel hundreds of miles in a day. The navvies who helped construct these lines were customers for local shops and pubs and lodging houses and some settled locally and worked in Lambeth all their lives. The larger railway stations repeatedly expanded.

Later there were horse trams and a new Underground railway. Commuting became a way of life. People in Lambeth didn't expect to know each other by sight any more. Shops learned to rely on passing trade, and the huge market stretching from New Cut almost to Vauxhall along Lambeth Marsh attracted customers from early morning until midnight. Big stores like David Greig's, for food, and Grove's, for clothes, came to Westminster Bridge Road and the Marsh.

From the 1870s, the new Albert Embankment was built out into the river to conceal Bazalgette's sewer system. The north bank having been similarly extended, the width of the Thames shrank by a couple of hundred feet.

RAILWAYS

Nine Elms is technically in Wandsworth; but from 1834 construction of its eponymous railway terminus put it firmly in Vauxhall, London's western outpost of urban pollution and squalor.

In 1838 the London & Southampton Railway Company opened its line from Nine Elms through Wandsworth, Wimbledon, Kingston, Ditton Marsh, Walton and Weybridge to Woking. This was extended to Southampton by 1840. Fast trains to Southampton and the ocean-going steamboats took three hours – compared with nine and a half hours by the fastest mail coach. Passengers must have felt they had entered a time machine.

The railway company also kept a goods yard

91. A horse tram passing St Mark's, Kennington c.1870. Lithograph, artist unknown.

and passenger wharf on the bend of the river next to Brunswick House, once the riverside retreat of Queen Caroline's older brother (the building was rescued from dereliction in 2006 by LassCo). Nine Elms Lane separated the station from the wharf because a railway next to the river was disallowed by law, and goods arriving by rail must be taken across it by horse and cart. An anonymous watercolour from the early days shows Nine Elms Wharf next to Windmill Pier on the river. The windmill was still in use, probably for grinding cement. There are goods sheds, cranes, sailboats, and the two paddle steamers used to ferry passengers to the City. These paddle-steamers belonged to different companies, and their rival touts would sometimes come to blows – 'a sight which the baser sort of the crowd ...enjoyed to their hearts' content.'

In the background can be seen a crowded industrial cityscape and a tall chimney belching smoke. There were small industrial sites and workers' cottages in the area already, as well as a few remaining market gardens. Nine Elms terminus and trainsheds were also a railway workshop – another local heavy industry, where throughout most of the nineteenth century locomotive engines were made and repaired and carriages and wagons built. The whole complex had been designed before the engineers really knew what they were doing, so the early turntables were small and the site was cramped. Since the works must operate on two sites separated by Nine Elms Lane, it was not efficient. Most of these disadvantages were overcome, and engineering expanded.

In 1848 Nine Elms station (next to the railway works) was closed and a branch line fanned out north-east from the main railway via Vauxhall to Waterloo. 253 railway arches now ploughed through land previously occupied by 700 houses. So thrilling was the new Vauxhall station that a visiting Russian delegation is said to have adopted the word 'Vauxhall' into their language as the generic term for a railway station.

Vauxhall, the first district to suffer, was typical.

92. *The first Waterloo railway station.*

It had been a modest old suburb at the start of the nineteenth century. There was a turnpike, and a pub near Cox's Bridge over the Effra; pleasure gardens with cold beer behind Brunswick House; shops on Bridgefoot, and more shops and pubs around the entrance to Vauxhall Gardens. In 1848 the whole village was cut through by the railway viaduct and thundering trains. Vauxhall Gardens and Kennington Lane and South Lambeth (and soon, the new gas-holders) were separated from the river, and the potteries, the breweries, distilleries and railway yard were strung along by the wharves. The whole place was redolent of steam, coal gas and smoke.

For City passengers from places like Woking, a through run to Waterloo must have been an improvement after daily confrontation with steamer touts or a sixpenny horse omnibus to the Bank. Only Queen Victoria fretted; she had part of the old Nine Elms station kept open for use by the Royal train whenever she stayed at Osborne, until 1854.

The Nine Elms terminus had gone, but engineering prospered. In 1870 about 1,250 people were employed in the yards. The carriage works was moved out of London in the 1890s, and locomotive building (including a class of engines promisingly named after volcanoes, like the *Stromboli*) was removed to Eastleigh before the First War. By then there were 25 tracks running into two vast sheds at Nine Elms works. It remained as a goods yard until the 1960s, when the site was redeveloped.

In 1864 the line from Kent was extended from Waterloo to the Strand. The sadly under-used Hungerford suspension bridge, which had been there for only 20 years, was removed. It was added to the Clifton bridge and the railway replaced it. Charing Cross Station replaced Hungerford Market. Once again, the environmental impact of track and viaduct building was extraordinary. Thousands of people lost their homes and the commercial dynamic of parts of Lambeth was changed.

WATERLOO STATION AND THE NECROPOLIS RAILWAY

The original, 1840s, plan had been a railway from Richmond that would terminate on the South Bank opposite Charing Cross. Trafalgar Square was being built and the Strand was still an important shopping street. But when the London and South Western Railway took over,

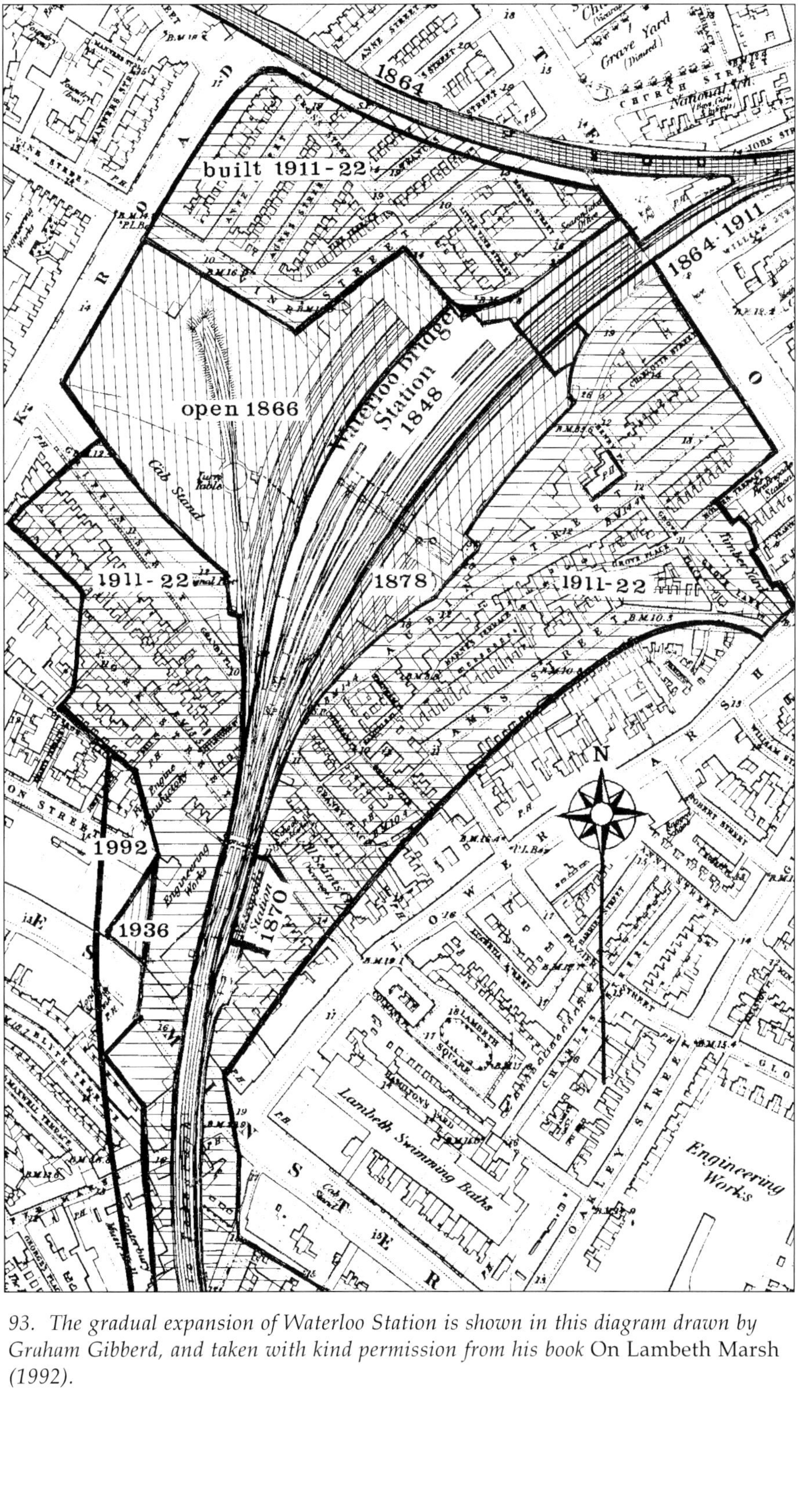

93. The gradual expansion of Waterloo Station is shown in this diagram drawn by Graham Gibberd, and taken with kind permission from his book On Lambeth Marsh *(1992).*

they bought more land, and redesigned the line to cut out Nine Elms and run through Vauxhall to a terminus more convenient to City commuters at Waterloo. It opened on 11 July, 1848. Steam trains puffed towards it at high level across Nine Elms, far above the west side of Vauxhall Gardens and behind the huge Doulton's works, over a demolished windmill. They chugged respectfully east of the Archbishop's lawn, ploughed straight across the old Lambeth Parochial School (which had to move to Westminster Bridge Road), dodged the Canterbury Music Hall, ran high alongside the market in Lambeth Marsh, and exhaled their final, noisy clouds of steam in a low-roofed shed built over four platforms at the new Waterloo station. From there passengers could take a hansom which would clatter, laden with luggage, down long ramps to the street; or a tuppenny omnibus to the City.

The first platforms were roughly where platforms 7 - 12 are today. For the next fifty years Waterloo station grew into a bigger and bigger mess. By an endless process of planning, aborted purchase, refusal, revision, and determined expansion it ended up with eighteen platforms in three separate sections and at least one line that came right onto the central concourse, the whole accessible by rickety ramps or smelly tunnels. It was all so confusing, and so inefficient, and so generally horrid, that something must be done.

There was also, from 1854, the Necropolis railway. This was a response to London's voracious consumption of burial space at a time of high infant mortality and high death rate. London suffered from mortally polluted air and water, unsafe working conditions and overcrowded slums. After the funeral in London, relatives would follow the horse-drawn cortège to the Necropolis line alongside Lambeth Marsh, where the coffin would be loaded onto a special train for transport to Brookwood Station, near Woking, and the cemetery. Trains left every twenty minutes.

By 1900 the Necropolis line was just one of

94. A virtually deserted Waterloo Station, probably in the early 1930s.

95. Waterloo Station in the 1920s.

many barriers to Waterloo's expansion and future efficiency, and people were grumbling. Waterloo station must be completely reconstructed. But that was a task for the twentieth century.

VICTORIANS GETTING BY

Kennington's fine merchants' houses of the later eighteenth century were as smart as north Lambeth got, and most of those (with a few exceptions near the parks or in West Square) were in multiple occupation by the mid-century. The 1841 census and later, Booth's poverty map tell much the same story: there were areas of extreme poverty, areas of 'getting by', and areas of 'keeping up appearances.' In Lambeth Walk, for instance, people were poor, but often did piecework at home or worked locally in trades that have died out since. People living in one or two rooms could be chair makers, frame makers or – if women, and unattached – straw bonnet makers, milliners, seamstresses or charladies. Men would be costermongers, coal-heavers, labourers, 'excavators' digging the dirt for railways or roads or buildings, lightermen or watermen. Close to the river – in Pratt Street and Lower Fore Street – there were numerous barge builders, and people who described themselves as waggoner, charwoman, sailmaker, pattern maker, bone chopper, tinman, hawker and 'cork cutter'. There were also at least a dozen fishermen, although back in 1828 a Royal Commission had pointed out 'the entire destruction of the fishermen's trade between Putney and Greenwich' because of pollution, and the last salmon was caught in 1833. Near the Clowes factory were compositors, 'readers to the press', and bookbinders. Occasionally, in the 1841 north Lambeth census, appears a cow-keeper, a farmer, a market gardener or a toll collector, like a blast from the eighteenth-century past.

It is hard to know who was running a cottage industry and who was going out every day to a place of work. In 1841 an 'engineer' could be working for Maudslay; Maudslay's early machine tools required finishing by craftsmen, who may have worked in their own back yards or at the factory. On the other hand, an 'engineer' could be tipping oil into pristine mechanisms in the railway yard at Nine Elms. Such a job description was vague, and as baffling to the general public as 'working in IT' is today.

Equally 'Ind' – independent – in the 'occupation' column on the census could mean an adult who was dependent on the family, looking for work, living on savings, thieving or in the sex trade (Waterloo being otherwise known as Whoreterloo). A person of independent means at a respectable address would be more likely to describe herself as an 'annuitant'.

Hercules Buildings held more people dependent on service industries and the provision of consumer goods, for this was a district with aspirations, where nearby pubs provided entertainment: french polisher, coffee house keeper, modeller, waiter, dressmaker, perfumer, hairdresser, jeweller, collar maker, tobacco pipe maker, musician, vocalist, comedian – a comedian could mean a straight actor, or it could mean a vaudevillian or music-hall performer who did comic turns; in Lambeth, with the Lord Chancellor's rules still prevailing, this latter was more likely. Lambeth's 1841 census boasts a number of chairmen. A chairman presided, from close to the stage, over acts performed in pubs and penny gaffs. He kept the show moving, and was a kind of go-between between audience and performer.

Local artisans were often potters or brass foundrymen or distillery workers; men who toiled in heavy industry along the river. A melodramatic, mid-century narrative painting by Augustus Egg depicts a young mother who has fallen on hard times – the inevitable result of immoral behaviour – and must sleep beneath the Arches at the Adelphi. Eyes brimming with remorse, she stares across the moonlit river at a hideous vista of smoke and shot towers, the Lion Brewery, factory chimneys and despair.

STREET LIFE

Those brave members of the propertied classes who went slumming in Lambeth were fascinated. Dickens and Thackeray visited the Canterbury Music Hall in the Westminster Bridge Road and saw a friendly, gutsy place, where working people forgot their daily grind in a cheerful pint of porter and a comic turn.

George Augustus Sala, writing in 1859, had rather more reservations after a night at the Royal Victoria (the Old Vic) and the gin palace opposite. Of the New Cut (the Cut) he wrote:

> 'It isn't picturesque, it isn't quaint, it isn't curious. It has not even the questionable merit of being old. It is simply Low. It is sordid, squalid, and, the truth must out, disreputable. The broad thoroughfare, which, bordered with fitting houses, would make one of the handsomest streets in London, is gorged with vile, rotten tenements, occupied by merchants who oft-times pursue the very contrary to innocent callings. Everything is second-hand, except the leviathan gin-shops, which are ghastly in their newness and richness of decoration. The broad pavement presents a mixture of Vanity Fair and Rag Fair. It is the paradise of the lowest of costermongers, and often the saturnalia of the most emerited thieves. Women appear there in their most unlovely aspect : brazen, slovenly, dishevelled, brawling, muddled with beer or fractious with gin. The howling of beaten children and kicked dogs, the

96. The crowd at the Old Vic c.1859, from Twice Round the Clock *by George Sala.*

> yells of ballad-singers, "death and fire-hunters," and reciters of sham murders and elopements; the bawling recitations of professional denunciators of the Queen, the Royal family, and the ministry; the monotonous *jodels* of the itinerant hucksters; the fumes of the vilest tobacco, of stale corduroy suits, of oilskin caps, of mildewed umbrellas, of decaying vegetables, of escaping (and frequently surreptitiously tapped) gas, of deceased cats, of ancient fish, of cagmag meat, of dubious mutton pies, and of unwashed, soddened, unkempt, reckless humanity: all these make the night hideous and the heart sick. The New Cut is one of the most unpleasant samples of London that you could offer to a foreigner.

The thoroughfare from today's Southwark Station, along the Cut, Lambeth Marsh and Upper Marsh and Carlisle Lane, and close to the railway viaduct as far as Lambeth Walk, was a mile of almost unbroken market trading, illuminated by gas burners at night; many of the stalls were open when the pubs and halls emptied. To this day, market traders keep their barrows in some of the railway arches.

Sala's distaste was understandable. The census's benign picture of the working class ignored reality, which was people who nudged, and occasionally joined, the criminal class or the underclass. But Sala was unreasonable. The vast mass of people slept several to a room in houses without bathrooms or anywhere to wash and dry clothes. Tap-water was often foul; it could give you cholera; so you drank beer. These things required municipal structures and government intervention which did not exist before the 1850s.

For a long time public houses were the only escape from miserable domestic circumstances into light and warmth. Astley's wasn't affordable every night. In the 1830s and 1840s there were penny gaffs, low haunts where lurid melodrama was improvised on a tiny dais and you got your pocket picked.

97. The New Cut market in the 1890s.

98. Run down Church Street c.1874. It became part of Lambeth Bridge Road. Watercolour by John Crowther.

MUSIC HALL

Astley's was still there, owned by the Ducrow family and later to become Sangster's - and since it continued to attract crowds to the Westminster Bridge Road, a young entrepreneur called Charles Morton decided in 1849 to take on a pub called the Canterbury Arms that backed onto Royal Street, on the river side of the newly-erected railway viaduct. There he provided a pleasant parlour and skittle alleys, and - since respectable women did not visit public houses - advertised Ladies' Nights with entertainment in the parlour. At last, men could take their wives or sweethearts out for a drink, a light supper at reasonable cost and, on Ladies' Nights, amusing turns supervised by a chairman with a gavel. It was a version of halls like Evans's, in King Street, Covent Garden, which were successful but had a raffish image.

Within three years Morton was able to extend the premises and open as the Canterbury Hall, where concert parties could attract 700 people. When some artistes performed extracts from plays he got into trouble as Astley and others had done. He was fined for contravening the 1737 Licensing Act although the magistrate was apologetic, and intimated that the Lord Chancellor's law had outlived its usefulness. After all, Canterbury evenings were reviewed in *The Times*.

The Times even accepted Morton's advertising. The Canterbury Hall was often packed, but Morton quickly recognised that too great a proportion of his takings was dry money. His appeal for lady guests had been only too successful, and as one songstress put it:

'She wouldn't call for sherry; she wouldn't call for beer;
She wouldn't call for cham, because she knew 'twould make her queer;
She wouldn't call for brandy, rum, or anything they'd got
She only called for Bovril - hot - hot - hot!'

It was the wet money Morton was after. So in 1856 he re-opened. This time the Hall was splendidly grand: horse-shoe shaped, with dozens of tables overhung by vast gasoliers, a platform stage with a piano and harmonium and a staircase swooping up from the foyer to a gallery perched on tall cast-iron columns. At the table, a young lady could accept a dozen oysters and bread and butter for a shilling, or chops and a baked potato; persuaded that she was unlikely to get tiddley with a hot dinner inside her, she might daringly indulge in a port and lemon (oh go on then). The smoke of a thousand cigars and the roar of conversation enveloped the crowds. A contemporary picture shows men in top hats (indoors) and overcoats, and women in shawls. Maybe there was no heating. But there was an adjoining art gallery with pictures by Frith and Maclise.

A few years later Morton sold the Canterbury to a new licensee and left to make a further fortune at the Oxford, on the corner of Tottenham Court Road, and other halls. But already Lambeth had become a showbiz district. Gatti's was close by – one of two: Gatti's under the Arches was

100. What remained of the entrance to the main hall of the Canterbury in 1947. Drawing by F.A. Evans.

99. Morton's Canterbury Hall in 1856.

today's Players' Theatre at Charing Cross and Gatti's in the Road was in the Westminster Bridge Road. It wasn't just the theatres that attracted The Profession, but the agents. The very first agent, a singer called Maynard, had an office in Waterloo Road in 1858 and moved later to York Road. Others who set up in the area included Maurice de Frece (whose son Sir Walter, the impresario, would later marry Vesta Tilley), Hugh Jay Didcott, and George Ware. The Westminster Bridge end of York Road became known as Poverty Corner. Stamford Street, another actors' haunt, was Misery Junction.

The Royal Victoria never had much success as a music hall after the Canterbury blew it away, and in 1880 it became the Royal Victoria Hall and Coffee Tavern, run by Emma Cons, who would later be remembered mainly as Lilian Baylis's aunt.

THE LAMBETH POISONER

The London & South Western Railway terminus at Waterloo did what railway termini always do; it became the centre of an immigrant world. When people come to a big city for the first time they revisit their arrival point as though following an invisible thread back to security. York Road was soon lined with the usual suspects: cheap hotels and lodging-houses, houses of assignation, brothels, pubs and prostitutes. Women's work was generally monotonous, ill paid, offering no prospects; marriage brought poverty and dependence. Prostitution offered variety and hope. A Stamford Street pimp, Joe Silver, took 25 girls, mostly Jewish immigrants from Poland, to South Africa when he was drummed out of Waterloo, and many must have looked forward to the adventure and opportunity so sadly lacking in Lambeth.

Waterloo Bridge linked south London, with its cheap accommodation, to the Strand and the theatres and bars and dining rooms from which men tumbled after an evening out. When the warrens around St Giles and Exeter Street were cleaned up in later Victorian times, more working girls came south of the river; they joined the quasi-amateurs and the foolish young women not long up from the provinces.

As night follows day, these girls sought drink and abortifacients. In the 1890s, Dr Thomas Neill Cream offered both. He had served a long sentence for murder in an American prison, from which he emerged addicted to morphine and obsessive about prostitutes. Not long after his release he turned up in London, which he knew well from earlier visits. Now he haunted the more raffish pubs of the Strand, bought bottles of Bass and glasses of porter for the girls, and escorted them back to their lodgings on the south bank. He told them he was a doctor; and they recognised his usefulness at once. He told them he had trained at St Thomas's. There was no greater recommendation – and he had indeed served there, after training at McGill University, in his youth. His residence had coincided with the strychnine poisoning of a young woman in Vauxhall by her bigamous husband, a railwayman.

Now, just over forty, Dr Cream seemed charming; not bad looking, handsomely moustachioed although losing his hair, but not short of a few bob and with the American accent, exotic. Perhaps the young lady's skin required a tonic? He had wonderful pills for that. Or perhaps, not to be too delicate about it, she had a minor obstruction? He had a quick and easy solution if things were not too far advanced…

Dr Cream was never present when his strychnine pills took effect. Other doctors were called to the lodging houses where his victims took hours to die screaming in agony.

Matilda Clover, an alcoholic recently deserted by her lover, with a two-year old son, died at her lodging in Lambeth Road after a date with Cream at the Canterbury. The child was sent to Lambeth Workhouse. Alice Marsh and Emma Shrivell, from Brighton and new to the game, were rushed to Tommy's by the police from their rooms in Stamford Street after a visit from 'Fred'; he had shared a can of salmon and some beer with them, and brought pills for both. Ellen Donwell, another woman on the game who lived with a soldier in Duke Street by the Clowes' works, was found in agony in the street one evening by a costermonger she knew. He got her to Duke Street and sent to the Canterbury for the soldier, who hurried back. She died on the way to St Thomas's.

The police were suspicious of Cream because he was at times obviously deranged, but at first they thought he was merely a blackmailer. Then his past emerged. He had murdered at least three women in America. He was a known abortionist. His first wife had died young in Waterloo in the 1870s. He was now engaged to a respectable girl from outside London. He was identified as the man seen with the victims.

Dr Thomas Neill Cream, the Lambeth Poisoner, was arrested, and during a sensational trial, pleaded insanity. He was hanged for four murders in 1892.

THE EMBANKMENT

A change bigger even than the railway took place in Lambeth between 1866 and 1870, and it began with the Great Stink: that summer of 1858 when the windows of the House of Commons were draped against the stench from the Thames with curtains soaked in chloride of lime, and Disraeli – hanky to nose – joined a mass exodus from the seat of government.

The Great Stink had been building up for over forty years. At the beginning of the century, in theory, rainwater drained off into open streams like the Effra or the Westbourne and human effluent was drained into covered cesspits which were periodically emptied. The night soil from the cesspits was borne upriver on barges for sale to farmers who used it as manure, or loaded onto ships at the docks and carried around the coast to farming communities in Essex and Kent.

By the end of the Napoleonic Wars this system had failed. For over a million inhabitants, there were only 200,000 cesspits. Many incomers could ill afford to pay for emptying and collection, and many absent landlords didn't care to pay. So filth piled up in the yards and cellars of houses.

And then there was Joseph Bramah's new patent WC. It used a lot of water, and flooded the cesspits.

To make matters worse, in 1815 connection of

101. Old houses along the Thames at Lambeth in 1867, demolished during construction of the Albert Embankment.

102. Fore Street, Lambeth in the 1860s, before the construction of the Embankment.

103. Upper Fore Street. On the right is Alfred Hunt's bone merchant warehouse.

house drains and cesspools direct to the sewers - which had been forbidden before - was suddenly permitted; the sewers became overloaded. In 1840 Thomas Cubitt wrote, disgustedly, 'The Thames is now made a great cesspool instead of each person having one of his own'. So when Isambard Kingdom Brunel built a well-designed pedestrian bridge, to be paid for by a toll, across the river to Hungerford Market on the Strand, it was ignored; people wouldn't pay to walk to market with pegs on their noses.

In 1842, Edwin Chadwick's report on sanitation in London included criticism of dismal building standards. Builders were unregulated and frequently incompetent (thank heaven that's changed). He reported a cellar solid with sewage to a depth of three feet, and backyards where people had to use stepping stones to get across. In his considered and well-meaning view, hygienists should consider the house first, the street next, and the river last in importance. So it was that just six years later, in 1848, the connection of house drains and cesspools to the sewers draining into the Thames became compulsory.

But guano imports had begun the previous year. Guano was a fantastic fertiliser, and cheaper than cess-pit contents. Night soil men went out of business and if you had a full cesspit in your yard, you couldn't find anyone to take the stuff away. What with that, and the new requirement to get drains connected to the sewers, pretty soon everything was getting dumped in the Thames.

In 1850 it became clear that because the river is tidal, sewers which had drained at low tide re-filled with sewage at high tide. London's river was mostly raw sewage. Its daily outflow and inflow were now so flocculent, so thick with muck, that the very house drains were now draining and re-filling daily. The Thames was where most water companies got drinking water for nearly three million people.

Enter the man who would save London from death by filth. This was Joseph Bazalgette, the son of a retired Naval officer and grandson of a wealthy French businessman who had taken British nationality before the Napoleonic Wars. As a young man (he was born in 1819), Bazalgette trained under a colleague of Telford's in Northern Ireland. He then returned to London, founded his own practice and worked on railway contracts in the 1830s.

104. *Duke's Head Court, c.1850, now replaced by the Embankment. Vignette watercolour by J. Findlay.*

105. *The Nag's Head in Fore Street. View looking towards the Thames and the Millbank Penitentiary on the other side. Watercolour by J. Findlay, c.1850.*

At that time, water engineers remained – in denial of their own eyes and noses – complacent about the state of the Thames. The dirt in water supply came, they said, from polluted cisterns; the water supplied for drinking was 'salubrious', as pure as spring water, and so on. In 1850 the Chelsea Water Company began to filter theirs, through sand. 'In 1853,' Simon Morris pointed out a century and a half later, 'the Lambeth Waterworks Company was the first to move its intake above the tideway... the death rate in its area fell to 37 per 10,000 compared with that of the Southwark and Vauxhall waterworks (which still drew from the Thames) which stood at nearly four times that figure.'

Doctors were smug too. The miasma theory of disease prevailed as it had done since the middle ages. This dictated that diseases were air-borne. If you smelled something bad, you could catch a disease from it. Hence the near-evacuation of Parliament.

Arguments had been put up against this for years, and were disregarded. Dr John Snow, who worked in Soho, was convinced that cholera at least was water-borne. He published a paper about it in 1849 but it was not until he was able to prove his case, with reference to cholera-bearing water from a local pump, in 1854 that anyone in authority stirred themselves.

Meanwhile Bazalgette had collapsed from overwork on railway contracts, taken a year off and in 1852 emerged as the engineer to the Sewers Commission, the previous incumbent having died of exhaustion. The Thames was getting stinkier daily, partly because the Great Exhibition had introduced water closets to hundreds of thousands of amazed visitors who were now ordering them for their own homes.

Bazalgette knew the urgency of the problem but so did a lot of people. The greatest of his many innovations was fierce quality control. An early victim of this was Mr Pilton, the manager of the Aylesford pottery in Belvedere Road. He

106. The old Lambeth waterfront, c.1860, before the Embankment was built. The first Lambeth Bridge is to the left, and Doulton's first pipe works are next to the Ship Tavern.

complained bitterly that Aylesford stoneware sewage pipes were just as good as Doulton's and 10% cheaper – they were good enough for Belgravia and Buckingham Palace, so how come they were not good enough for the Commissioners of Sewers? In front of an enquiry Bazalgette patiently explained, with reference to experiments carried out, that Aylesford pipes were more porous and less resistant to chemicals than Doulton's. The salt glaze made the difference.

He did not argue about theory; he simply acted upon truths that now seem obvious. Yet vested interests stood in the way of progress; the water companies, the 'select vestries' like the one in Lambeth, even campaigners for personal freedom against the nanny state. Nobody would invest. It was clear that action must come from a central authority with its own funds and powers of enforcement.

At long last, in 1855, the Metropolitan Board of Works was created and Bazalgette was appointed its Chief Engineer. Following the Great Stink two years later, he had a free hand to effect street and sewer improvements. He knew exactly what to do because he had been thinking about it for years. He submitted designs for a revolutionary system which would carry London's effluent largely by gravity, and where necessary via a pumping station, out to the Thames Estuary in huge underground tunnels built right across both north and south London. New embankment roads, and ultimately bridges, would be constructed along with the outfall scheme. A clean, efficient city was to be the culmination of his life's work and his enduring monument.

He drove it hard, insisting on expert workmanship and only Portland Cement, every batch tested by his own people, in the brick-built tunnels. After 1865 the sewer systems out to Crossness and Abbey Mills were opened; and then came the easy stuff – the Embankments, which on the northern bank would hide underground lines as well as sewers and services. Part of Albert Embankment was the first, in 1869; then Victoria and Chelsea. The river was 200 feet narrower by 1875.

The Albert Embankment was opened with little fanfare because it was in Lambeth, an

107. Above is the construction of the Albert Embankment near Lambeth Palace in 1868.

108. Lambeth Waterworks, 1825. Watercolour, artist unknown.

unfashionable area. It was erected, not to conceal sewers (which flowed inland) but as flood protection, because most of Lambeth lay below the high-water mark. It also provided a wide thoroughfare to replace cramped Fore Street. Old barge houses and cottages were demolished along Bishop's Walk, and so were the cottages and quays, alleyways and courts off Fore Street as far as Vauxhall. Caissons – big tanks to be filled with rubble – were sunk beyond the shoreline and water pumped out from behind them; the resulting ditch was filled with more rubble and the Embankment road laid. Tolls were gone from all the Thames bridges within ten years.

The Archbishop of Canterbury's land would, of necessity, be bisected by a curve of the Albert Embankment so that it could join the road sloping up to Westminster Bridge. Most of the resulting triangular plot next to the bridge was sold to St Thomas's Hospital, which also paid for some reclaimed land along the Embankment. This helped to defray the cost of Bazalgette's work in Lambeth.

109. St Thomas's Hospital, rebuilt on the Albert Embankment.

TOMMY'S

St Thomas's Hospital was founded in Southwark in the middle ages and Guy's, added by Thomas Guy in the eighteenth century, had slowly overwhelmed it. It must find a new home; and Lambeth offered the perfect site, opposite the Houses of Parliament. Between 1868 and 1871 nine handsome 'e-blocks' were built, exactly the length of Parliament, with a central quadrangle, the river side of which led under colonnades down wide steps to the new Embankment. Six of the blocks housed wards, treatment rooms and an operating theatre; there was also a small Home for Paying Patients. The central block housed the administrators and there was nurses' accommodation and a medical school.

110. The entrance hall of the new St Thomas's Hospital.

For many years the nurses wore floor-length gowns, snowy aprons and caps. Florence Nightingale herself had trained at the Southwark site and founded the nursing school at the new St Thomas's. At first, outpatients were either medical cases or surgical ones; there was no dedicated children's unit, no specialist unit for any condition. There was no A & E as we know it either, although victims of violence or murderous attack were brought in often enough and there must have been a lot of road accidents in streets tangled, dangerous and crowded with thundering drays, horse-buses and fast hansom cabs.

As a hospital reliant on voluntary contributions, Tommy's struggled for money. Certain city livery companies and individual donors were its most devoted contributors. Somerset Maugham was a young doctor there in the 1890s, and his *Liza of Lambeth* brought the hardships of this impoverished part of London to wider attention.

GOOD WORKS

Henry Mayhew had found squalor in Lambeth and Charles Booth reported whole streets full of people struggling for money. George Peabody, the great philanthropist, built estates near Waterloo; Millicent Fawcett, wife of the inventive blind Postmaster-General Sir Henry, carried out his dying wish to have Vauxhall Park constructed on the site of their home; for two hundred years the people of Lambeth were given ragged schools, charity foundations, almshouses, orphan asylums and blind schools, not to mention the Lying-In Hospital. It wasn't that wealthy people did not see, and try to ameliorate, the conditions in which the poor lived. It was simply that housing and health, fresh air and education were too important to be left to piecemeal organisation. But by the end of the nineteenth century the Welfare State was still a long way off and the LCC in its infancy.

One of the many facilities lacking was accommodation for poor travellers. By law, licensed lodging-houses must take in only permitted numbers, segregate men and women and supply certain sanitary arrangements. But there was scant inspection or enforcement and licences were easy to obtain. Cheap lodgings were usually sordid.

Lord Rowton, who was related to Lord Shaftesbury and had been Disraeli's private

111. *The Peabody Estate off Blackfriars Road, pictured in 1872.*

112. Lord Rowton.

113. The Rowton House at Bondway.

secretary, decided to take action. He was friendly with Lord Iveagh, of the Guinness family Trust, and asked his advice about raising finance. Then he thought about the accommodation he would provide. He would open six hostels, conveniently located for commercial travellers or men coming to London to look for work, in which beds could be taken at reasonable cost. For his first Rowton House he chose Bond Street, Vauxhall, near the bridge foot and close to the tram stops and railway station.

At home in Berkeley Square he planned clean, airy dormitories. In 1891 his niece laid the foundation stone in Vauxhall and building proceeded. Rowton watched, but something was wrong. He had misgivings about the soullessness of the place; maybe it reminded him too much of school, or maybe, for he became ill at this time, he was struck by the importance of privacy, comfort and companionship in times of trouble. Or maybe he was influenced by his friend, Mr Farrant of the Artisans' Dwelling Company. Anyway he told the workmen to stop, produced new plans and had part of the building torn down and rebuilt. He wanted it to offer dignity, as well as shelter.

Cubicles would be provided, not dormitories, each with its own window and lock, and glazed brick would be used indoors (Mr Farrant was at the time engaged with construction of the Central Line, where this was used). Smallpox outbreaks were still quite frequent and hygienic surroundings would prevent the spread of disease. There would be concrete floors throughout, a barber's shop, smoking and reading rooms, and a tobacconist. Men would have hot water and tubs, partitioned off, in which to bathe. Rowton prescribed every detail down to the size of the sheets, the pictures on the walls, the turnstile and an electric bell at the door with which to summon the porter. The Rowton House would be an hotel, rather than a doss-house.

It cost £30,000 to build and opened on New Year's Eve, 1892. Accommodation cost sixpence a night and in the first year, the 484 beds achieved average weekly occupancy of about 80%. Each cubicle contained a bed, chair, chamberpot, shelves and hooks; clean sheets were provided and hot water pipes ran through each room. A man could lock up the tools of his trade in a special tool-room. He would not be thrown out at the crack of dawn but could stay for as many nights as he paid for, and do his own washing in troughs in the laundry room or pay for a service wash. There was a dressing room where guests could change out of dirty work clothes, next to 40 washbasins, footbaths and clothes lockers. Visitors could sit at the back outside on a paved promenade. Lodgers could cook in their own kitchen, where four ranges provided constant facilities and hot water, and eat in one of two dining rooms - or they could buy a cooked meal. As for the rules, there was no gambling and no alcohol, but no prayer readings, either.

Regulations were tightened after the first year. A supervisor was employed to keep vagrants out and warn off vandals, and the books and soap were released to visitors only on request. (There had been a lot of pilferage). Rowton Houses became a company and within a decade, most of the sites, the Lambeth one especially, were pretty well constantly full. Today it is Centrepoint's Bondway hostel.

THE TUBE

The first underground railway in London ran from Paddington to Farringdon in 1863. It was built to house steam trains, and was constructed by the cut and cover method - the road was dug up, the track laid down and then roofed over, meaning of course that road traffic in that area was entangled for years. It was some years before technology, invented by James Greathead, could allow deep tunnels to be constructed, without the need for cut and cover, and for electric traction to supersede steam locomotives. The route chosen for the first genuine tube railway ran beneath the pleasant residential backwater which stretched from Stockwell through the Oval to Kennington, Newington (the Elephant and Castle stop for

114. Three locomotives prior to the opening of the tube line.

Tarn's grand department store), and through the Borough to the City. The area was already built up, well served by trams and horse omnibuses, and too crammed with valuable property for a cut-and-cover operation anyway.

The City and South London line opened on 18 December 1890 from Stockwell to King William Street. The Prince of Wales, who would later be Edward VII, opened Stockwell station and the line. The first nervous passengers entered stations designed by Mr T. Phillips Figgis that looked much as Kennington Station does today, except that Kennington's original entrance was in Braganza Street. The travellers were welcomed by ticket collectors and descended in wood-panelled hydraulic lifts which could carry 50 people. The lift mechanism at Kennington is still in its lead dome.

Most of the original line had tracks travelling in opposite directions on adjacent platforms. Island platforms, no place for the nervous at rush hour, were built at Stockwell and still exist further south. Above them was a row of gas lamps topped with crowns. Electricity was generated from the Stockwell terminus but there wasn't enough of it to supply electric light as well as power and light for the trains, so platform walls and pedestrian areas were tiled in white to reflect the flaring, flickering glow.

The Siemens locomotive rolled out of the tunnel mouth into the station pulling a line of ominously sealed carriages. A railway guard ushered passengers from the platform onto a 'balcony' at the end of each one. The carriages were hardly commodious, but they had banquettes along either side and were opulently upholstered to eye level, where there was a slit the size of a letter-box for ventilation. *No windows*. There had been much discussion about this at the design stage, but reason (and maybe economy) prevailed over convention. Windows were redundant if you were hurtling at speed through a tunnel, were they not? At each stop the guard called out the station name and helped ladies down to the platform from the balcony.

The carriages were, of course, nicknamed 'padded cells', but the City and South London line was a huge success despite claustrophobia and competition from the trams above ground. Its profits shamed directors of the older lines north of the river, then run by two rival tycoons whose race for territorial enlargement was costing shareholders a fortune.

Within twenty years, the carriages had windows, the King William Street station was closed, replaced by one at London Bridge, Otis electric lifts were installed, and the line took people to Moorgate and Angel; it joined up in 1907 with interchanges at King's Cross and Euston, so all its track had to be widened to match the conventional gauge.

In 1898 Greathead's Waterloo to Bank system, the Drain, was opened. It was never connected to the rest of the tube network, and in the 1980s, it was still possible to take a nostalgic ride along it in rattling 1930s' carriages with hardwood detailing and knee-crushing rows of high seats. It has been upgraded since and is at the time of writing (2006) being updated further.

THE OVAL

When the nearby tube station was opened, Kennington Oval cricket ground was already a popular destination.

Thomas Milne's 1800 Land Use map shows a circular market garden on roughly the same site. In 1845, when the Duchy of Cornwall's trustees were thinking of letting this go for development, they were persuaded by the Treasurer of the Montpelier Cricket Club, of Walworth, to let his club have it on a 31-year lease. There was a game plan behind his thinking; Surrey had no rival to the Middlesex Cricket Club and it was time it did. Subscriptions came in after a couple of big fund-raising dinners at the Horns, and Surrey County was formed. The Oval became the Surrey ground and so it remained.

In the early days, a laurel hedge separated the pitch from carriages and drays passing around the perimeter curve between Camberwell and Vauxhall Cross. At the east end, a two-storey pavilion was converted out of an old house, and there was a dressing hut, Mr Lillywhite's specially made scoreboard and a shed.

115. Cricket at the Oval in 1848.

The Surrey club was run in a businesslike way from the start, which the MCC was not. The pitch was booked by local businessmen, a few titled enthusiasts, and motley public-school types for practice, as well as for County games. Surrey could afford to offer 'talent money' to those semi-professionals who attracted spectators. Professional cricketers, mostly from the north of England, grumbled about this and demanded proper wages, but Surrey preferred incentives and it worked. The club attracted more than just the carriage trade; shopmen and clerks paid to watch crowd-pleasers at the Oval. The Australians came to play for the Ashes; W G Grace scored centuries; and the Surrey ground was not reserved exclusively for cricket. All but the second of football's Cup Finals were held at the Oval until 1893, besides the first-ever 'home' soccer international and the first rugby international.

In 1869 the five decorative gasometers were built nearby, of which four remain. They would become a much-loved backdrop, a kind of icon for cricket at the Oval. Big cricket matches could attract audiences of up to twenty thousand who sometimes couldn't be made to go home - one summer evening, in 1889, by the time when bad light should have stopped play action had reached such a nail-biting pitch that it carried on. This was talked about for years afterwards as 'the gas-lit match', although one doubts that the Oval's facilities actually did include gas-light over the pitch.

At the end of the century, the great days of Jack Hobbs, the Bedsers and Jim Laker were yet to come.

CHAPLIN

Charlie Chaplin is Lambeth's most famous son. He was born in 1889, spent his sad childhood in Kennington, and by 1902 had moved on (mentally, although not yet physically), with his sights set on provincial tours, West End shows, and finally, America.

His father was an alcoholic vaudeville singer also called Charles, a favourite at the Canterbury, whose family had pubs in Lambeth. In the 1880s he married a Walworth girl, also a music-hall singer, who had come back from South Africa with her small son, Sydney, after a brief liaison with a man who proved no good. They lived near her parents close by East Street market, and there Charlie was born.

116. Charlie Chaplin.

Charles snr wasn't around much but his wife and little Sydney and Charlie got on fine without him. They lived in style in West Square. She had lots of friends in the business, and sang on the halls in the evenings. Decades later Chaplin wrote:

> 'London was sedate in those days. The tempo was sedate; even the horse-drawn tram-cars along Westminster Bridge Road went at a sedate pace and turned sedately on a revolving table at the terminal near the bridge. In Mother's prosperous days we also lived in Westminster Bridge Road. Its atmosphere was gay and friendly with attractive shops, restaurants and music halls. The fruit-shop on the corner facing the Bridge was a galaxy of colour, with its neatly arranged pyramids of oranges, apples, pears and bananas outside, in contrast to the solemn grey Houses of Parliament directly across the river.'

In the 1890s successful artistes took 'an engagement' or 'an appointment' on the halls. A tenant might be 'a lady with connections to the stage.' It was all terribly refined, and show folk were everywhere locally. You were only a step away, in Kennington, from bright lights and the promise of financial security for life. Miss Bessie

117. Lambeth Workhouse pictured in The Builder *in January 1874.*

Wentworth, a stout girl of a type much admired at the time, was born here and lived all her 27 years around Kennington; she dressed in men's clothes like Vesta Tilley and had nationwide success with her 'coon songs', sung in a rich contralto. (She died in 1900, having only just paid a deposit on the Mason's Arms, Canterbury Place.) There were lodgings for theatricals and assistance funds for Artistes.

Kennington was still a passable address, which is more than you could say for the rest of inner south-east London. George Robey, the son of a civil engineer, spent his earliest years in a smart family flat on Kennington Park Road. E Nesbit, the writer, had been born in Lower Kennington Lane in a house from which her father and grandfather had run an agricultural college. The son of the Vicar at St Mark's was a young officer who would later become Field Marshal Montgomery. Most of Kennington's Georgian terraced houses were in multiple occupation now, but there were no obvious slums and clerks and shopkeepers liked living so conveniently along a tram route.

So Charlie and his older half-brother Sydney were strong, cheerful, much-loved little boys. Then their mother lost her voice. It started to give out in mid-song and the poor woman got pelted with orange peel.

She retired from the stage, stopped seeing her friends and took in sewing for which she was badly paid. Charles snr had disappeared and they lived in various lodgings around Kennington Road, returning several times to the attic of 3, Pownall Terrace. Their mother began to attend church for comfort, but she was increasingly depressed and her sons were taken away to Lambeth workhouse in Renfrew Road. Quite soon they were moved to a boys' home at Hanwell where they stayed for over a year. She got them back for a while to Kennington; Charlie must have been about six then. He was a watchful child, and always retained a memory of the 'vaudevillians' posturing and loudly talking outside the Tankard, on Walcot Place, 'as it was their custom on a Sunday to take a final 'one' before going home to the midday meal.'

Money was an endless problem. Once again her sons were taken, this time to Norwood workhouse, and in their absence their mother was committed to Cane Hill Asylum, twenty miles from Kennington.

In all this time Chaplin had met his father only once, outside 287 Kennington Road 'coming down the garden path with a lady'. This was a worn-out, resentful dipsomaniac called Louise who also had a little boy by Chaplin.

On their release from Norwood, Sydney and Charlie went to live with his father and Louise, who, predictably, was only occasionally around. He was doing quite well, even going to America to work, but Louise neglected the children. She sent Sydney and Charlie to Kennington Road Schools. Sydney rarely came home because she hated him, but Charlie was expected to stay in and do the chores.

One day Charlie came home and found himself locked out, with no one in. Often both parents were drunk. Finally, when Charlie and Sydney were found asleep by a watchman's fire at 3am, the Society for the Prevention of Cruelty to Children arranged the release of their mother from Cane Hill.

They went to live near a pickle factory at Kennington Cross. Charlie's mother inspired him, for she loved stories and pictures and the rhythms of language, but his education was otherwise neglected. School was boring until he learned that by reciting comic rhymes he could make other children laugh.

He joined 'the Eight Lancashire Lads' and played the halls. But his mother nagged the man who ran the troupe and he was sent home. Living again at Pownall Terrace – Charlie was about nine now – he and his mother spent a couple of idyllic weeks with an old friend of hers, at the friend's well-appointed house on Lansdowne Road in Stockwell. Here, less than a mile from home, he was briefly introduced to another kind of life, with spacious rooms, a garden, a piano, and servants.

In 1899, he came across his father sitting in the Three Stags in Kennington Road. Chaplin snr had grown enormous. He had lived on booze,

118. A house in Pownall Terrace in which Chaplin lived. It has since been demolished.

punctuated by a pre-performance dose of raw eggs in port, for years, and was swollen from dropsy. He died in St Thomas's three weeks later. Albert, one of his brothers, was wealthy and lived in Africa; Spencer, another brother, had several pubs, including the Queen's Head on the corner of Black Prince Road and Vauxhall Walk, which is still there.

Some of the Chaplin relations gave Charlie a lift back to Kennington after the funeral, dropping him off when they stopped to go into one of Spencer's establishments. The connection, a new one, ended there.

Sydney, by now about thirteen, got a good job on a cruise liner and for a while they were in the money. Charlie and his mother then entered 'our recessional period'. There wasn't enough for the rent, even at Pownall Terrace, and they had to go and stay at Grandpa's in Walworth, where they seem to have lived on porridge made flavoursome with onions. Charlie's maternal grandmother had died of drink long before. Years ago there had been a long separation from her husband and the birth of an illegitimate boy.

Charlie kept trying to make money. Once he sold junk from the Pownall Terrace garret on the pavement at Elephant and Castle. This was a bad time; they had not heard from Sydney – he was in hospital in Cape Town – and their mother was suffering from malnutrition. When she became delusional she was sent to Cane Hill once more. Charlie stayed, hungry, in Pownall Terrace, and at last Sydney came back – with twenty pounds saved.

They resolved to go on the stage. Charlie got two acting parts and went on tour while Sydney, having had no luck, became a barman at the Coal Hole in the Strand. When Charlie returned to London he and Sydney got themselves rooms in Kennington Park Road and later, with their mother back, in Chester Street. Sadly, she lost her mind again and eventually the boys put her into a private care home.

As young swells, Charlie and Sydney would take bachelor apartments on Brixton Road, near the Oval. He rehearsed a troupe upstairs at the Horns, at one stage, with his own script, until the producer pulled out. He fell in love with a girl called Hetty Kelly. He never forgot the romance of an evening walk with Hetty along the Embankment. But America beckoned, and long before the First World War, he had answered the call.

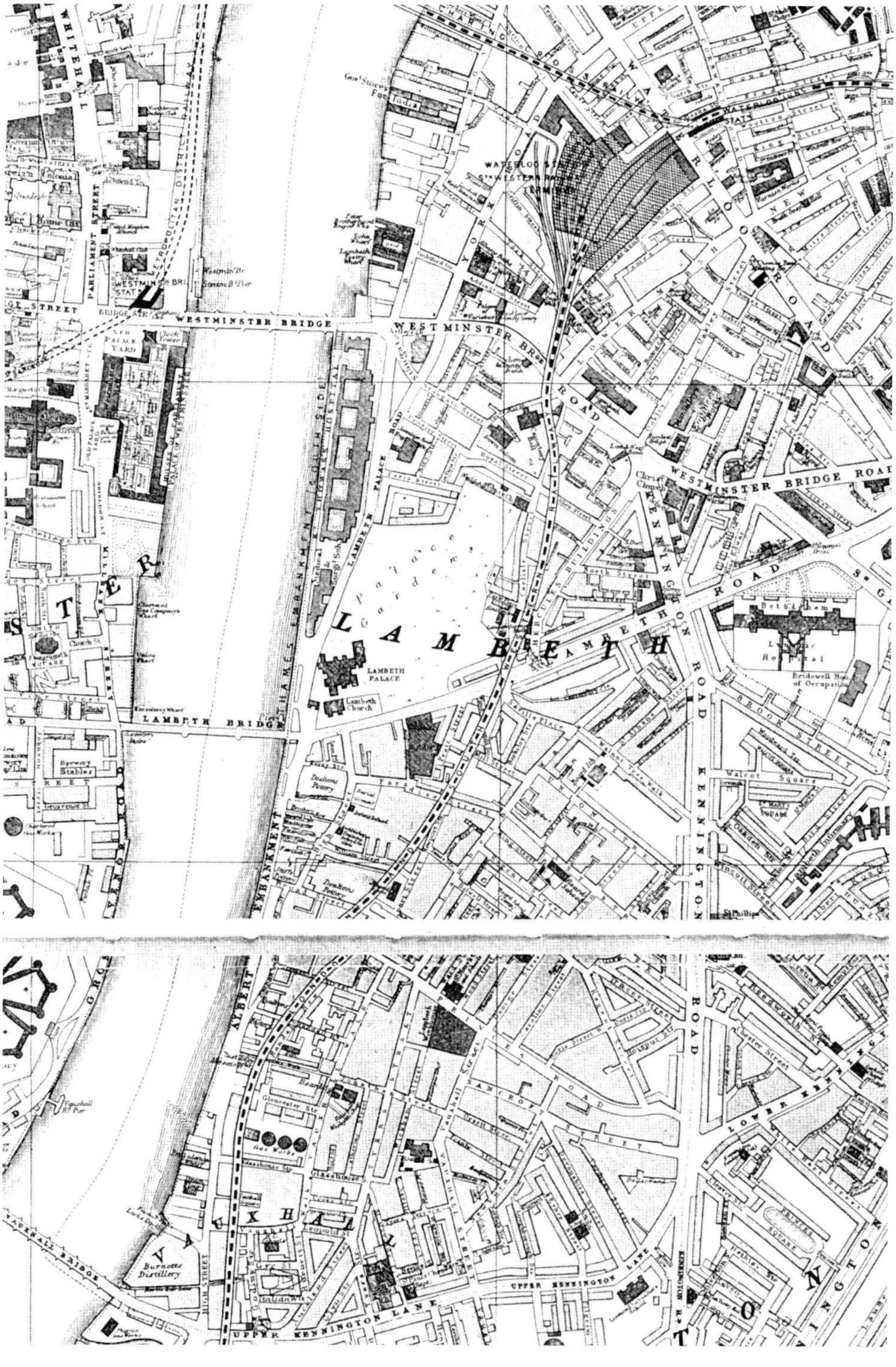

119. Detail from Bacon's map of London, published in 1888, showing the main Lambeth area.

The twentieth century

Lambeth in 1900 advertised the ugly side of capitalism. Most of it was insanitary, overcrowded, and smelly, fogbound in winter since its air was both damp and polluted, and full of ill-fed people with terrible teeth. Rickets, tuberculosis and parasites were common and the din from the factories, trains and streets was overwhelming.

You spent your entire adult life trying to keep ahead of the pawnshop and the soot, only to have some toffee-nose like Walter Besant (in 1899) stroll by and opine 'The place is dull; in parts it is dirty; everywhere it is without character or distinction.' South London obtained its living from trade and the City. 'One feels there must surely be some artistic disadvantage in being separated from the literary and artistic circles whose members, it must be confessed, reside for the most part in North London.' The Newington and Kennington area 'consists principally of lodging-houses for clerks'.

The very worst dirt and poverty have gone. Even some of the snobbery. It would be heart-warming to think that human benevolence and creativity were entirely responsible, but the following brisk overview, written at the very start of the 21st century, shows that Lambeth has been equally improved by a hurly-burly of war, economic necessity, and greed.

In the beginning came an exciting development.

THE MOTOR CAR

A photograph of Westminster Bridge Road in 1905 shows the bridge approach busy with horse-drawn carts and hansom cabs. A man called Lawson wanted to change all that. He had founded BMS – the British Motoring Syndicate – to promote petrol-driven vehicles. He had patents from Daimler for the technology and wanted to license it to manufacturers. The London to Brighton run was his brainwave and at the first race in 1904, 33 horseless carriages crossed Westminster Bridge.

The people of Lambeth were probably blasé about this. There had been a brief craze for steam-driven cars and there were electric cabs in London, though both steam and electricity were unsatisfactory for different reasons. Motor cabs were already on the streets; between 1900 and 1910 the British Motor Cab company was based at the junction of Camberwell Road and Brixton Road, by the Oval, in a building which remained a taxi depot until recently.

There was engineering expertise in Lambeth, but the great British love affair with steam, inevitable in a country well supplied with coal, meant that French and German makers had the advantage in petrol-driven transport. English manufacturers had to pick an imported de Dion Bouton, Panhard or Daimler apart and work out how to make their own. Nonetheless there were 296 motor manufacturers in Greater London by 1914, and five of them were still in Lambeth. Others had already left.

The Brush Electrical Engineering Company of Belvedere Road made petrol-engined Brush cars there until 1904, when it moved production to Loughborough for lack of space. This would be the pattern.

The firm that made Napiers began in Lambeth *(see ill. 77)*. David Napier, an early pupil of Henry Maudslay, had located his own works here in the 1830s and made printing presses, steam engines, astronomical telescopes and machines for numbering and printing banknotes. Napiers were originally in Vine Street, but when the area was bought up by the railways they moved to York Road. A young blade, Montague Napier, inherited the firm in 1895 and in 1898 began producing petrol engines for marine use. With the encouragement of S F Edge, a super-salesman and former racing cyclist, he turned to motor cars. The first Napier car was sold in 1899 and in 1902 a Napier won the Gordon Bennett trophy. Napiers made motor-driven charabancs and there were plans for a motorised and steerable balloon. The partnership of Edge the salesman, and Monty the manufacturer, had made and sold 396 Napiers out of Lambeth in 1904 when they, too, were forced by lack of space to move. In Acton, they expanded fast until the Government took them over in 1915 to produce the Napier aero engines for which they would gain lasting fame.

In 1857 a marine engine builder - like David Napier, a Scot - called Alexander Wilson had established the Vauxhall Ironworks in Wandsworth Road, (pretty much where Sainsbury's garage is now). He sold marine engines to the Admiralty, and steam and - later - petrol engines for river tugs, under the Vauxhall brand. His logo was the wyvern, which the *OED* defines as 'a winged two-legged dragon with a barbed tail'. The wyvern symbol had been used on the gates of Vauxhall Gardens, just closing for good when Wilson came to Vauxhall (one wonders whether he bought the gates). The wyvern had been Fulk de Breant's heraldic sign.

Wilson left for the City to be a consultant in 1894, leaving the firm in control of his assistant, F W Hodges. Hodges bought a car and stripped it down to find out how it worked. Like Napier he tested his efforts in a river launch, and then built, tested and started selling a small car. In 1904 he sold 76 cars, including a bigger version of his original. But that was the year the Vauxhall Ironworks' lease ended.

The firm set up on three acres in Luton and thrived, producing army staff cars in World War I. Coincidentally, Luton had been a manor awarded by King John to Fulk de Breant. His wyvern symbol survived Vauxhall Motors' sale to General Motors in 1925.

In 1926 the building at 1-3 Brixton Road, by the Oval, which had once housed the British Motor Cab company was taken over for production of the Marendaz Special until 1932. Later on the same building became the British depot for Bugatti.

THE FIRST WHITE COLLARS

Engineering firms, breweries and printers typically found that they'd outgrown Lambeth. There was no room for mass production, the workforce had to live in slums or commute, and transport was no longer so desperately river-dependent as it been before the days of steam locomotion and tarmacadam. Also, land was cheaper elsewhere. Of the big firms, only Clowes and Doulton's, both of which had moved part of their production outside London, were still at work in Lambeth in 1939.

In due course white-collar jobs would come to Lambeth in quantity, but construction of County Hall and other offices was delayed by the 1914-18 war. Until then, clerks found work only in factories, small offices and the larger local stores. For book-keepers and 'type-writers' lodgings in Kennington were affordable, but many commuted from further afield to work in the West End or the City. A photograph of Vauxhall Station taken at about 6pm on a sunny June evening at 1912 shows empty motor trams returning to Victoria and packed ones leaving for Tooting and Brixton and Camberwell. Most of the men are wearing boaters and starched collars with dark suits, and the few women are in white with wide hats and leg'o'mutton sleeves which must have been almost impossible to keep clean.

ROUND ABOUT A POUND A WEEK

The 1912 picture of Vauxhall Station shows those who travelled through, not those who actually lived in the poverty that still disfigured the south bank from Blackfriars to Nine Elms. Maud Pember Reeves published a report in 1913 which suggested that readers might:

> 'Take a tram from Victoria to Vauxhall Station ... from either end of the [railway] arch comes a close procession of trams, motor-buses, brewers' drays, coal-lorries, carts filled with unspeakable material for glue factory and tannery, motor-cars, coster-barrows, and people.'

If you crossed the new Vauxhall bridge (the old one hadn't lasted) and got off your tram under the railway, and turned left onto the site occupied only sixty years before by Vauxhall Gardens, you came across streets of back-to-backs occupied by the working class. 'The poorest people - the riverside casual, the workhouse in and out, the bar room loafer – are anxiously ignored by these respectable persons.' Dull lives were lived here on between eighteen and thirty shillings a week. This was net-curtain land, with an 'atmosphere of criticism', where people kept themselves to themselves. Housewives hearth-stoned the step and looked worn out at thirty. Money went on rent, burial insurance, coal and light, cleaning materials, clothing, and food. They shopped in 'the Walk' – Lambeth Walk market which extended a lot further north than the 1970s' excuse for a market does now. Wood, soap, lamp-oil, tea, sugar, margarine, tinned milk and jam were their essential purchases.

The men were lucky enough to be regularly, rather than casually, employed. They rarely drank more than once a week. They couldn't afford to, once they'd paid union dues and the sick club. Overtime money went on boots for the children. Many families had four or five that had survived, and the youngest wore hand-me-downs.

The essential diet was bread and scrape (margarine) and potatoes, with sweet tea. Most people got a stew and a suet pudding a couple of times a week. Fortunately, nutritious herrings and liver were cheap. Less fortunately, there were no fridges and often no oven, just a gas burner paid for by meter. Coal could not always be delivered, and if there was no other way, the women would think nothing of carrying home a stone of coal or potatoes, or wheeling it back in an old pram if they had one.

The women were sub-literate and 'culturally impoverished' whites. Mostly, they were the children and grandchildren of the thousands who had poured into London in the nineteenth century from Ireland and the provinces. They could see no way out of this endless grind because they had learned not to hope. If by some miracle they got money to spare, they must put it away for the rainy day which would surely come.

There was a cinema as close as Kennington Lane in those days, and Lilian Baylis was already thinking about bringing culture to her aunt's teetotal Coffee House at the Old Vic. (Full length plays would not be allowed until the Lord Chancellor relaxed the two-hundred-year-old ban after the First War). Lambeth housewives didn't enthuse about silent films or excerpts from Shakespeare. They had no joy, no further horizons in their lives at all.

THE GREAT WAR

Medical boards examining volunteer soldiers in the years leading up to August, 1914, were dismayed by the urban poor. Too many were stunted or underweight or had rotten teeth. And although the Great War forced many changes, better nutrition wasn't one of them; food was rationed to some extent, but not redistributed with anything like the severity or efficiency of rationing in World War II.

At the end of the Great War, the *Daily Mail* printed a map showing where Zeppelin and aeroplane bombs had hit London over the four-year period. There was heavy bombing near Waterloo. Most of Lambeth's bomb-sites, black spots on the map, run along the old Roman road from Streatham Hill through Brixton to Stockwell, the Oval and Kennington – and there the line diverges and heads up Kennington Road to Waterloo and Charing Cross. Approaching blacked-out London from the south at night, the Kaiser's pilots could not follow railway lines but could trace trams along the main road, where 'arc-ing' between faulty contact points often made a bright flash.

Between 1914 and 1918, bombs landed close to the motor garage in the Brixton Road, by the Oval; just north of the Oval tube; and south of Kennington Park near St Mark's. There were hits in the Walnut Tree Walk area, and close to St George's Circus. On the corner of South Lambeth Road and Harleyford Road, and at Gun House Stairs, the railway must have been the target. Three bombs landed on or near the railway works in Wandsworth Road. There were several near-misses at Westminster Bridge.

Eighty-odd years later, a TV programme broadcast the recollections of Madge Maindonald, who was waiting for her brother outside Vauxhall station in 1917 when a bomb hit the gasworks on the riverbank. "I heard this

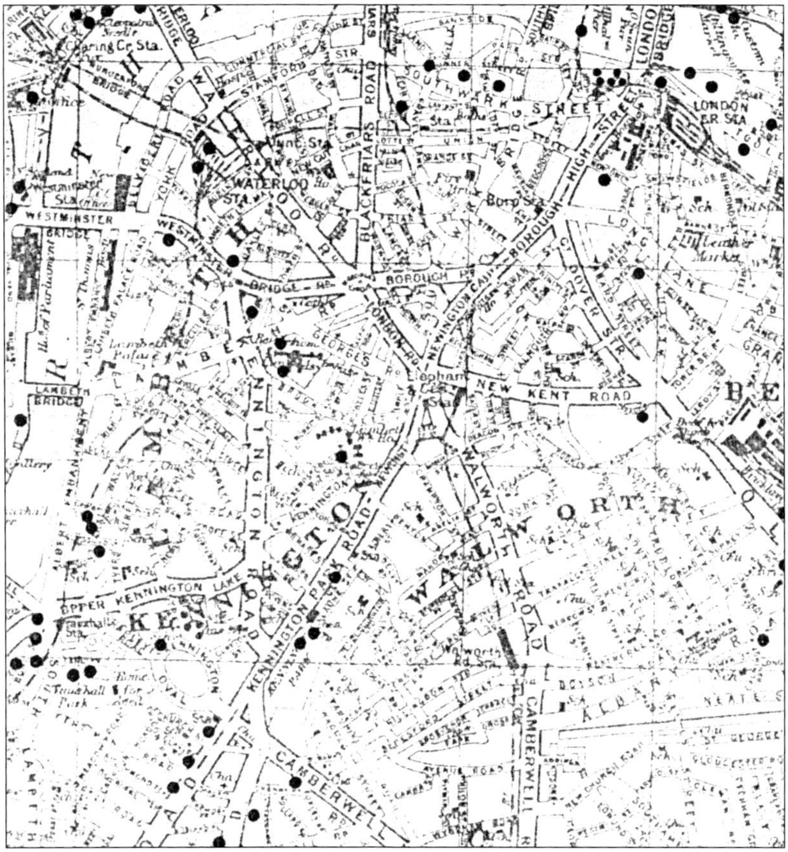

120. A map showing bomb damage in Lambeth during the First World War.

dreadful bang," she said. "People began rushing past me to get into the station, but I didn't move because my brother had said Stand There ... People were crying and screaming and praying." There had been five bombs and people she knew had been killed in the flats nearby.

There was no siren before bombs fell, Madge said. "To begin with, a policeman came round on a bike with a notice on him saying TAKE COVER and ringing his bicycle bell." People rushing into the station ran under a glass roof; they knew no better, then.

For food, you had to queue. In Walworth, 3000 people queued for margarine one freezing day in December 1917. Madge Maindonald confirmed the pre-war findings of Maud Pember Reeves. "People starved" she said, but "if you were hungry, you didn't tell anybody... People were too proud."

Competent Lambeth women who had someone to look after their children were liberated. They got men's jobs as bus conductors or postal workers, or worked in hospitals, shops or munitions factories. But you couldn't get a porter at Waterloo, and there weren't any delivery boys, so the well-shod ladies of Kennington had to carry their own cases and parcels.

At Waterloo, as at other London termini, there was a YMCA hut where returning soldiers could get a bed, a meal and a bath. Waterloo was unique in having also a YMCA annexe where wives could say goodbye. Across Waterloo Road, the Union Jack hostel for wounded soldiers had been opened in 1907 by voluntary subscription, and was extended in 1917. A writer in *The Times* in February 1917 was scandalised by the honeypot that emerged out of all this:

'Waterloo Station, perhaps the most important station in London from the military point of view, is situated in the very centre of a poor working-class district which, in point of bad housing, excessive drinking, immorality and general low standard of living has for many years had a bad reputation. Into this area of overcrowded and insanitary dwellings, low-class public houses, dirt, and general degradation pour troops on leave from the front or from Aldershot... Night after night the short stretch of road between Stamford Street and the Old Vic is thronged by women who are unmistakably pursuing the traffic of prostitution...'

He described young women accosting 'victims' with whom they would disappear into the side streets.

'There is ample evidence that the black streets which spread like a net between Westminster Bridge Road and Blackfriars Road are honeycombed with 'houses of accommodation' and 'shebeens.'

"You want a drink? My mother will get you one. She lives just round the corner. I'll show you," small boys would tell the soldiers. Some men were robbed, a Canadian soldier was murdered. Others were comforted, and one hopes that most of them ended up in the 'houses of accommodation' rather than the tumbledown, bug-ridden shacks of which photographs remain in the Lambeth archive.

121. Emma Cons. A chalk drawing by William Rothenstein.

THE OLD VIC

The Old Vic was set on its feet by Lilian Baylis during the First World War, but it was already nearly a century old then. It had been the Coburg Theatre when it was founded after the Napoleonic Wars, and is said to have stones from the demolished Savoy Palace (a mediaeval palace, not a theatre) in the Strand in its foundations. It began with high ideals. Kean and Kemble acted there in the early years. In 1833 it was renamed to honour the Princess Victoria. According to *The Times* on the occasion of its centenary in 1916, 'aborigines' - meaning the low types of Lambeth - took over soon afterwards and the place went downhill, with performances of cheap melodrama and finally music hall. An evening there, described by George Sala, is noted in the previous chapter. The theatre was on its last legs when Emma Cons came along.

The well-educated daughter of a piano case maker, she was artistic, religious and pushy: a friend and associate of Ruskin, Charles Kingsley and Octavia Hill. After several years as a volunteer social worker in Marylebone she raised money from the Duke of Westminster and others to set up a model housing scheme in north Lambeth. It was while she was working on this that her attention was drawn to the Old Vic, which she would re-open as a 'coffee music-hall'. There were lectures on scientific and other subjects as well as concerts and operatic performances.

It didn't make money, but staggered along

122. Lilian Baylis. A chalk drawing by William Rothenstein.

123. The Old Vic in the 1920s.

thanks to generous donations, not least from Samuel Morley MP, who had made a fortune from socks. (Morley College, now in Westminster Bridge Road, originated in classes given in the theatre's dressing rooms in the 1890s.)

By 1899 the eccentric Emma Cons (the code used in the *Dictionary of National Biography* is 'tomboyish', while adding the information that even in evening dress, she kept a knife and a piece of string to hand), was staggering along herself, for she was over-committed to causes besides managing the theatre. She cast about for someone who might share the burden.

Her sister, a singer, had married a violinist called Baylis and with their grown-up children they formed a touring troupe, which was then in South Africa. It was the elder daughter, 25-year-old Lilian, to whom Emma Cons sent her cry for help. Lilian returned to England, worked as manager of the Old Vic until the death of her aunt in 1912, and set about raising the professional standards and changing the programme. Like her aunt, she was adept at extracting money from benefactors. She was determined to present all the Shakespeare plays and many other classics besides continuing the operatic repertoire. It was still difficult to present plays, but there were ways to get around the Lord Chancellor's rules and she knew them. During the Great War, when theatres were often dark in the West End, the best actors were glad of any work they could get. The Old Vic became a destination of the fashionable rather than a huge success with the locals.

In the twenties, Lilian Baylis promoted cinema performances for children until she decided that much of the available material was unsuitable. She was also instrumental in setting up Sadler's Wells as the Old Vic's sister theatre. She died in 1937.

COUNTY HALL

The powerful London County Council had taken over from the Metropolitan Board of Works as the supreme local authority. It was bursting out of offices on various sites, at least one of which, at Spring Gardens off Trafalgar Square, it would

124 and 125. *The old Surrey Chapel in the 1920s had been turned into a boxing hall called The Ring. This would, no doubt, have much dismayed Rowland Hill.*

126. The site of County Hall in 1906.

like to sell for a big profit; and it needed a prestigious County Hall. The site of the old Lion Brewery on Pedlar's Acre was chosen in 1908. Fortunately, or perhaps presciently, the builders of the Bakerloo Line had designed their tubes from Waterloo to zig-zag down to the Elephant via a nearby stop at Lambeth North which opened in 1907.

A 29-year-old architect called Ralph Knott won the competition to design County Hall in the 'English Renaissance' style specified by the LCC. Not counting the cost of the land, it should come in at around £850,000. That's what he said.

The North block caused unforeseen expense. Messrs Holloways, the builders, had taken a 77-year lease on that land in 1900 and required proper compensation, resolved by a court case. Then there were alterations to the design. And extra land reclamation (County Hall took up 6.38 acres of which, in the end, 2.38 acres was reclaimed). And Pedlar's Acre was owned by a charitable trust and compensation must be claimed on behalf of the trust, but by whom? The Vestry of St Mary's, disempowered under recent legislation by the local Council, claimed that Pedlar's Acre was an ecclesiastical charity, and the income from it should pay for church repairs. But Lambeth Council claimed that it took over Pedlar's Acre when it took powers from the Vestry, and therefore, it was entitled to claim funds for the trust. The Judge chose in favour of Lambeth. The LCC forked out more legal fees.

The contractors set to like snails. In 1912 Mr Edward Smith pointed out at an LCC meeting that 'when a deputation visited the site last week only 62 persons were at work there. At the present time for its various offices in 37 different centres the Council was paying £1000 a week in rent. At the present rate of progress they would not be in the new Hall by 1926.'

In 1916 construction ceased, and then the habitable, finished part of County Hall was occupied by the Ministry of Food instead. At the Armistice the Ministry couldn't be winkled out, and Edward Smith – now Sir Edward – fulminated that it had become a 'repository for Government clerks' and would the LCC ever get it back?

It was officially opened in 1922 by the King, who arrived with the Queen and an escort of the

127. Belvedere Road in 1909, demolished to make way for County Hall. Crosse & Blackwell's factory is on the left.

128. The great river frontage of County Hall in the 1920s.

129. The Council Chamber in County Hall.

Household Cavalry. They processed home, cheered by crowds, along Kennington Road and Upper Kennington Lane and Vauxhall Bridge in time for a late lunch at Buckingham Palace.

Opened, yes, but County Hall was not actually finished until 1933. It had cost at least £4 million, but it marked the start of Lambeth's resurgence as a centre for white-collar workers. Indeed by now there were so many of them working for the LCC that the Council decided to keep Spring Gardens after all, as an annexe.

THE GERALDINE MARY HARMSWORTH PARK

When, in the 1920s the Royal Bethlem Hospital closed up and moved to Beckenham, the building was taken over as the first national home for a scattered collection of valued artefacts, documents and painting which, together, would form the Imperial War Museum. Planning began for the adaptations required. The fourteen acres of parkland that surrounded the building – all that remained of St George's Fields – were to be sold by Bridge House Estates for development.

Fortunately for us, Viscount Rothermere, newspaper magnate and brother of the late Lord Northcliffe, paid £155,000 for the park and presented the land to the LCC. It would benefit local children, for whom the nearest green spaces were otherwise in Southwark or at Kennington, and it would be named in honour of his mother, Geraldine Mary Harmsworth, who had had fourteen children and lived to be 86. Opening the park in 1934, Rothermere said she was 'a woman of great intellect and grace of mind' and hoped that her spirit might descend on the spot to aid the splendid struggling mothers of Southwark in the training and upbringing of their children.

A jolly spirit certainly did descend in the pre-war years. There was a toddlers' Lido in summer, 90 feet long and deepening from eight inches to three feet. Admittance was reserved to those under 12. And the LCC employed children's entertainers – clowns and conjurers – to give performances here as they did at Victoria Park and elsewhere.

The war put an end to it all. Today there is no Lido, and perhaps it should be revived. The Spaw is long gone, the duckpond too, and the source of the Neckinger remembered only in the name of Brook Drive. Beneath the lush green park lurks a proper pond, waiting to bubble up from the depths and splash rudely all over our health and safety legislation.

BETWEEN THE WARS

The roaring twenties passed Lambeth by. On the whole, Lambeth women didn't become flappers and Lambeth men didn't save up for crystal wireless sets. This wasn't night-club land, although undoubtedly some of the girls went Up West and brought their earnings back to spend in the Walk. Some things changed – Bedlam moved out and the Imperial War Museum moved in, put a library in the asylum's dome and planted a cannon in front of the building. Tommy's, the hospital that had saved so many lives during the war, struggled for money. The Licensed Victuallers' School left, and the Naafi, which provided catering for the armed forces, took over their school in Kennington Lane and opened tea

130. The Licensed Victuallers' School in Kennington Lane, in 1828.

131. The school, rebuilt in 1836, here photographed in the 1960s and then renamed Imperial Court and occupied by Naafi, the catering organisation for the armed forces.

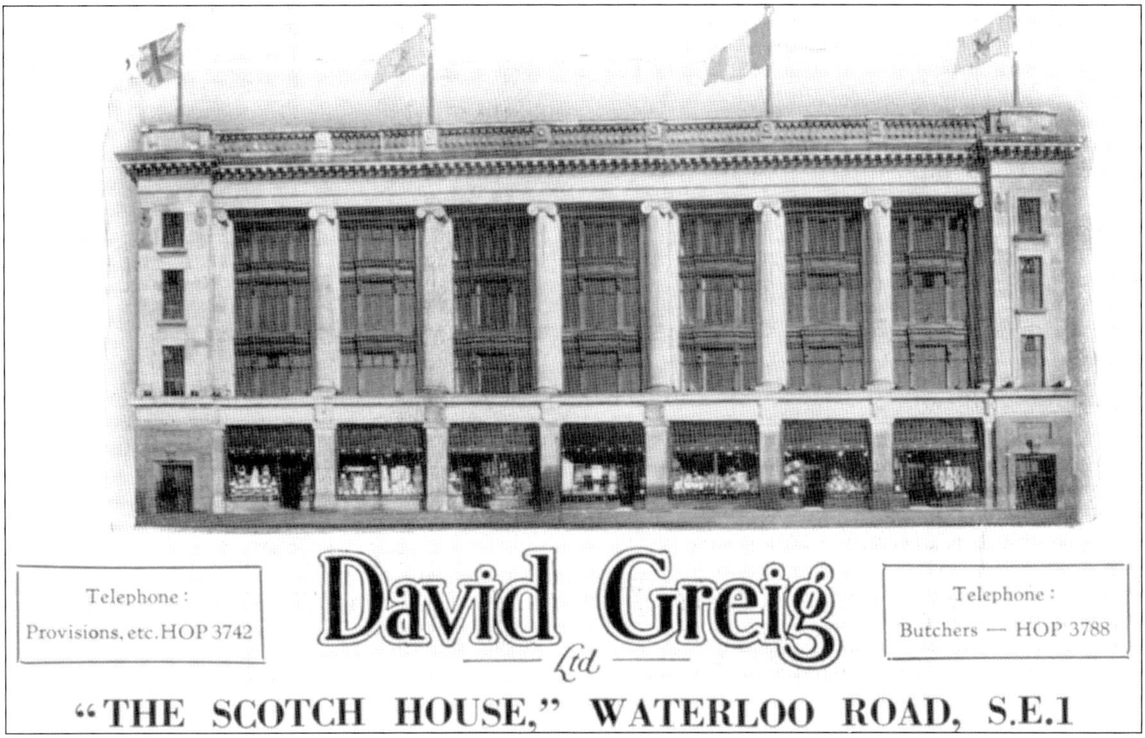

132. A big local employer was the grocery firm, David Greig in the Waterloo Road, by the Old Vic. It had a shop on many high streets.

and cheese warehouses, together with a printing factory, off Kennington Park Road. Waterloo Station – having undergone a modernisation programme that began in 1900 – was at last finished off with a Victory Arch as memorial to railwaymen who had died for their country.

Housing remained disastrously inadequate, but efforts were made by the new, go-ahead municipal authority. Nikolaus Pevsner, and Bridget Cherry who took up Pevsner's baton in documenting the buildings of south London, having described how Lambeth became 'slummier and slummier' in the nineteenth century now wrote with resignation:

> 'In the early twentieth century the Duchy of Cornwall took the lead, and Adshead & Ramsay's neo-Regency cottages and flats in Kennington remain a model of their kind, one which unfortunately had little impact between the wars on the LCC, whose straggling amorphous estates of dreary four-and five-storey walk-up blocks recur all over Lambeth.'

This is the view of someone who had never had to share a single room with a wife and four children, or a single lavatory with three other families. In the 1990s, a retired midwife who had trained at Tommy's during World War II told this author that she remembered being taken out on call to women in labour in local houses and being mystified by her mentor's immediate demand for boiling water and newspaper. The steaming kettle, she learned, was to give the husbands something to do; the newspaper was to give the bugs somewhere to land. When you lit a fire in a Lambeth bedroom as late as 1944, bed-bugs teemed out from behind the wallpaper and landed, tick, tack, tick, tack on the newsprint. Sneer as the middle-classes might, the 'amorphous estates' were much appreciated by people who had lived in piggeries like this before.

Others didn't sneer at the way the workers had to live, but romanticised it. In 1937 Lupino Lane (a descendant of that Signor Lupino who had

133. J J Sainsbury, founder of the supermarket chain, was born at 5 Oakley Street, now Baylis Road, in Lambeth on 12 June 1844. By 1851 the family was living near the New Cut where he had his first job in a grocer's shop. In 1864, when his father died, they were living in Belvedere Road. Sainsbury and his wife opened their first shop in Drury Lane in 1869, but the firm after his death returned to his roots in 1936 when it opened its factory off Stamford Street and became large a local employer. This poster is of the between-the-wars era.

worked with De Castro, and himself a contemporary of the De Castro sisters who became stars in America) popularised a dance from a West End musical called *Me and My Girl*.

Any time you're Lambeth way
Any evening, any day,
You'll find 'em all
Doing the Lambeth Walk....

Not everybody was a Pearly King, of course. Norman Collins wrote a book, later made into a film, called *London Belongs to Me*. His subjects belong to the innocent lower-middle class of Kennington in 1938, with war on the horizon. Small families, with a regular wage coming in and plenty to eat, occupied 'rooms' in eight or ten-roomed Regency houses, behind lace curtains that revealed 'the red mahogany wardrobe, the wash-hand-stand, the chest-of-drawers, the dressing-table.' The women took their pin-curls out when company came. The men could afford a ticket for the cinema or the Oval if they felt like it. In Kennington, by living carefully and offending no-one, you could earn a kind of security.

THE SECOND WORLD WAR

In the summer of 1939, sandbags went up round the War Museum. People remembered the Zeppelin raids, and evacuated their children. They found out where the air-raid shelters were and how to use a gas mask. Those who had gardens built blast-resistant Anderson shelters in them. At first nothing happened, and some of the children returned.

One sunny afternoon in September 1940, Luftwaffe raids began over Silvertown. Soon after, Lambeth began to get hit. This was the Blitz. Only just over half the borough's pre-war population were around to suffer it, since the rest had removed to the suburbs or were in the armed forces.

At first nobody was allowed to shelter in the deep tubes. The authorities thought that they'd stay down and refuse to come out, as had often happened in the First World War. When the Blitz began, the authorities – prompted by a Government minister called Herbert Morrison – had the courage to change their minds. Morrison was the son of a Brixton policeman and knew how working people needed those shelters.

From September to May, 1940-41, the Luftwaffe dropped high explosive bombs and showers of incendiaries. Until the New Year, London was free from air attack on only three nights. Some buildings were hit twice. With so many people bombed out, the housing that remained got more crowded than ever. Ambulance and rescue services, many of them manned by volunteers, kept going on adrenalin, cigarettes and sweet tea, and the hospitals were in a permanent state of emergency.

Since most of the LCC architects' department had to spend night after night in rescue work, they didn't organise hit-counting until the bombing slackened off in January, 1941. In May, the Luftwaffe turned away to the Eastern front. Bombing continued sporadically until July '41, and then there was a lull.

When calm descended that summer, Lambeth emerged as the fifth worst-hit London borough, with 36 kilos of bombs per acre and 178 houses lost per thousand of population. Lambeth had 3423 houses destroyed and 5281 damaged – together 18% of the housing stock. 2,722 people were dead or wounded; this was more casualties than any other borough.

Throughout the bombardment, 30,000 Civil Defence volunteers had been busy carrying out emergency repairs and fixing broken gas mains. Now they set about clearing sites. Visible destruction was bad for morale.

1942 was quiet. A picture *(ill. 135)* taken one sunny day in Lambeth Walk shows a group of women using 'emergency washing facilities'. Nearly all are shabby and a bit overweight, with a fag hanging out of a mouth here, and a cross-over pinny there; they could be living in the 1930s. There is a child in hand-me-down stack-heeled shoes that are too big for her and a woman, younger-looking than the rest, who has a smart frock – an overall? – and her hair in a Victory roll. The surroundings – the propped tarpaulins and sagging washing line – are reminiscent of a

134. Children playing on a bomb site in 1948. They are using the remains of Field's Candle factory and a burned out train from the old Necropolis station at Waterloo.

135. Women sharing the laundry facilities and washing line during the war.

136. A flying bomb damaged the Pilgrim Glassworks, a gasometer and Hayward's pickle factory in July 1944.

refugee camp in Africa today. All these women are clearly unfazed by a mangle, a washboard and a washtub – a stick in a half-barrel on legs, vintage around 1910. By the look of it, the vagaries of fate were nothing new, and rationing and a regular income were an improvement on what had gone before.

Up the road at Lambeth Palace, brass hats from the War Office in Whitehall played tennis in the Lambeth Palace garden.

In July of 1943 the bombing started again and gradually worsened until, in June, 1944, the first of hundreds of V1s came over. V1s were the unmanned buzz bombs, known also as doodlebugs, that droned ominously through the sky before cutting out. "Everyone in the restaurant stopped eating and froze, knives and forks in the air, until we all looked like statues..." wrote a woman years afterwards. If the drone stopped directly above you, you'd had it. The bomb would drop, explode and sear all within a wide radius with its blast. A cartoon of the time showed a parrot speaking to a contented cat: 'Purr if you must, but for heaven's sake don't cut out.' 71 V1s fell in Lambeth between June and September of 1944. Many houses were hit for a second time, and at the south end of Kennington Park, a V1 hit a shelter with huge loss of life.

In September, the chairman of the government's Counter-Measures Committee, which knew all about German secret weapons, announced that the Battle for London was pretty well over. The following day, a terrific explosion was heard. Then came others just like it. For weeks the authorities muttered about gas mains before finally admitting that V2s were hitting London. These were long-range rockets with 2000lb warheads that made a deep crater. Having a tendency to fall short of their target, most fell in Camberwell or Lewisham and only three in Lambeth.

By the end of the war, the force of 30,000 tidiers-up had grown to 145,000. Damage to Lambeth itself had been caused only partly by attack on strategic local targets such as railway lines and stations, goods yards and gasometers. Often, Lambeth's bombs were meant to hit the Thames bridges, the Houses of Parliament, Whitehall or Charing Cross, but fell short.

PICKING UP THE PIECES

Before the Blitz began there is no doubt that a 'Come, friendly bombs' attitude prevailed in some quarters; a few direct hits would at least get rid of the Victorian slums. LCC architects were much attracted by notions about high-rise machines for living in with green spaces in between, and the influential town planner Sir Patrick Abercrombie was keen on separating traffic from people – should the opportunity arise.

From January 1941 the LCC Architects Department received damage reports from borough surveyors, house by house and street by street, graded according to the degree of devastation from 'total destruction' through 'severely damaged, probably repairable' to 'blast damage, not structural' and minor damage of the broken-window type. The point was to pinpoint areas for clearance post-war.

Lambeth Baths, at the end of Lambeth Walk, had been seriously damaged, as had sites along the river such as the one where MI6 now stands. A section of Lambeth Walk close to Newport Street and the railway had gone. St Thomas' Hospital had been badly damaged on several occasions, on the north side by a V1, and much of it had to be pulled down; in Royal Street a

137. The South London Industrial Exhibition held at Lambeth Baths in February 1865. The building was destroyed in the Second World War.

factory and Gatti's Cinema, which had once been the Canterbury Music Hall, were reduced to a flooded pit; the Necropolis station was not worth repairing. The old link from Albert Embankment to Westminster Bridge was wiped out (St Thomas's later extended its site to cover it). The early nineteenth-century grid of streets and factories from the river to York Road was seriously damaged, partly obliterated. A V1 had landed on York Road and another on Hungerford Bridge.

Buildings on the site of mediaeval Norfolk House were destroyed. Across the road, Lambeth Palace was already badly damaged. The thirteenth-century crypt – embellished by Laud, desecrated by soldiers during the Commonwealth, used as an air raid shelter in the First War and a shelter and bookstore in the second – was already burned out by incendiaries; north of its garden and Archbishop's Park, other buildings were now reduced to rubble by a V1.

Comparing bomb sites in Lambeth with present-day buildings, it is possible to see that much repair and restoration was carried out, as well as demolition and replacement with sixties blocks or green spaces.

But before this could happen there was a decade or more of austerity, relieved by one big party.

THE FESTIVAL OF BRITAIN, 1951

There is no doubt that people *did* enjoy themselves at the Festival of Britain. They paid their ten bob (50p) and walked into a world that was colourful, light and clean and expressed hope for the nation. There were good reasons to be cheerful. Britain's new Welfare State – especially the National Health Service – guaranteed a safety-net if ordinary people were sick or destitute and their children could, because of the grammar schools, hope to get on in life. The Conservative party were glum about the whole thing, astutely perceiving that the Festival was in fact a political statement.

Of course it was run by a committee. The Central Office of Information, the British Film Institute, the Arts Council, and the Council of

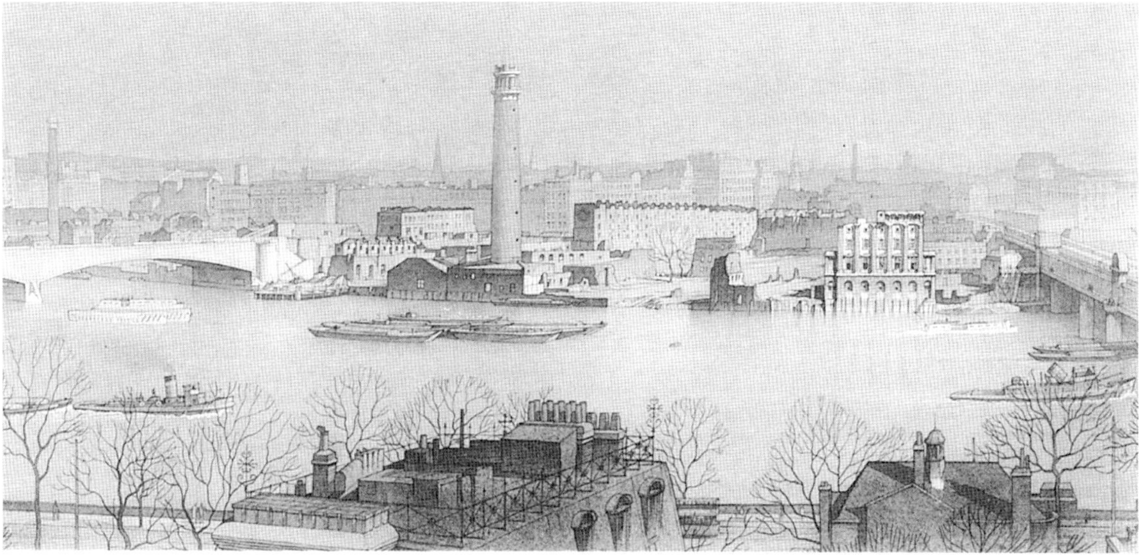

138. The site of the Festival of Britain in 1949. Watercolour by Lawrence Wright.

Industrial Design were involved. Sir Patrick Abercrombie, Lady Megan Lloyd George and Herbert Morrison were among the worthies; Morrison (Lord Morrison of Lambeth) devoted so much time to the Festival that he neglected his day job as Foreign Secretary. (Which neglect probably changed the course of British history more than any Festival.) Ideas were contributed by committee members like T S Eliot, Sir Malcolm Sargent and Kenneth Clark, and the creative drive to get the image and the look right came from architects such as Hugh Casson and Misha Black.

The main exhibition was set up on cleared ground, much of which had been bombed, between Westminster Bridge and Waterloo Bridge. Another 600 yards of riverside were embanked, and the site extended inland to York Road. There was also an architecture and town planning exhibition at Poplar, a sponsored funfair at Battersea, craft exhibitions at South Kensington, about thirty approved festivals or arts festivals up and down the country, and a travelling festival. People in 2,000 towns and villages also set up their own celebrations. The BBC made nearly 3,000 related broadcasts. And all this – from South Bank clearance in 1949 – was achieved within two years.

The Shot Tower, with a flashing beam on top, was the only structure that remained on Lambeth's Festival site from before the war. Where south Hungerford Bridge is now, the rocket-like Skylon soared up 91 metres to the heavens. Behind it the Dome of Discovery boasted the widest unsupported span in the world. Huge enthusiasm went into every aspect of the Festival, although the only building designed to be permanent was the Royal Festival Hall.

The look of the thing is what has endured; the fifties aesthetic – the ubiquitous icon (the streamlined Britannia), the designs of Robin and Lucienne Day on fabrics and furnishings, and the unmistakeably 1950s' south side of the Royal Festival Hall. The South Bank riverside, crowded with outdoor cafés in photos of 1951, even now retains its sense that this is a place where you come to stroll about and enjoy yourself, not to work or to shop.

It wasn't, as the 1851 Exhibition had been, intended to promote British industry and achievement. The Festival aimed to achieve pride in national identity through a history that was presented, in exhibitions and films, as white, egalitarian, and morally robust, of Anglo-Saxon men who had all somehow worked for the common good since about 1066. The Chinese,

139. *Aerial view of the Festival of Britain, dominated by the Dome of Discovery, with the Royal Festival Hall to the left.*

140. *The Royal Festival Hall with the remaining shot tower to the left.*

141. The striking private boxes at the Royal Festival Hall.

Irish and Jews, the Indians, French, Italians and Poles, the black British Victorians (one thinks of Robert Wedderburn the Methodist preacher, Coffey the Chartist and Vesta Victoria of the music hall, who had all worked in Lambeth) and the very few West Indians so far here, were left out of the picture. Their numbers were presumably too small to have made much impact.

Perhaps it was the earnest appeal to nationalism that made aspects of the Festival so *square*. Across the river, people were propping up bars in Soho and talking about Ferlinghetti, Sartre and Thelonius Monk; down the road, boys and girls were snogging in the picture house and sometimes, girls were getting Up the Duff. None of them could have got the Festival together. But they were a reminder that even the British were not all singing from the same copy of *Land of Hope and Glory*.

So the Festival expressed a notion of 'ordinariness' which had a lot to do with clean-living white conventions. However, a good time was had by all.

In 1952 all 27 acres were cleared, except the riverside restaurant, the Telekinema (which begat the National Film Theatre) and the Royal Festival Hall. Most of it became a garden and a car park, until later, the theatres, concert halls and art galleries of the South Bank were added; then the enormous, sprawling Shell Centre along York Road.

MEANWHILE, UNNOTICED...

River buses ran for the duration of the Festival of Britain, but stopped afterwards. George Reid's photographs of the Thames taken in the twenties and early thirties show that the Thames from Blackfriars to Nine Elms was still busy, before the war, with sailing barges and lighters, salvage boats and tugs. All the way along Lambeth's foreshore there were working wharves, with jetties and cranes and derricks serving the flour mills and distilleries, garbage collectors and coal merchants. Something was always going on there, there was something to see; but once the industries had gone, the river seemed to dwindle in London's consciousness. The Thames was too mucky for fish and too shallow for shipping. As a commercial thoroughfare it was moribund. The dockers' protests took place further east. In Lambeth, the river reached its nadir in the 1960s and 1970s. It was a barrier, and except for the odd tourist boat or garbage barge, not much else.

PLANNING AND REBUILDING

In 1943 Professor Abercrombie had produced the County of London Plan, which proposed that north Lambeth should become a Comprehensive Development Area. And so it came to pass.

Pevsner, or Bridget Cherry, wrote in 1983:

> 'By 1952 it was already possible to say of North Lambeth ... that there was no other area in London which showed so clearly (and not very encouragingly) what a future inner London with everybody living in council flats might look like.'

This passage bemoans the continuing trend, under Chief Planner Hollamby of the Greater London Council which replaced the LCC in 1965, towards wholesale clearance. In 1981 almost half the households in the entire borough of Lambeth lived in council housing. This was 'thirty years of rebuilding which has altered Lambeth more drastically than at any time since the spread of the nineteenth century suburbs' (although the council also housed people in existing buildings, never demolished).

Geoffrey Fletcher, whose lively drawings of a London fast vanishing were much loved by nostalgia buffs, visited Brunswick House in 1966. This was a fine Georgian mansion once part-owned by the Duke of Brunswick, Queen Caroline's older brother, later a pleasure garden and tea-room, at Vauxhall Cross. At the time of Fletcher's visit it retained some dignity, but 'wharves prevent access to the river for most of the way, and the landscape is grim and industrialised.' He wandered around Vauxhall Gardens, didn't find anything quaint enough to draw, and left, saddened (having missed the grim sign BAGWASH outside a laundry at the Oval, which would have been right up his street; it is still there).

In 1971 the Victoria Line was extended from Oxford Circus through Vauxhall to Brixton. But it seemed that Lambeth in general had got to get worse before it got better. The Clean Air Act of the 1950s got rid of the soot and fog, but on still days, a haze of traffic particulate descended much as soot had done before.

And then there was the smell. Waterloo, with the South Bank, County Hall and the Shell Centre playing host only to white-collar workers, didn't have it, but an industrial pong overhung Vauxhall all the way to Battersea – nobody knew where it came from; some said it was the distilleries, others the Marmite factory, or Lucozade, or Price's Candles, or the gasworks. It persisted until the early 1980s.

As to planning, locals rightly described it as criminal, by which they meant that the anonymous expert responsible should be jailed. The South Bank complex was a windswept muddle of outdoor walkways and threatening tunnels. A cliff of tall office blocks barred Vauxhall and Kennington from the river. Vauxhall's town centre, so busy in that 1912 photograph, was demolished in favour of a roaring traffic intersection where pedestrians must climb steps – impassable by baby buggies or wheelchairs – to cross six lanes of cars and buses.

Local authority developers seemed to have the best of intentions. Occasionally, planning worked; demolished streets on the Vauxhall Spring Gardens site were replaced by 1950s' flats around a park and a city farm. But most 'improvements' proved uninspired. A GLC annexe, an octagon in pebbly brown concrete of such hideousness that it was regularly voted London's worst eyesore, seemed to have landed from space, inaccessible except by underpass, in the middle of the Westminster Bridgefoot roundabout. Since the abolition of the GLC it has remained derelict and a disgrace. At the other end of York Road, the sunken concrete pit of the Waterloo Bridgefoot roundabout slowly became a vast open-air doss-house for vagrants.

The Duchy of Cornwall disposed of its bomb sites to police and security services and Government offices like the COI, who promptly

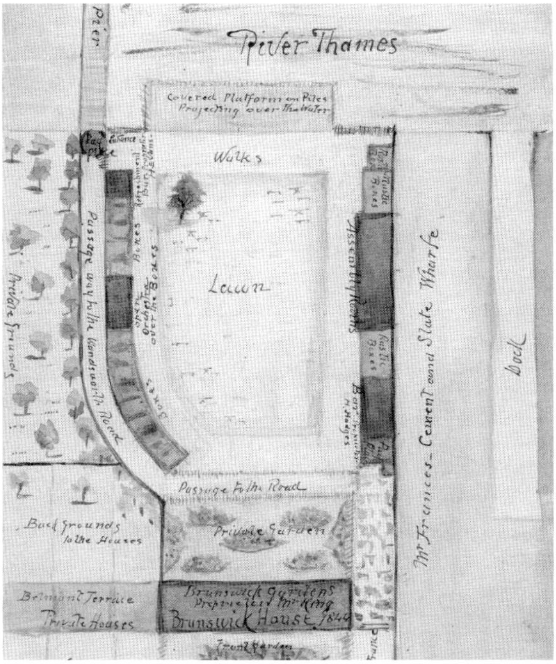

142. *Brunswick House gardens in the 18th century.*

put up more slabs. In the seventies the railway yards finally disappeared from Nine Elms under New Covent Garden market; surrounding housing was replaced by service depots. St Thomas's filled in its quadrangle and built a sixties slab of new wards where bombs had wiped out the old ones. British Telecom built more office blocks. None of the slabs worked at ground level. The Albert Embankment was usually empty of pedestrians, the concrete-dominated South Bank much the same, and strung about with pedestrian walkways some of which had a decidedly temporary feel.

For local people, the worst of this was the shops: they'd all gone. Business rates and high commercial rents had a lot to do with that. The people who were rehoused out of the slums into council flats didn't have cars and they relied, as their forebears had done, on the Marsh, the Cut, the Walk, Vauxhall Walk, and even Westminster Bridge Road. These had been replaced by a

143. *The city farm at Vauxhall Park in 2006.*

shopping centre miles away at the Elephant, and later, a Sainsbury's supermarket at Nine Elms. This too was useless to the 81% of Lambeth council tenants who in 1981 had no access to a car. The GLC, Lambeth Council, the Government and the economy between them had killed Lambeth street life.

There was, of course, a backlash. Hippies squatted in Victorian Bonnington Square, pulled up the paving slabs and planted palm trees, made remaining bomb-sites into gardens and opened a community café. Angry residents of Coin Street and its environs, who lived between Stamford Street and Belvedere Road, battled for ten years from 1974 against plans to redevelop the whole South Bank for offices. Destruction threatened the remaining warehouses and the Oxo Tower at Upper Ground, and council tenants were likely to be shipped out to some suburb they would hate. Today, since the developers gave up, the GLC was dissolved, and Coin Street Community Builders were able to buy the freehold of the site, they have formed a housing co-operative and provide intelligent and creative support for the local enterprises, gardens and festivals that have brought the South Bank to life.

In the meantime, but rather disengaged from general Lambeth life, the Old Vic entered upon a heyday period when, having been repaired after war damage and other alterations since, it reopened in 1963 as a temporary home for the National Theatre under the direction of Sir Laurence Olivier. In 1982 the building was bought by the Canadian Ed Mirvish and generously refurbished to splendour. Recently it has been under the direction of the American actor, Kevin Spacey.

MIXED BLESSINGS

In the late 1980s, Margaret Thatcher closed down the GLC, and this summary execution coincided with a short-lived property boom. A new, more enlightened and respectful generation of architects and developers took a hard look at the mess and decided to go no further. Victorian buildings would be restored and converted wherever possible, mixed use was in favour, and new office blocks would be... well, not slabs. The most ambitious development was Terry Farrell's MI6 at Vauxhall Cross, a fortress and instant symbol of the Government's secret services.

Margaret Thatcher's government made it quite easy for existing council tenants to convert rentals to purchases, but made it almost impossible for councils to build new council homes. A lot of local people bought and stayed; others bought and later sold, to move out of London; still more bought, and rented their properties out; some simply hung on and sub-let when they had no further need for the accommodation. The poorest families found it more difficult than ever to get decently housed. In the late 80s and again in the late 1990s, residential property in Lambeth became a profitable investment. Its proximity to the West End and the City made it attractive and once London had its first Mayor in 2000, public transport improved. However the great street markets have not reappeared and most of the small shops have closed.

As the Millennium approached, Eurostar trains from Paris glided into Waterloo beneath Nicholas Grimshaw's snaking glass canopy – a service which will cease in 2007 in favour of St Pancras. The threatening wasteland where the old Gas, Light and Company had stood at Vauxhall Bridge, and the nightmarish empty bulk of the Nine Elms Cold Store next to the river, were replaced by green glass apartment blocks. Ugly office towers along the river were re-clad and re-furbished as apartments with atria, porterage, and high service charges. Offices on the Albert Embankment became hotels, and a lot of money was spent on new trees.

Lambeth's riverside, once home to wharves and mills, munitions factories and glassworks, has been reborn as a leisure destination. The scruffy Hungerford footbridge has been demolished and Lifshutz Davison, architects, has put up two graceful walkways, one on either side of the railway bridge to Charing Cross. The London Eye, designed by David Marks and Julia Barfield, is a 443-foot (135m) ferris wheel outside County Hall. It is a magical addition to London's skyline, and fascinated thousands of onlookers

144. *The MI6 building at Vauxhall, designed by Terry Farrell.*

145. *The new face of Vauxhall – futuristic flats by Vauxhall Bridge.*

146. A renovated and peaceful Cleaver Square, 2006.

when it was being assembled, flat on its side, in the river.

Lambeth's almost-completed section of the Thames Path results from insistence that developers provide pedestrian access along the riverbank. It is a triumph. Runners and cyclists can travel along it off-road from Nine Elms beyond Blackfriars to Bermondsey and they do, dodging the tourists; it has become a commuting route to the City via the Millennium Bridge. The river itself is newly accessible. The Jubilee pier is in regular use at last and a riverboat between the two Tate galleries links Waterloo to Pimlico and the Borough.

Lambeth has become desirable – if you can afford to live in it. Waterloo has good communications, an improving South Bank and some decent restaurants. Vauxhall has been partly central for a ragbag of sub-cultures for years; and inland, much of Kennington has become stylish again. The Imperial War Museum wins awards as a national resource.

St Thomas' Hospital's bright new Children's Wing has verve, inside and out. There are small, well-tended parks and unexpected local galleries and museums, community activities, under-funded but well-attended libraries, and good children's playgroups run by Lambeth Council.

However, Lambeth is two nations. The community is socially polarised. There are major social problems, crime and depression. There is cultural *anomie*, drug dependence and ignorance. Lambeth's improvements will remain cosmetic until there is radical action on education, and this is a national problem, worse in Lambeth than in many other places.

THE START OF THE 21ST CENTURY

Newcomers have done a lot to transform Lambeth, mostly for the better, since 1970. The Festival of Britain in 1951 brought crowds to a white Anglo-Saxon Lambeth where immigrants had been absorbed. There had been Dutch incomers and Huguenots in the seventeenth century (a Dollond cousin, brought up and educated in Kennington, went on to take over the prestigious family firm of optical instrument makers that would become Dollond & Aitchison.) Jewish show folk and craftspeople lived in Lambeth from the eighteenth century onwards, and shopkeepers and Jewish residents in Kennington, but late-nineteenth-century refugees from the pogroms generally stayed in the east end. The Lambeth poor were insular and

147. Roupell Street, one of the old streets, with the London Eye in the distance.

148. The London Eye, 2006, with County Hall and the Shell Centre in the background.

suspicious, and if you too were poor and didn't speak their language, there was every reason to avoid them.

However, newcomers did somehow manage to break these barriers, remaining separate from the English only in half-remembered family customs. To Kennington came French people in the later nineteenth century, political refugees, often teachers; there were a few shopkeepers from Germany, Irish families, Poles and Cypriots after the second war. Probably some Indian or West Indian or Chinese people had settled in Lambeth. But in pictures of troops going off to the front, schoolchildren, or market scenes, the faces are generally white European.

North Lambeth as we know it didn't begin until the first generation of black Londoners was born here. A picture of schoolchildren in 1972 shows quite a lot of kids whose parents were probably West Indian; everybody else is white. Now those children have grown up in Lambeth, as have many people of Bangladeshi, Indian or Pakistani origin.

Since the early 1990s, thanks to numerous factors including political upheaval abroad, demand for labour at all levels in health, construction and IT, and EC expansion, north Lambeth has successfully absorbed much larger numbers of immigrants. Barely a single country goes unrepresented; your neighbours, your in-laws or your parents probably come from Korea or Vietnam, Brazil or Colombia, Portugal or Poland, Romania or France or Somalia. The book-keeper may be Malaysian, the barmaid from South Africa, the doctor Nigerian. When there are enough people from the same place, they get together and contribute to Lambeth's new identity. Some communities have regenerated the churches, others have formed local football teams or produce music festivals or summer shows. They work, they achieve, and many families tell heroic stories of struggle and survival.

The divide between Lambeth's two nations is a divide of income and education, just as it was in the nineteenth century. Everybody needs to get involved in what happens next in this ancient part of London – its housing, jobs, health and above all, schools. The newcomers are enriching Lambeth, but will they stay here when they have children? Will those children have a sense of the place? The future looks uncertain.

Further Reading

1 Beside the river

'Aspects of Archaeology and History in Surrey', *Cotton, Crocker & Graham, Surrey Archaeological Society 2004*
Celtic Britain, Charles Thomas, Thames & Hudson 1986
Cross-Channel trade between Gaul and Britain in the Pre-Roman Iron Age, Macready and Thompson, Society of Antiquaries of London 1984
Digging the Dirt with Time Team, Tim Taylor, Channel 4 Books 2001
Effra: Lambeth's Underground River, Ken Dixon, The Brixton Society 1993
London Bodies, ed. Alex Werner, Museum of London 1998
Notes on the Map: Map of the Geology and Contours of London & its environs, R W Mylne (1856), introduction by Eric Robinson and topographical notes by Simon Morris, London Topographical Society 1993
On Lambeth Marsh - The South Bank and Waterloo, by Graham Gibberd, publ. Jane Gibberd 1992
Pre-Roman roads T G Newcomen, a talk to the Institution of Highway Engineers, 2nd February 1951
Roads and tracks for historians, Paul Hindle, Phillimore 2001
South London, Walter Besant, Chatto & Windus 1899
The prehistory and topography of Southwark and Lambeth, Jane Sidell *et al*, MoLAS Monograph #14, Museum of London Archaeology Service 2002
Treasures and Trinkets: Jewellery in London from pre-Roman times to the 1930s, Tessa Murdoch. Museum of London 1991

2 Mediaeval Glory

A Domesday of Crown Lands, Sidney Madge, Frank Cass 1938
England's population, a history since the Domesday survey to 1939, Andrew Hinde, Andrew, Hodder Arnold 2003
Historical Particulars of Lambeth Parish and Lambeth Palace in addition to the histories of Dr Ducarel, Rev. Samuel Denne MA, Vicar of Wilmington & Darenth, John Nichols 1795
History and Antiquities of Lambeth Palace, Dr A. Ducarel, in *Bibliographica Topographica Britannica: Antiquities of Middlesex and Surrey* Vol. IV, John Nichols 1795
History of the Origin and Progress of the Company of Watermen and Lightermen Vols I-III, Henry Humpherus, Prentice 1887
Lambeth Palace, a photographic record, H C Stacy, Society for the Promotion of Christian Knowledge 1958
Lambeth Palace, a short guide, Dorothy Mills, Church House Information Board 1951
Lambeth Palace, C R Dodwell, Country Life Ltd 1958
Lambeth Palace, Gordon Huelin, Church Information Office 1974
Lambeth Palace, Mary Cryer, Churchman Publishing 1988
Mediaeval London, www.britannica.com article 10107; also article 9039313 (*King Harold II*), Encyclopaedia Britannica Premium Service 2005
Pevsner's Buildings of England, London 2. South, Bridget Cherry & Nikolaus Pevsner, Penguin 1994
Swein Forkbeard's invasions and the Danish conquest of England, 991-1017, Ian Howard, Boydell Press 2003
The Black Prince, Richard Barber, Sutton 2003
The Black Prince's Palace at Kennington, Surrey, British Architectural Reports 26, 1976
The builders of Lambeth Palace, an historical lecture delivered by the Rev H Bedford Pym, MA, Church House 1898
The Surrey Domesday, Alecto Historical Editions 1989

3 Turbulence: 1500 - 1700

A Domesday of Crown Lands, Sidney Madge, Frank Cass 1938
A letter from Dr Ducarel to William Watson MD upon the early cultivation of Botany in England; and some particulars of John Tradescant, a great promoter of that Science....in the last Century, Bowyer & Nichols, 1773
Ark to Ashmolean, Arthur MacGregor, Ashmolean Museum 1983
Connoisseur and Diplomat - the Earl of Arundel's embassy to Germany in 1636, Francis C Springell, Maggs Bros Ltd 1963
Elias Ashmole FRS, C H Josten, Ashmolean Museum & Museum of the History of Science1978
Dictionary of National Biography on George Villiers 1st Duke of Buckingham and George Villiers 2nd Duke of Buckingham
Great Villiers, Hester W Chapman, Secker & Warburg 1949
Historical Particulars of Lambeth Parish and Lambeth Palace in addition to the histories of Dr Ducarel, Rev. Samuel Denne MA, Vicar of Wilmington & Darenth; John Nichols 1795
History and Antiquities of Lambeth Palace, Dr A. Ducarel, in *Bibliographica Topographica Britannica: Antiquities of Middlesex and Surrey* Vol. IV, John Nichols 1785
Huyghens and his telescopes, paper given by Peter Louwman of the Louwman Collection of Historic Telescopes of Wassenaar at the conference *Titan: from Discovery to Encounter*, European Space Agency, Noordwijk, Netherlands, April 2004
Lambeth Churchwardens' accounts 1504-1645 and Vestry book 1610, Surrey Record Society Volume XVIII (1941)
London in the 1690s : a social atlas, Craig Spence, Centre for Metropolitan History, University of London 2000
London Maps, various, including those of Ogilby and Morgan, John Oliver and *A plan of the cities of London & Southwark as fortified by the order of Parliament in the years 1642 & 1643*, George Vertue 1738. King's Topographical Collection Vol. XX 1-55, British Library
Mistresses of Charles II and politics at the Restoration Court, unpublished thesis, Sonya M Wynne, Corpus Christi College Cambridge 1997
Monopoly and Competition, Hermann Levy 1911; Batoche Books, Ontario, reprint of 2001 downloadable from website of McMaster University, California
On Lambeth Marsh - The South Bank and Waterloo, by Graham Gibberd, publ. Jane Gibberd 1992
Oxford Dictionary of National Biography on Sir Noel Caron
Roads and tracks for historians, Paul Hindle, Phillimore 2001
South London, Walter Besant, Chatto & Windus 1899

The A to Z of Elizabethan London compiled by Adrian Prockter and Robert Taylor, London Topographical Society 1979
The Big Smoke, a history of air pollution in London, Peter Brimblecombe, Methuen 1987
The Century of Inventions, The Marquis of Worcester's 1655 text with introduction by Henry Dirks, 1864, online at www.history.rochester.edu/steam
The Development of English Glassmaking 1560-1640, Eleanor S Godfrey, Clarendon Press 1975
The John Tradescants, Prudence Leith-Ross, Peter Owen 1983
The man who drew London, Gillian Tindall, Chatto & Windus 2002 (on Wenceslaus Hollar)
The Marquis of Worcester and Calthoff, Transactions of the Society Vol. XXVI, G Doorman, 1947-9
The Marquis of Worcester and Vauxhall Transactions of the Newcomen Society, Vol. XIII 1932-5, W H Thorpe; additional comments from Mr Clowes of the Duchy of Cornwall archives, with plate showing location of works.
The Tradescants, Mea Allen, Michael Joseph 1964
www.londoncrownglass.co.uk
www.nazeing-glass.com
www.pepysdiary.com

4 Lambeth in the 18th Century

A new and accurate map of the countryside 25 miles around London, Andrews 1777
A plan of streets, roads &c between Blackfryers Bridge, London Bridge, Westminster Bridge, Lambeth Newington Butts and St Margaret's Hill as they now are, together with the new intended streets roads and communications, c1770
Old Lambethans Past and Present, J H Goodfellow, 1906 (a privately printed history of Lambeth Parochial/ Archbishop Temple's School)
The Girls' Charity School Lambeth supported by Voluntary Subscriptions and Benefactions, 1794 (a privately printed history of Archbishop Tenison's School)
The Memoirs of J De Castro, Comedian, ed. R Humphreys, Sherwood Jones 1824
Windmills in Lambeth, an historical survey, Michael Short, London Borough of Lambeth 1971
The Times Digital Archive for numerous references to Astley's c.1800-1811
Incidents in the life of Joseph Grimaldi, Giles Neville, Cape 1980.
Historical Particulars of Lambeth Parish and Lambeth Palace in addition to the histories of Dr Ducarel, Rev. Samuel Denne MA, Vicar of Wilmington & Darenth, John Nichols 1795
The much-lamented death of Madam Geneva, Patrick Dillon, Headline 2002
London maps, views and plans of the eighteenth century (Boydell's view, 1752, Faden's map 1785, Cary's map 1797, Hulsbergh's drawings c. 1724 for a bridge at Vauxhall, &c). Most are from the King's Topographical Collection XX 1-55 at the British Library.
Leaves from a beech-tree, Gwendolyn Beaufoy, privately printed 1930
Colonel Mark Beaufoy FRS 1764-1827, paper written c.1980 by Jean Martin & deposited in the Lambeth Archive
Blake Records, second edition, GE Bentley Jnr, Yale University Press 2004
The Times Digital Archive and *Dictionary of National Biography* on Sir Joseph Mawbey
Canaletto, Antonio Paolucci, transl. Diane Goldrei, Thames & Hudson 1971
A warning for bad wives, or the manner of the burning of Sarah Elston on Kennington Common, for murthering her husband Thomas Elston ... and likewise the execution of John Masters, for robbing on the highway, &c. Anonymous pamphlet, London, 1678.
London's River, Geoffrey Fletcher, Hutchinson 1966
The Life of John Dollond FRS, Inventor of the Achromatic Telescope, John Kelly, privately printed 1808
Catalogue of the plants growing wild in the environs of London, publ. William Curtis, 1774
The Gentleman's Magazine, August 1910, article on William Curtis by Mr Urban
www.vauxhallsociety.org for an article based on *Beaufoys Vinegar Yard* by Rachel Gaunt, 1978
Mrs Coade's Stone, Alison Kelly, the Self Publishing Association Ltd, Upton on Severn, in association with the Georgian Society, 1990
Eleanor Coade – Artificial Stone Manufacturer born Exeter 1733 d London 1821 John Havill, privately printed 1986
Etchings of Coade's Artifical Stone manufacture Narrow Wall Lambeth Near Westminster Bridge, Catalogue produced by John Bacon, sculptor, with etchings by William Blake, 1777-79
History of the Vauxhall and Ratcliff Glass Houses and their Owners 1670-1800, William Henry Bowles, privately printed 1926
A history of the General Lying-in Hospital York Road Lambeth 1765-1971, Philip Rhodes, Davis-Poynter 1977
English Pottery and Porcelain, W B Honey, A & C Black 1969
English Delftware Tiles, Anthony Ray, Faber & Faber 1973
www.geocities.com on Handel's career in London
Springs, Streams and Spas of London, Alfred Stanley Foord, Fisher Unwin, 1910
Plan of a Society Established in London Anno Domini 1785 For the Support and Encouragement of Sunday-Schools in the different counties of England, pamphlet, 1785
History of Telegraphy, Ken Beauchamp, Institute of Electrical Engineers 2001
Dictionary of National Biography on John Dollond
William Curtis Botanist & Entomologist 1746-1799 with notes on Samuel Curtis FLS, by W Hugh Curtis, Warren (Winchester) 1941
The Botanical Magazine, early editions, Linley Library, Vincent Square London SW1

5 Great machinery of Empire: 1800-1900

1841 *Census of Population*
A brief history of St Thomas's Hospital, G Q Roberts CBE, Photochrome Company of London and Tunbridge Wells, 1920
A Family Business 1803-1953, W B Clowes, William Clowes and Sons, Ltd 1953

A prescription for murder: the Victorian serial killings of Dr Thomas Neill Cream, Angus McLaren, Chicago, University Press 1993
Address to the Ladies and Gentlemen Subscribers of the Licensed Victuallers' School, Kennington Lane Lambeth, 1825
Bessie Wentworth, article in *Music Hall* issue # 38, 2000
Bethlem Hospital 1247-1997: a pictorial record, Patricia Allderidge, Phillimore 1997
British Music Hall, a story in pictures, Raymond Mander and Joe Mitchenson, Studio Vista 1965
Darling old Oval, Eric Midwinter, Cricket Ltd 1995
E Nesbit, Doris Langley Moore, Benn 1967
George Robey and the Music Hall, James Harding, Hodder & Stoughton 1990
Henry Maudslay and the Pioneers of the Machine Age, John Cantrell & Gillian Cookson, Tempus 2002.
Henry Maudslay, 1771-1831, and Maudslay, Sons & Field, Ltd, The Maudslay Society 1949
Industrial Biography, Samuel Smiles (1863), reprint by David & Charles 1967
King Cholera, Norman Longmate, Hamish Hamilton 1966
Lambeth Palace, C R Dodwell, Country Life Ltd 1958
Liza of Lambeth, W Somerset Maugham, Jubilee Edition, Heinemann 1947
London's Underground stations, Laurence Menear, Midas Books 1983
Map of the Geology and Contours of London & its environs, 1856, by R W Mylne, with introduction by Eric Robinson and notes by Simon Morris, London Topographical Society 1993
Metropolitan Commission of Sewers – a report by Mr Bazalgette, Engineer-in-Chief to the Commission, on the comparative suitability of Lambeth Stoneware and Aylesford Pottery pipes, July 1855
My Early Years, Charles Chaplin, Chivers Press, Bath 1979
On Lambeth Marsh, Graham Gibberd, publ. Jane Gibberd 1992
Railways of Waterloo, J N Faulkner, Ian Allen 1994
Robert Owen, Ian Donnachie, Tuckwell Press 2000
Rowton Houses, 1892-1954, Michael Sheridan, Rowton Houses Ltd 1956
Scenes from Bedlam: a history of caring for the mentally disordered at Bethlem Royal Hospital and the Maudsley, David Russell, Baillière Tindall 1997
Self-Help, Samuel Smiles, introduction & notes by Peter W Sinnema, Oxford World Classics 2002
Socialist Infidels & Messengers of Light, Anna Davin, from *The Streets of London – from the Great Fire to the Great Stink,* ed. Tim Hitchcock & Heather Shore, Rivers Oram 2003
South London, Walter Besant, Chatto & Windus 1899
St Thomas's Hospital, E M McInnes, George Allen & Unwin 1963
The Doulton Lambeth Wares, Desmond Eyles & Louise Irvine, Richard Dennis 2002
The Great Stink of London: Sir Joseph Bazalgette and the cleansing of the Victorian Metropolis, Stephen Halliday, Sutton 2001
The Life of Henry Stephens FRCS 1796-1864, by his daughter Martha Walsh (1925), The Stephens Collection c.1990
The LSWR at Nine Elms: the Works and its Products 1830-1909, Barry Curl, KRB Publications 2004
The Much-lamented death of Madam Geneva, Patrick Dillon, Headline 2002
The Rights of Conscience in Danger, by A Lambeth Elector, published by the Author (1857, price 3d) on William Roupell MP
The Roupells of Lambeth: politics, property and peculation in Victorian Lambeth, Judy Harris, The Streatham Society 2001.
The story of London's Underground, John R Day, London Transport Publications 1978
The Story of the Oval, Louis Palgrave, Cornish 1949
The Terracotta Revival, Michael Stratton, Gollancz 1993
The Times Digital Archive on Chartists at Kennington, March & April 1848
Thomas Milne's land use map, 1800, London Topographical Society 1976
Twice Round the Clock, or The Hours of the Day and Night in London, George Augustus Sala, reprinted by Victorian London Publications
Vauxhall Gardens, J G Southworth, Columbia University Press 1941
Victorian Diaries, Ed. Heather Creaton. Mitchell Beazley 2001
www.vauxhallsociety.org

6 The twentieth century

'The autobiography of a nation': the 1951 Festival of Britain, Becky E Conekin, Manchester University Press 2003
All quiet on the home front, Richard van Emden & Steve Humphries, Headline 2003
British Car Factories from 1896, Paul Collins and Michael Stratton, Veloce 1993
Dictionary of National Biography on Sir Patrick Abercrombie & Lord Morrison of Lambeth
Festival of Britain 1951 Information Summary, Information Office, Festival of Britain 1951
Growing up in Lambeth, Mary Chamberlain, Virago 1989
How we lived then. A history of everyday life during the Second World War, Norman Longmate, Arrow 1973
Locating offices near rail termini in central London: a comparative analysis of Shell Centre staff travel surveys, John Parker, pcl School of Environment Occasional Paper #4, May 1979
London belongs to me, Norman Collins, Collins 1945
London's river, Geoffrey Fletcher, Hutchinson 1966
Pevsner's Buildings of England, London 2. South, Bridget Cherry & Nikolaus Pevsner, Penguin 1983
Round about a pound a week, Maud Pember Reeves (1913), Virago 1979
The British Motor Industry 1896-1939, Kenneth Richardson, Macmillan 1977
The Home Front in the Great War, David Bilton, Leo Cooper 2003
The LCC Bomb Damage Maps, 1939-45, London Topographical Society 2005
The Times Digital Archive 1908-33 on the building of County Hall, & prostitution in Waterloo during the First World War

INDEX

An asterisk denotes an illustration or caption